THE BEST OF CORDON BLEU

*In preparation

THE BEST OF

Cordon
Bleu

*Rosemary Hume
and
Muriel Downes*

J M Dent & Sons Ltd

LONDON   MELBOURNE   TORONTO

First published 1979
© The Constance Spry and Cordon Bleu Group Ltd 1979

Phototypeset in 11pt Monophoto Baskerville by
Northampton Phototypesetters Ltd
Printed in Great Britain by
Billings Ltd, Guildford, London & Worcester for
J. M. Dent & Sons Ltd
Aldine House, Welbeck Street, London

British Library Cataloguing in Publication Data

Hume, Rosemary
  The best of Cordon Bleu.
  1. Cookery
  I. Title II. Downes, Muriel
  641.5 TX717

ISBN 0-460-04405-2

Contents

Introduction

A question we are so often asked is 'What is Cordon Bleu Cooking?'

The answer is certainly not so-called 'fancy' cooking but rather in our methods and approach to good food.

We attach great importance to basic principles. Every student is trained to cook plain every-day food well, before going on to more elaborate dishes. This she (or he) cannot do until certain methods have been mastered and well understood. No one can run before they can walk and this is especially true in cooking.

Another answer is the care and attention to detail given at every stage of the preparation and cooking of any dish. Only in this way is it possible to build up, or teach, the necessary techniques that a cook must acquire, whether a student or a house-wife. Good technique, i.e. the right way to set about work in the kitchen, gives speed and confidence so that cooking is an enjoyment and not a chore.

The addition of mixers and other pieces of equipment in the kitchen has helped not only to lighten the load but also to enlarge the scope of the housewife, without any drop in standards.

As an example a well-trained Cordon Bleu student will instinctively take the right knife or pan for the job in hand.

When cutting brown bread and butter to accompany a first course, she will reach for a palette knife or round-bladed table knife with which to spread the soft butter to the edge of the crust before thinly slicing the bread with a saw-edged bread knife.

This may seem to many a small and unimportant point but it is this sort of detail, if not properly carried out, that can spoil the presentation of a meal.

For over thirty years particular emphasis has been given to keep the School, recipes and teaching up-to-date and in line with the changing times and fashion in food.

We have been conscious that a balance must be struck between economy and the necessity to keep as much variety and interest as possible in the recipes, both for entertaining and every day. At the same time it must be recognized that the classic dishes have changed little.

The growth of the School and the constant and successful watch on standards has been largely due to the enthusiasm and loyalty of our staff.

The recipes in this book have been favourites with our students and readers for many years. You will find some for everyday and many for entertaining.

First Courses

Tomates Farçis Nantua

Like all tomato first courses or salads, make when the tomatoes are at their best and full of flavour. This is an ideal dish for a buffet.

6–8 even-sized ripe
    tomatoes
4–6 oz (125–185 g)
    picked prawns or
    shrimps
¼ pint (150 ml)
    mayonnaise
1 rounded teaspoon
    gelatine
1 large tablespoon
    tomato juice
1 level teaspoon tomato
    purée
Lemon juice to taste
Small rounds of brown
    bread and butter,
    stamped out to fit
    tomatoes
Watercress to garnish

Scald and skin the tomatoes, slice off the tops and scoop out all the seeds. Turn them upside down to drain. Dry the shellfish well and chop prawns or leave shrimps whole.

Dissolve the gelatine in the tomato juice, add the purée and fold into the mayonnaise. Season and add lemon juice to taste. When thickening, stir enough into the shrimps to coat them nicely. Fill into the tomatoes and replace the tops. Set each tomato on a round of bread and butter and garnish with the watercress.

Serves 4–6

Tomates Farçis Carmel

6 large firm tomatoes
3.03 oz (85 g) packet
    Philadelphia cream
    cheese
1 ripe avocado
1 rounded teaspoon
    gelatine dissolved in 2
    tablespoons tomato
    juice strained from the
    seeds
Salt, pepper and a
    squeeze of lemon juice
French dressing
Watercress or cress

Serves 4–6

Scald and skin the tomatoes. Cut off the tops from the flower end and carefully scoop out the seeds and core. Turn the tomatoes upside down onto a paper towel to drain. Work the cheese until smooth, peel and crush the avocado lightly with a fork. Gently heat the gelatine and tomato juice, then add to the cheese. Fold in the avocado, season well and sharpen with a little lemon juice.

Fill into the tomatoes with a teaspoon or bag and plain pipe, once the mixture begins to stiffen. Chill slightly and dish. Spoon a little French dressing over each and garnish with cress.

Artichauts Vinaigrette Milanaise

4–6 artichokes

Dressing:
2 shallots, finely chopped
2–3 oz (84 g) each of
  ham and tongue
2–3 tomatoes
6–8 tablespoons
  (105–140 ml) salad oil
3–4 tablespoons
  (53–70 ml) white wine
2 tablespoons (35 ml)
  white wine vinegar
1 tablespoon chopped
  parsley or chopped
  mixed herbs

Trim and cook the artichokes as in the following recipe.

Prepare the dressing. Sauté the shallots slowly until tender in 2 tablespoons (35 ml) of the oil; turn into a bowl and leave until cool. Cut the ham and tongue into julienne strips; scald and skin the tomatoes, remove the seeds and cut into shreds. Add seasoning to the shallots, then whisk in the wine, vinegar and the remaining oil.

Pull out the centre leaves from each artichoke and scrape away the choke. Mix the dressing with the salpicon of ham, tongue and tomato; add the herbs. Put a spoonful of the mixture in the centre of each artichoke. Serve cold.

Serves 4–6

Artichauts Vinaigrette Provençale

A dish for a summer lunch party which looks good and tastes good.

As most globe artichoke dishes tend to be rather messy to eat, you might like to have finger bowls or a bowl of water on the table.

6 globe artichokes
4 large ripe tomatoes
3 oz (42 g) large black
  olives

Vinaigrette:
2 tablespoons (35 ml)
  cider vinegar
Salt, pepper from the mill
3–4 tablespoons
  (54–70 ml) oil
1 tablespoon freshly
  chopped parsley
1 dessertspoon chopped
  herbs; savory, basil
  and thyme

Trim the artichokes and plunge them into a large pan of boiling salted water. Boil for thirty-five to forty-five minutes according to size. When a leaf can be pulled out easily the artichokes are done. Drain, refresh and dry thoroughly. Pull out centre leaves and remove choke. Set in individual plates.

Scald, skin and remove tomato seeds and stalk. Cut flesh into shreds, halve olives and shred also. Combine ingredients for vinaigrette and taste for seasoning or additional oil. Add tomatoes and olives. Spoon this mixture into the artichokes and serve slightly chilled.

Serves 6

Artichauts Farçis

4–6 artichokes
4 oz (113 g) white crab
  meat
4 oz (113 g) prawns

Dressing:
½ or 1 small green
  pepper, chopped
Salt, black pepper from
  the mill
2 tablespoons (30 ml)
  white wine vinegar
8 tablespoons (120 ml)
  salad oil
Squeeze of lemon
Caster sugar to taste
2 tablespoons snipped
  chives or spring onion

Serves 4–6

Trim off the points of the leaves of the artichokes with a pair of scissors and trim the stalk from the bottom. Cook the artichokes in boiling salted water until a leaf can be pulled out, about 35–40 minutes. Drain, refresh and leave until cold.

Meanwhile, prepare the dressing. Drop the green pepper into boiling water, cook for one minute, then drain and rinse well with cold water; drain and dry. Mix a large pinch of salt, add twice as much of the ground pepper with the vinegar and whisk in the oil. Sharpen with lemon juice and add a little sugar to taste. Add the green pepper and chives or spring onion to the dressing.

Pull out the centre leaves from each artichoke and scrape away the choke. Mix the flaked crab meat with the prawns and moisten with the dressing. Put a spoonful of the crab mixture in the centre of each artichoke. Serve cold.

Avocats Trianon

A 'starter' for a special lunch or dinner. The best of the smoked salmon trimmings can be used for this. Make sure that the dressing is well sharpened with lemon, and serve with brown bread and butter.

3 ripe avocados
2 oz (56 g) smoked
  salmon
3 oz (84 g) prawns

Dressing:
¼ pint (150 ml) thick
  mayonnaise, using
  lemon juice in place of
  vinegar to sharpen
1 small teaspoon grated
  lemon rind
1–2 tablespoons tomato
  juice to thin
A dash of Tabasco

Prepare dressing in the order given.

Shred smoked salmon. Have ready the prawns, thawed out and patted dry in a paper towel. Split the avocados and remove the stones. Set each half in individual dishes. Combine prawns and salmon and moisten with a little of the dressing. Using a teaspoon scoop the flesh to loosen in each skin, folding in the prawn mixture. Top with the rest of the dressing.

Serves 6

Avocats Sevillienne

Serve this in late summer when English tomatoes are at their best. It is good for lunch or dinner, accompanied by thinly sliced white bread with crusts removed, spread generously with anchovy butter, rolled tightly and baked until brown and crisp.

2 avocados

Dressing:
1 small onion
Juice and grated rind of
    1 orange
Juice of ½ lemon
½ lb (225 g) ripe
    tomatoes
½ clove garlic
½ bay leaf
Salt and pepper
3 tablespoons (50 ml)
    salad oil
½ teaspoon sugar
½ teaspoon tomato purée
1 tablespoon chopped
    fresh basil

Prepare the dressing. Chop the onion finely, pour over the orange and lemon juice, add the orange rind, cover and set aside. Scald and skin two of the tomatoes, and keep on one side. Wipe the rest of the tomatoes, cut out the small core at the stalk end, squeeze gently to remove the seeds and slice roughly. Place the tomatoes and garlic, uncrushed, in a small pan, add bay leaf, seasoning, sugar, oil and tomato purée; bruise the tomatoes with a wooden spoon, cover and simmer gently until the tomatoes are soft and pulpy. Remove the piece of garlic, and then rub through a strainer; allow to cool.

Cut the reserved tomatoes in shreds, removing the core and seeds. Strain the juices from the onion, whisk it into the tomato mixture and adjust the seasoning; add the shredded tomato and basil. Halve the avocados, remove the stones and spoon the tomato mixture into the cavities.

Serves 4

Fresh Salmon Pâté

¾ lb (340 g) salmon
6 oz (170 g) fresh
    haddock fillet
Salt and pepper from the
    mill
2 tablespoons (35 ml)
    dry sherry
4 tablespoons fresh white
    crumbs
1 egg yolk
1 oz (28 g) butter
1 tablespoon (18 ml)
    thick cream
1 spray fresh dill or
    1 bayleaf

Cut half of the raw salmon into fingers, sprinkle with salt, black pepper and the sherry and leave to macerate for one to two hours; turn from time to time.

Remove all skin and bone from the remaining raw fish, both salmon and haddock, and work in a blender or Magimix until smooth. Add the breadcrumbs, egg yolk, melted butter, the sherry marinade and cream; mix well and season to taste.

Cover the bottom of a small terrine with a layer of the mixed fish mixture, cover with a layer of the marinated salmon meat and repeat until all the ingredients are used, finishing with the mixture. Smooth the top and lay the dill or bay leaf on top, cover with foil and lid and set the dish in a roasting tin of warm water. Bake in a gentle oven, 170°C/325°F/Gas Mark 3 for forty minutes.

Remove the lid and when cool, press lightly – a weight of about 2 lb (1 kg) is sufficient – and leave overnight in a cool larder.

Serve cut in fingers with toast and plenty of butter. We think it is best served with a bowl of whipped herb butter. To make this: take 4 oz (113 g) of a blended Continental butter and beat it in a warm basin until soft and light, add one to two tablespoons white wine or dry Vermouth a little at a time. Season with salt and freshly ground black pepper and a squeeze of lemon. Stir in one tablespoon of chopped parsley and dill or chives and a spoonful of cream.

Serves 6

Smoked Salmon Pâté (No. 1)

This is for a special occasion; rich and delicate in flavour. Serve individually or whole for a buffet with a cucumber salad, brown bread and butter or hot brown rolls.

If home made aspic is not available dissolve one rounded teaspoon of gelatine in four to five tablespoons of white wine.

8 oz (226 g) fresh
  haddock
8 oz (226 g) smoked
  salmon pieces
2 tablespoons mayonnaise
¼ pint (150 ml) white
  sauce made with:
  ¾ oz (20 g) butter
  ¾ oz (20 g) flour
  4 tablespoons liquid
    aspic
4 tablespoons (70 ml)
  double cream
Lemon juice and freshly
  ground pepper

Oven poach the fresh haddock in a buttered dish with a squeeze of lemon and cover with a butter wrapper or foil. When cold drain well and pound with the twice-minced smoked salmon until smooth.

If using a Magimix work the cooked white fish and all ingredients except the aspic together until smooth, taking care not to get it oily through over-mixing.

Stir the cool, but still liquid, aspic or the gelatine dissolved in the wine into the fish mixture and add the cream. Season with the lemon juice and pepper.

Turn into six ramekins or a 6-inch soufflé case and leave until set.

Serves 6

Smoked Salmon Pâté (No. 2)

The following recipe is an excellent way to use smoked salmon trimmings. It is rather laborious to make unless you have a Magimix, but the result is very elegant for a special luncheon or dinner party.

¾ lb (339 g) smoked salmon
½ lb (225 g) fresh haddock fillet
4 tablespoons fresh white crumbs
3 egg whites
¼ pint (150 ml) thick cream
Juice ½ lemon
Freshly ground white pepper
A pinch of ground mace

To finish:
¼ lb (113 g) unsalted butter
Tabasco and lemon juice
Sliced cucumber

Remove all the skin from the fresh haddock and any hard pieces from the smoked salmon; mince the two fish together and place in a bowl over ice. Beat the egg whites with a fork until frothy and add to the fish a little at a time; stir in the crumbs. Rub through a wire sieve or work in a blender or better still, in a Magimix, to a fine purée. Beat in the cream a little at a time and when it is all absorbed add the pepper. Stir in the lemon juice very slowly.

Turn into a small buttered loaf tin, cover with foil and cook in a bain-marie in a moderate oven until firm. Allow fifteen to twenty minutes at 180°C/350°F/Gas Mark 4.

When cold press lightly in the same way as the fresh salmon pâté and chill well.

Cream the butter until very soft and smooth and season with a few drops of Tabasco and the juice of a quarter to half a lemon. Put in a forcing bag fitted with a vegetable rose pipe.

Turn the pâté onto a long dish, decorate with the savoury butter and surround with sliced cucumber and fresh dill. The pâté is cut in slices for serving; hand Melba toast and curls of unsalted butter separately.

Serves 6

Asparagus Mousse

Though under the heading of a starter, this mousse makes a delicious main course for a summer lunch or supper dish. The mixture can equally well be turned into small cocottes for individual servings as a first course for lunch or dinner. Double up on the recipe and it is good for a fork lunch when it will give ten to twelve portions.

The aspic over the top does help to preserve the colour and fresh taste. For convenience the commercially

Make Béchamel sauce and allow to cool. Prepare mayonnaise.

Trim asparagus, boil until tender, drain and refresh. Cut off about six to eight of the green tips, split in two if fat and set aside on a paper napkin for decoration. If using canned asparagus, drain off the liquid, tip out the stalks carefully and cut off the same number of tips and set aside.

Put all the tender part of the asparagus through a mouli sieve or liquidize to reduce to a purée. Measure and add sufficient stock to make one pint.

Add four to five tablespoons of the remaining stock to the gelatine and allow to soak.

prepared aspic may be used, though home-made aspic made from a well-flavoured chicken stock is really the best, adding to the delicate flavour of the mousse. But time dictates here and it may be feasible only in the summer months when other dishes calling for aspic are 'on the go'. Make the mousse with fresh asparagus when possible, though the canned green is an excellent substitute. This means that this dish can be on the menu for six to eight months in the year.

Accompany with rolls of thin brown bread and butter well filled with chopped seasoned prawns or small shrimps.

When fresh asparagus is available and the green tender part only is used, keep the harder green and white stalks. Well scrubbed they make excellent stock for an asparagus or green soup.

This mousse is not suitable for freezing.

1 large bundle, 1 lb ($\frac{1}{2}$ kg)
    fresh green asparagus or
    sprue, or 1 × 15 oz can
    Green Giant asparagus
1 pint (600 ml) good chicken
    stock, free from grease

Béchamel sauce :
$\frac{1}{2}$ oz (15 g) butter
$\frac{1}{2}$ oz (14 g) flour
$\frac{1}{4}$ pint (150 ml) milk,
    flavoured with a slice of
    onion and $\frac{1}{4}$ bay leaf
$\frac{1}{4}$ pint (150 ml) mayonnaise
$\frac{3}{4}$ oz (21 g) gelatine
$\frac{1}{4}$ pint (150 ml) whipping or
    double cream
2 egg whites
Salt and pepper
6-inch soufflé case or cocottes

Stir the asparagus purée gradually into the Béchamel and when smooth fold in the mayonnaise. Season well.

Warm gelatine until dissolved and add to the mixture.

Partially whip the cream and fold into the mixture. Whisk the whites until stiff and when the mousse begins to thicken, fold in carefully.

Turn into the soufflé case or cocottes, cover and leave to set in the refrigerator.

Decorate top with the asparagus tips and run a little cool aspic over the top. When set, spoon over a little more aspic. Return to refrigerator to chill slightly before serving.

**Serves 4–6 as a 'starter';
4 for a main course**

Pineapple with Tarragon Cream Dressing

Use for a first course or as a side salad with cold ham or chicken. When possible use fresh fruit. Try it in summer with ripe Victoria plums, halved and stoned.

1 medium sized pineapple
Caster sugar
Paprika pepper

Dressing:
1 large egg
2 rounded tablespoons caster sugar
3 tablespoons (45 ml) tarragon vinegar
Salt and white pepper
¼ pint (150 ml) double cream

First prepare the dressing: break the egg into a bowl and beat it with a fork. Add sugar and, gradually, the vinegar. Stand the bowl in a pan of boiling water. Stir the mixture until it begins to thicken, then draw off the heat and continue to stir. When the mixture has the consistency of thick cream, take the basin out of the pan, stir for a few seconds longer; season lightly and leave till cold. Partially whip cream and fold into the dressing. Set aside.

Cut the peel from the pineapple and cut into slices about half an inch thick. Stamp out the core and halve the slices. Dust lightly with caster sugar.

When ready to serve, arrange two halves on individual plates and coat with a spoonful of the dressing. Dust with paprika.

Serves 6

Tartelettes de Champignons Bonne Femme

This delicious hot first course will make an excellent light luncheon dish – allow two tartlets per person and serve with a mixed green salad.

Short crust pastry:
6 oz (169 g) plain flour
4 oz (113 g) butter
1–2 tablespoons water

Filling:
½ lb (225 g) mushrooms
3 oz (84 g) gammon rasher
2 shallots
½ oz (15 g) butter

Béarnaise sauce:
3 tablespoons white wine vinegar
A slice of onion

Prepare the pastry; chill and then line eight tartlet tins and bake blind. Wipe and trim the mushrooms and slice thickly. Cut the gammon into fine shreds, cover with cold water and blanch; rinse and drain well. Melt the butter, add the shallots finely chopped and after a few seconds put in the bacon. Frizzle gently for two to three minutes, add mushrooms, cover and cook until the juice begins to run, remove the lid, season lightly, increase the heat to drive off any liquid, then draw aside and allow to cool.

Prepare the Béarnaise: reduce the vinegar with flavourings to about a dessertspoonful. Work the egg yolks with a nut of the butter and a pinch of salt in a small basin and strain on the vinegar. Thicken carefully in a bainmarie and add the rest of the butter a small piece at a time, stirring continuously with a wooden spoon or small whisk. When thick adjust the seasoning and add the herbs and meat glaze.

Fill the mushroom mixture into the pastry

A blade of mace
6 peppercorns
2 egg yolks
4 oz (113 g) unsalted
 butter
1 teaspoon fresh tarragon
 and chervil
Meat glaze, a small piece
 the size of a hazelnut or
 ⅛ teaspoon of meat
 extract

cases. Top each with a spoonful of Béarnaise.
Five minutes before serving slide the tartlets
into a moderately hot oven, 190°C/375°F/
Gas Mark 5. Serve at once.

These tartlets freeze well and should be
packed after the Béarnaise sauce has been
spooned on top of the mushrooms. Allow to
thaw at room temperature while preparing the
salad and setting the table and heat at 200°C/
400°F/Gas Mark 6 for ten minutes.

Serves 4

Salade d'Avocats et Poires

A particularly delicious
and refreshing salad, well
suited to precede a roast
or grill for lunch or
dinner.

It is essential that the
pears are just 'à point' so
choose August or early
September when
Williams are at their best
or late autumn for
Comice. If Comice pears
are really large, one will
be enough if each
quarter is halved again.

2 ripe avocado pears
2–3 ripe William or
 2 Comice pears

Dressing :
1 large green pepper,
 seeded and chopped to
 give 2 tablespoons
2 tablespoons spring
 onion, chopped
2 tablespoons freshly
 chopped parsley
1½–2 tablespoons
 (20–30 ml) white wine
 or cider vinegar
Salt, good pinch of sugar,
 and pepper from the
 mill
Lemon juice to taste

Prepare dressing: blanch pepper and spring
onion for one minute. Drain and refresh.

Mix all the ingredients in the order given,
and add lemon juice to taste. Set aside.

Halve the avocados, remove the stone and
cut again into quarters, removing the peel.
Peel and quarter the dessert pears and cut
away the core. Place a quarter of each kind
of pear in an individual serving dish and
spoon over one to two tablespoons (15–30 ml)
of the dressing. Chill slightly before serving.

Serves 8

Flageolet, Tunny and Tomato Salad

This salad makes a good main course for a summer lunch. Serve with hot French bread.

1 can (14 oz/390 g) green flageolet beans
½ lb (226 g) ripe tomatoes
1 can (7 oz/198 g) tunny fish
Salad oil
Salt, and pepper from the mill
Lemon juice or white wine vinegar
1 tablespoon chopped fresh basil or marjoram

Serves 4

Drain the beans thoroughly, dress with three tablespoons (45 ml) oil, salt and pepper and 1 tablespoon (15 ml) lemon juice and leave to marinate while preparing the other ingredients.

Skin the tomatoes, remove the core, cut in thick slices and dust lightly with sugar and salt.

Turn the tunny fish onto a plate, DO NOT DRAIN, but break carefully into large flakes. Prepare 4 fluid oz French dressing using one part lemon or vinegar mixed with salt and freshly ground pepper and three parts of oil.

Mix the beans and fish together and turn into a serving dish; surround with the tomato slices. Whisk the dressing well, add the herbs and spoon over tunny, beans and tomatoes. Chill for an hour before serving.

Mousse aux Fruits de Mer

A quick and simple mousse to make, excellent for those who do not like mayonnaise or if the main course of the meal is rich. The fish can be varied depending on season and availability and firm white or smoked fish can replace some of the shell fish.

½ lb (225 g) flaked white crab meat
½ lb (225 g) fresh prawns or 4 oz (113 g) peeled frozen prawns
½ head celery
½ green pepper
2 level teaspoons gelatine
2 tablespoons (35 ml) light stock

Shell the prawns and if large split in two and mix with the crab or any other chosen fish. Remove the stringy side of the celery with a speedy-peeler, finely chop enough of the celery to fill a tea cup and add it to the fish.

Remove any core or white seeds from the green pepper, dice and blanch in boiling water for two minutes. Drain, refresh with cold water, drain again and dry well on paper towelling.

Soak the gelatine in the stock, add half the wine and dissolve over gentle heat and stir carefully into fish and celery. Add the green pepper and season well. Lightly whip the cream, fold it into the mixture and as it begins to thicken pour into a lightly oiled ring mould or soufflé case and leave to set.

For the mousse set in the ring mould, pick over and wash the watercress for garnish, if set in the soufflé case slice the cucumber, sprinkle lightly with salt and press between two plates for ten to fifteen minutes. Drain and dry well. Grind black pepper over the cucumber, dust with ¼ teaspoon caster sugar

1 wineglass (115 ml)
    white wine
Salt and pepper
Cayenne or Tabasco
¼ pint (150 ml) double
    cream

Garnish:
Watercress or ½ cucumber

and sprinkle with one dessertspoon white wine
and a squeeze of lemon juice.

Turn the mousse out of the ring mould and
fill the centre with watercress or just spoon the
cucumber salad on top of the mousse in the
soufflé case. Serve with brown bread and
butter.

Serves 4

Petites Timables de Fromage

Small cheese and
cucumber mousses. They
are delicious for a warm
spring or summer day.
This recipe is best freshly
prepared – it can be
stored overnight in the
refrigerator but do not
freeze.

1 large cucumber
6 oz (170 g) cream
    (Philadelphia) or curd
    cheese
1 teaspoon onion juice,
    pressed from finely
    grated onion
Salt and white pepper
¼ pint (150 ml) water,
    vegetable or chicken
    stock
½ oz (14 g) gelatine,
    soaked in 3 tablespoons
    (45 ml) cold water
2 tablespoons (30 ml)
    white wine vinegar
1 tablespoon caster sugar
Pinch of ground mace or
    coriander
¼ pint (150 ml) double
    cream, lightly whipped
Approx. ¼ pint (150 ml)
    French dressing

Dice the cucumber very finely, sprinkle with
salt and leave it pressed between two plates for
thirty minutes. Work the cheese with the onion
juice and seasoning. Pour boiling water (or
stock) on the soaked gelatine, stir until it is
dissolved, then add it to the cheese.

Drain the diced cucumber thoroughly and
mix it with the vinegar, sugar and spice.
When the cheese mixture is quite cold, fold
in the cucumber and the cream. Pour into the
prepared moulds and leave to set.

Wash and pick over the watercress. Turn out
the mousses, and garnish with watercress. Add
the chopped herbs to the French dressing and
serve this separately with the brown bread and
butter.

To garnish:
1 bunch watercress
1 tablespoon chopped
    parsley
1 tablespoon snipped
    chives
Brown bread and butter
6–8 dariole moulds,
    lightly oiled.

Serves 6

Cauliflower and Prawn Salad

Make this salad when cauliflowers are at their best and most abundant – in the early summer and autumn. Add a bayleaf to the cooking water.

1 large cauliflower
6 oz (185 g) shelled
  prawns

Mayonnaise :
2 egg yolks
Salt, pepper
8 fluid oz (235 ml) olive
  or salad oil
Wine or cider vinegar
  to taste
1 teaspoon Grey Poupon
  mustard
1 tablespoon (15 ml)
  boiling water or single
  cream

Paprika pepper

Sprig cauliflower, leaving on any tender green leaves. Boil in salted water until just tender, drain and refresh. When quite cold, arrange in a serving dish with the prawns.

Work egg yolks with seasoning; then beat in the oil very gradually at first and then more quickly as the sauce thickens. Sharpen slightly with the vinegar. Thin to a flowing consistency if necessary with the water or cream.

Spoon the sauce over the cauliflower and prawns. Dust well with paprika pepper.

Serves 4

Crab and Water Chestnut Salad

This salad is especially suitable for an autumn or Christmas party.

½ lb (226 g) white crab
  meat
1 can (7 oz/198 g) water
  chestnuts
3 sticks tender celery
4 tablespoons (60 ml)
  French dressing
2 tablespoons (30 ml)
  thick cream
1 tablespoon (15 ml)
  freshly chopped parsley

Drain the water chestnuts and slice finely. Cut the celery into 1½-inch lengths and slice each piece finely along about half the length; soak in ice-cold water for one hour. Drain and dry on kitchen paper.

Prepare the dressing, add the cream and mix into the crab; add the water chestnuts, celery and parsley. Adjust the seasoning and turn into a salad bowl for serving.

Serves 4

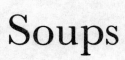

Soups

Potage Crème de Cresson

Choose to make this when the watercress is at its best, dark green and juicy. Swish the bunches well in a bowl of cold water before chopping. It should not be necessary to remove any of the stalks.

If freezing the soup, it is best to add liaison when heating, after it has been thawed.

1 onion, finely chopped
1 oz (30 g) butter
2 bunches watercress, chopped
1 oz (28 g) flour
1¾ pints (1 litre) milk
Salt and pepper

Liaison:
2 egg yolks
2½ fluid oz (70 ml) cream

Melt the butter in a large saucepan, add the onion, cover and cook slowly for one minute. Then add the watercress, cover again and cook gently for five minutes. Draw aside and stir in flour off the heat. Bring milk to boiling point, pour on gradually and season. Simmer gently for fifteen minutes.

Pass through a mouli sieve or work in a blender. Return to a clean pan. Mix the yolks and cream together and add to the soup. Reheat gently, stirring continually, then serve, if wished, with fried croûtons.

Serves 6

Potage Crème de Champignons

½ lb (225 g) mushrooms
1 small onion, finely chopped
1½ oz (45 g) butter
1 oz (30 g) flour
1¾ pints (1 l) strong well flavoured chicken stock
2 egg yolks
¼ pint (150 ml) cream

Serves 6

Wash the mushrooms well but do not peel; chop them roughly and set aside. Melt ½ oz (15 g) of the butter, add the onion, cover and cook very gently for ten to twelve minutes until golden but not brown and add to the raw mushrooms with ¼ pint (150 ml) of the cold stock and work to a fine purée in the liquidizer.

Melt the remaining butter in the pan, blend in the flour and cook lightly until straw coloured. Tip on the stock, stir until boiling, season and simmer for ten minutes; skim if necessary.

Add the mushroom purée, simmer for two to three minutes and add the liaison of egg yolk and cream. Adjust the seasoning and thicken the soup without boiling.

Potage de Tomates à l'Orange

A Cordon Bleu classic that can be made all the year round. For perfection use fresh ripe tomatoes, but when these are not available the Italian canned plum tomato is very good. Remember these are concentrated in flavour so one 14 oz (400 g) can should be enough.

The orange juice and rind should be added at the last, and the soup not allowed to boil afterwards. See that the rind is cut across into short shreds; it can be embarrassing to eat them if they are too long! Like most soups, this freezes well.

2 lb (1 kg) ripe red
    tomatoes
1 onion
1 carrot
1 strip lemon rind
1 bayleaf
4–6 peppercorns
2 pints (1 l) chicken or
    light stock, free from
    grease
1 level teaspoon salt
1½ oz (42 g) butter
1½ oz (42 g) flour
¼ pint (150 ml) single
    cream
Thinly pared rind and
    juice of half an orange

Serves 6–8

Halve the tomatoes and squeeze to remove seeds. Slice onion and carrot thinly. Put into a pan with the tomatoes, lemon rind, bayleaf, peppercorns and stock. Cover and simmer for half an hour until the tomatoes are very soft. Pass all through a mouli sieve.

Rinse out the pan, melt butter in it and stir in the flour. Blend in the tomato liquid and stir until boiling. Simmer for five minutes and season to taste with salt, pepper and sugar. Add cream. Shred orange rind, blanch and add to the soup with the strained juice.

Bisque Aurore

1 oz (28 g) butter
1 medium onion
  (2 oz/56 g)
1 potato (4 oz/113 g)
½ teaspoon paprika
  pepper
½ oz (14 g) flour
1½ pints (900 ml) chicken
  stock
4 oz (113 g) fillet of
  whiting or fresh
  haddock
2 ripe tomatoes
A pinch of ground mace
2 oz (56 g) prawns,
  coarsely chopped
2–3 tablespoons
  (35–53 ml) cream

Melt the butter, add the sliced onion and potatoes and cook slowly until soft but not coloured, draw aside and blend in the paprika, flour and stock. Stir until boiling and simmer gently for ten minutes.

Meanwhile, scald and skin the tomatoes, squeeze to remove the seeds and slice, add to the pan with the ground mace and the skinned fish and continue cooking very gently for ten to fifteen minutes.

Work in a liquidizer or pass through a mouli sieve. Reheat, add the prawns and cream and adjust the seasoning.

Serves 6

Potage St Jacques

4 scallops
1 glass (115 ml) white
  wine or 2 teaspoons
  lemon juice
½ bayleaf
6 peppercorns
1 shallot, sliced
½ pint (300 ml) water
5 leeks
3 small potatoes, 6 oz
  (170 g) in weight
2 oz (60 g) butter
1 pint (600 ml) milk

Liaison:
2 egg yolks
¼ pint (142 ml) single
  cream

Fried croûtons

Serves 4–6

Wash the scallops and place in a pan with wine or lemon juice, shallot and water and poach gently for five to seven minutes. Keep on one side.

Slice the white part of the leeks thinly and cut the green part of two leeks into shreds. Blanch these well, refresh and set aside. Slice potatoes thinly.

Melt the butter in a stewpan, add leeks and potatoes. Cover and simmer gently for six to seven minutes. Pour on the milk and bring to the boil. Simmer for fifteen to twenty minutes. Add the liquid from the scallops and season to taste. Pass through a mouli sieve or work to a purée in the blender. Slice the scallops thinly.

Return to a clean pan, blend the yolks and cream together and add this liaison to the soup by degrees. Stir over gentle heat until thickening creamily, draw aside, add scallops and the blanched green leek.

Turn into a hot tureen or casserole and serve with fried croûtons.

Spicy Tomato Soup

Another Cordon Bleu classic; it was adapted from an early nineteenth-century recipe. This was described as 'a nourishing soup for invalids', and had then more port than spices! It is particularly suitable for a cold winter's night.

1¼ lb (566 g) ripe
   tomatoes, halved and
   squeezed to remove
   seeds
1 medium sized onion,
   sliced
1 oz (28 g) butter
¾ oz (22 g) flour
1 rounded teaspoon
   paprika
A small pinch ground
   mace or a blade of
   mace
1 clove
1½ pint (900 ml) chicken
   or light stock
A bouquet garni
1 level dessertspoon sago
1 glass port

Melt butter, add the onion and cover pan. Soften without colouring then add the flour and spices. Pour on the stock, blend and bring to the boil. Season, add herbs and simmer for twenty to twenty-five minutes. Rub through a strainer and return to the rinsed out pan. Stir in the sago and simmer for ten minutes, stirring occasionally. Adjust seasoning and add the port.

Serves 6

Potage Rognons de Coq

½ lb (225 g) red beans
   (known as Rognons de
   Coq or Dutch Brown
   Beans)
1 carrot
1 onion
2 oz (56 g) butter
Salt and pepper
1 dessertspoon tomato
   purée

Soak the beans for twelve hours, then drain. Melt the butter in a casserole, add the sliced vegetables, the beans, and the seasoning. Toss over the fire for a few moments, then add the tomato purée and herbs. Pour on the stock and simmer until the beans are tender (approximately two hours).

Meantime, skin, depip and shred the tomatoes. When the beans are ready, remove the herbs, add the prepared tomatoes and

Bouquet of herbs
4 large tomatoes
3 pints (1.8 l) light stock,
   vegetable, veal or
   chicken
Grated cheese

simmer gently for seven to ten minutes.

Just before serving, stir in one to two table-spoons of thick cream and serve with grated cheese.

Serves 8

Soupe des Pêcheurs

This is one of those dishes that form a complete and satisfying meal. Ideal for an After Theatre supper.

The quantity given here can easily be increased by the addition of more fish and vegetables. Serve with crisp French bread, and have small bowls of garlic mayonnaise, croûtons, chopped hard-boiled egg and parsley to accompany.

1 medium sized carrot
1 large leek
2–3 sticks celery
2 medium sized potatoes
3 ripe tomatoes, skinned
2–2½ pints (1–1¼ l)
   chicken stock, free
   from grease

Fish:
2–3 kinds of firm white
   fish such as rock
   salmon or eel, bass,
   cod steak in season,
   totalling about 1–1¼ lb
   (453–566 g) in all
Shellfish such as scallops
   or prawns can be
   included
Salad oil

Slice the carrot into thin rounds and cut the leek and celery into pieces. Halve the tomatoes, squeeze to remove seeds and chop.

Put 2 pints (1 l) of the stock into a large pan, season lightly and bring to the boil. Add the carrot, leek and celery. Cover and simmer for six to seven minutes, then slice and add potatoes with the tomatoes. Continue to simmer for a further six to seven minutes.

Meantime, prepare the fish. Skin and cut into square pieces, dry thoroughly. Heat a large frying pan, add three to four large tablespoons of oil. When just smoking, put in the fish and fry briskly for a few minutes until coloured. Lift out with a draining spoon and drain well on paper.

Slip the pieces into the soup and add more stock if necessary, though the soup should be thick with vegetables and fish. Simmer for three to four minutes, adjust the seasoning and serve.

Serves 4–6

Potage Paysanne

A rich looking and tasting soup – one that would make a good lunch on a cold day.

2 onions
2 carrots
1 small head or half a head celery
2 leeks
Quarter of a small head of firm cabbage
1 × 7 oz (198 g) can tomatoes
1 × 7 oz (198 g) can red kidney beans
4 oz (100 g) garlic sausage in one piece
4 oz (100 g) Polish sausage
1 Frankfurter sausage
3–4 pints (1¾–2½ l) good beef or light ham stock
2 tablespoons freshly chopped parsley

Halve the onions and slice across downwards. Slice the other vegetables in thin rounds and put into a large pan with the tomatoes broken up with a spoon. Add stock, season lightly, cover and simmer for one hour. After forty minutes add beans drained from their liquid. Continue to simmer until the hour is up.

Have ready the garlic sausage diced. Blanch the Polish sausage and the Frankfurter, then slice and add all to the soup. Simmer for a further fifteen minutes then add the parsley. Adjust the seasoning and serve.

Serves 4

Potage Crème d'Asperges

This soup can be served iced or hot, and is suitable for freezing. In this case freeze without the liaison and use this to bind the soup once it has been thawed and on re-heating.

This is an ideal soup for a dinner party.

1½ lb (678 g) fresh 'loose' asparagus or 2 cans (15 oz/400 g) Green Giant asparagus

If using fresh asparagus scrape and well wash the stalks. Cut off about a dozen of the tips and set aside. Cut the rest of the asparagus into inch lengths and put into a pan with the stock. Salt lightly and simmer for about twenty to twenty-five minutes until tender.

Pass all through a mouli sieve. Melt the butter in the same pan, add the onion, cover and allow to soften without colouring. Stir in the flour and pour on the liquid. Stir until boiling and simmer for about ten minutes.

Meantime boil the reserved tips in water until tender. Drain and refresh. Draw soup aside, combine yolks and cream for the liaison and add gradually to the soup. Thicken slowly

2 pints (1 l) well
    flavoured chicken stock
1 medium sized onion
    finely chopped
1 good oz (30 g) butter
1 oz (28 g) flour

Liaison:
2 egg yolks
¼ pint (150 ml) cream

without boiling and strain into a bowl to cool. Add the tips and chill in the refrigerator.

If using canned asparagus, drain off liquid and add asparagus to the stock.

Melt the butter, add onion and cook as before. Stir in the flour and pour on the stock. Bring all to the boil, simmer for five to seven minutes, then pass through a mouli sieve or blender. Bind with the liaison or freeze if wished.

Serves 6

Potage de Santé

A delicious soup that can be served hot or cold. In early summer when salads are the order of the day, this soup can be made with an even wider choice of greenery.

Outside leaves of 2 lettuce
1 large handful of spinach,
    sorrel or young nettles,
    well washed
Stalks of 2 bunches
    watercress
Green tops of 1 bunch
    spring onions
1½ oz (42 g) butter
1 pint (600 ml) well
    flavoured chicken
    stock, free from grease
¼ pint (150 ml) creamy
    milk
2 teaspoons arrowroot

To finish:
2–3 tablespoons
    (35–50 ml) whipping
    cream
Fresh garden mint

Shred the lettuce and spinach and chop the watercress stalks and spring onions. Melt the butter, add all 'the greens' and stir over gentle heat for eight to ten minutes, pour on the chicken stock, season and simmer about ten minutes.

Work to a fine purée in a liquidizer or pass through a mouli sieve and mix the arrowroot with the creamy milk. Return the soup to the rinsed pan, reheat and adjust the seasoning; add the slaked arrowroot and stir to boiling point.

Streak in the lightly whipped cream and freshly chopped mint just before serving the soup.

Serves 6–8

Potage Palestine

A delicious vegetable soup, light and delicate in flavour. Like most soups it will freeze well. Serve with croûtons, lightly sprinkled with salt.

1 lb (453 g) good Jerusalem artichokes
2 medium sized onions, about 4 oz (113 g) in all
1 oz (30 g) butter
1 pint (600 ml) water drained from boiled potatoes
1 pint (600 ml) milk
Salt and pepper

To finish:
1 oz (28 g) cornflour
4 tablespoons (70 ml) creamy milk or single cream
¾ oz (20 g) butter

Small fried croûtons

Thinly peel the artichokes, slice. Thinly slice the onions, put into a pan with the butter, cover and cook very gently for five to six minutes. Add artichokes and continue to cook for a further six to seven minutes.

Season very lightly and add the water. Bring to boil and simmer until both vegetables are tender. Pass through a blender. Rinse out the pan, add milk and bring to the boil. Pour half onto the purée and return this to the pan.

Mix the cornflour with the milk or cream and stir into the soup. Stir until boiling, adjust seasoning and simmer for three to four minutes. Draw aside and add the butter in small pieces, stirring well.

Serves 8

Potage Crème Constance

This particular soup was named after Constance Spry and was a favourite at summer parties in the early days at Winkfield.

To be perfection the chicken stock must be strong and well flavoured and the finished soup delicately flavoured with curry.

1 medium sized onion (2–3 oz/56–84 g)
1½ large tablespoons (30 ml) oil

Chop onion. Heat oil in a saucepan, add onion, cover and cook gently for five minutes. Add curry paste and after one to two minutes stir in the flour and pour on the stock. Add bayleaf and lemon rind. Simmer for twenty minutes, then remove bayleaf and lemon rind. Add a little of the liquid to the coconut cream and when dissolved blend into the soup. Season.

Thicken with a little slaked arrowroot, about a dessertspoon to two to three tablespoons (35–53 ml) stock or water. Reboil, cool and pass through a blender. Pour into a bowl, cover and leave until cold.

Lightly whip the cream and set aside. Blend the wine with the curry paste, turn into a small pan and reduce to half quantity. Add the purée

32

1 tablespoon curry paste
1 tablespoon flour
2 pints (1 l) chicken
   stock, free from grease
½ bayleaf
A strip of lemon rind
1 tablespoon (18 ml)
   coconut cream
Arrowroot to thicken

Curry cream:
¼ pint (150 ml) cream
1½ wineglasses (70 ml)
   port or red wine
1 teaspoon curry paste
1 tablespoon apricot
   purée or jam
Squeeze of lemon juice

or jam, mix well and strain. When cold fold by degrees into the whipped cream.

To serve, whisk the soup for a few seconds and pour into bowls. Add a spoonful of cream to each bowl and 'streak' it in with a fork. Serve well chilled.

Serves 6

Potage Crème d'Or

One of the best of cold soups. For perfection use the outside red part of the carrot only, the core can be used for stock.

1 medium sized onion,
   finely chopped
1 lb (453 g) good carrots,
   weighed when peeled
   and sliced
1 oz (30 g) butter
1½ pints (900 ml) chicken
   stock, free from grease
2 heaped teaspoons
   arrowroot
½ pint (300 ml) fresh
   orange juice, strained
7½ fluid oz (220 ml)
   whipping or single
   cream
Salt and pepper
2 teaspoons snipped
   chives

Melt the butter in a saucepan, add onion and the carrots. Cover the pan and cook gently for five to six minutes without colouring. Pour on the stock, season lightly and simmer for twenty to twenty-five minutes until the vegetables are tender.

Pass all through a mouli sieve or blend until very smooth. Return to the pan and reheat. Slake the arrowroot with two tablespoons of cold water, add to the soup and stir until boiling. Pour into a bowl, cover and leave until cold.

Stir in the orange juice. Whip the cream lightly and whisk into the soup.

Serves 6–8

Potage Crème d'Oignon or 'Le Thourin'

The original recipe for this soup comes from the Isle de France. One of the simplest and quickest to make of the onion soups, with a delicate flavour.

2 medium sized onions
1½ oz (42 g) butter
1 oz (28 g) flour
1¾ pints (approx. 1 l) creamy milk
8–12 small rounds, about 1¼ in. (3 cm) in diameter cut from 4–6 thin slices stale bread

Liaison:
2 egg yolks
2 large tablespoons single cream

Peel and halve the onion lengthways. Cut across into thin slices. Melt the butter, put in the onions, cover and cook slowly until completely soft. Draw aside, stir in the flour and add salt and pepper. Bring the milk to the boil and pour on gradually, stirring continually. Return pan to heat and stir until boiling. Simmer gently for ten to fifteen minutes.

Meantime bake bread to a pale golden colour in a slow oven, 130°C/250°F/Gas Mark 2.

Mix yolks and cream together for the liaison. Pour a little of the hot soup onto this, blend and return to the pan. Taste for seasoning.

Put the rounds of bread into the bottom of a soup tureen. Stir soup over slow heat until thickening creamily, then pour into the tureen.

Serves 4–6

Potage Crème d'Avocats

A quickly made soup with a delicate flavour. It is ideal served before a simple dish of grilled cutlets of new season's lamb or small spring chicken roasted or grilled.

2 good sized avocado pears, or 3 small
12½ fluid oz (375 ml) V8 juice
¼ pint (150 ml) whipping cream
½ pint (300 ml) natural yoghurt
1 pint (600 ml) good chicken stock
Salt, white pepper from the mill
A dash of Tabasco or cayenne

Peel the avocados, remove stones and crush the flesh with a fork or potato masher or blend in a liquidizer with the V8 juice until smooth. Lightly whip the cream and stir in the yoghurt.

Remove any trace of fat from the chicken stock with kitchen paper and blend with the avocado mixture.

Stir in the cream and yoghurt, season to taste, cover and chill. Serve in chilled soup bowls.

Serves 4–6

Egg
Dishes

Oeufs en Cocotte Arnold Bennett

An ideal first course for lunch. This is our version of the famous 'Omelette Arnold Bennett', geared to the cook-hostess.

1 lb (453 g) Finnan haddock on the bone or 12 oz (340 g) smoked haddock fillet
7 new laid eggs
¼ pint (142 ml) cream
1 tablespoon each finely grated dry Cheddar and Parmesan cheese

Cover the smoked haddock with cold water, bring slowly to the boil, draw the pan aside and leave for ten minutes. Flake the fish, removing skin and bones. Separate one egg and mix the yolk with four tablespoons of the cream, add to the fish, season with a little white pepper and spoon into six buttered cocottes.

Lightly whip the remaining cream, add the cheese and seasoning. Stiffly whisk the egg white and fold into the cheese mixture.

Break an egg into each cocotte, cover with the cheese mixture and bake for five to six minutes in a hot oven, 200°C/400°F/Gas Mark 6.

Serves 6

Oeufs Meulemeester

The eggs are soft boiled, crushed and heated with cream, prawns, Gruyère cheese and fresh herbs. It makes an excellent first course for a lunch party, *not* inexpensive but well worth it for a special occasion.

6–8 new laid eggs
2–3 oz (56–84 g) butter
7½ fluid oz/⅓ pint (220–300 ml) double cream
6–8 oz (169–225 g) shelled prawns
1 tablespoon (18 ml) Dijon mustard
2 teaspoons chopped tarragon
2 teaspoons chopped parsley
2 oz (56 g) grated Gruyère cheese

Prick eggs on the rounded ends and put carefully into boiling water. When the water reboils, boil for five minutes, then lift into a bowl of cold water. Leave for seven to eight minutes. Crack gently all over with a spoon then peel off the shell. Slip back into luke-warm water and set aside.

Have the prawns well thawed if using frozen ones and pat dry in a paper towel.

Take out the eggs and drain and dry well. Put on a warm plate and cut up roughly. Melt butter in a shallow saucepan, add the eggs and cream, season and stir over gentle heat for two to three minutes.

Add the prawns, mustard and herbs. Continue to stir, using a metal spoon, until the mixture is thickening slightly. Turn into a gratin dish, scatter over the cheese and brown quickly under the grill.

Serves 4–6

Oeufs Farçis Aux Anchois

Almost the best of the cold egg dishes; delicious for a first course for a lunch party or as a supper dish.

The eggs are stuffed with butter and anchovies, then coated with mayonnaise flavoured with fresh herbs.

5 eggs, hard boiled
4 fillets of anchovy
2½ oz (70 g) unsalted butter
1 tablespoon mixed chopped fresh herbs, parsley, marjoram or mint, chives
½–1 bunch watercress

Mayonnaise:
2 egg yolks
Salt and pepper
½ pint (300 ml) salad oil
1 tablespoon (18 ml) wine or cider vinegar

Serves 8

First prepare the mayonnaise. Work yolks with the seasonings, then add the oil very slowly at first and then more quickly as the sauce thickens. When half the oil has been added, sharpen with a little of the vinegar. Continue adding the oil and finish with the rest of the vinegar. Adjust seasoning and bring the sauce to a coating consistency by the addition of a dash of boiling water. Cover and set aside.

Peel the eggs and split in two lengthways. Carefully push out the yolks and slip the whites into a bowl of cold water. Cream the butter and sieve the yolks onto this. Beat until smooth. Chop and crush the anchovy fillets well. Add to the mixture with ground pepper from the mill.

Take whites from the water and drain well on a paper towel. Fill each half with the mixture, smoothing the top with a palette knife dipped in warm water, so that it resembles a whole egg.

Add the herbs to the mayonnaise and spread a little on the bottom of a serving dish. Arrange the eggs on this and coat with the remainder of the mayonnaise. Garnish with a bouquet or two of watercress.

Note: Unless the anchovies are preserved in brine there is no need to soak them in milk to remove excess salt. They are now usually preserved in oil.

Oeufs Florentine

This can be either a first course or a supper dish. Choose spinach when at its best. The combination of the soft eggs, leaf spinach and rich cheese is delicious.

5–6 new laid eggs
2 lb (1 kg) fresh leaf spinach

French poach or soft boil (mollet) the eggs. Slip either into cold water and set aside until wanted.

Wash the spinach thoroughly and cook for five to six minutes in plenty of boiling salted water. Drain well.

Put the butter into the pan and cook to a 'noisette'. Add the spinach, stir and shake up with a fork, adding the nutmeg, salt and pepper. Keep warm in the pan.

Prepare the sauce. Melt the butter, stir in the

1 oz (28 g) butter
A grating of nutmeg
Salt, and pepper from
the mill

Mornay sauce made with:
1 oz (30 g) butter
1 oz (30 g) flour
12 fluid oz (good ½ pint/
370 ml) milk
1½ oz (42 g) Cheddar
cheese
½ teaspoon French
mustard
1 tablespoon (18 ml)
cream

flour off the heat then pour on the milk. Blend, season and stir until boiling. Cook for one minute, draw aside and add 1 oz (28 g) of the cheese gradually. Finish with the mustard and cream.

Reheat the spinach and arrange down the centre of a fire-proof dish.

Lift out the eggs with a draining spoon onto a paper towel and pat dry. Set on top of the spinach. Coat with the sauce. Sprinkle rest of cheese over the top and brown under a pre-heated grill. Serve at once.

Serves 4–5

Soufflé d'Epinards et Champignons

2 × 8 oz (225 g) packets
frozen chopped
spinach *or* 1½ lb (680 g)
fresh spinach, boiled,
drained and sieved
1½ oz (40 g) butter
1 oz (25 g) or 1
tablespoon flour
A pinch of ground mace
or nutmeg
¼ pint (150 ml) milk
2 large tablespoons
(70 ml) cream
3 egg yolks
4 egg whites

To layer:
10 oz (280 g) mushrooms
¾ oz (21 g) butter
Salt and pepper

To finish:
Browned crumbs
Grated cheese

Size No. 1 soufflé case

Place the frozen spinach in a covered pan on a low heat to thaw out completely. Remove lid and increase heat to drive off surplus moisture, adding ½ oz (15 g) of the butter. Then draw off the heat and stir in the rest of the butter. Add flour and seasoning, blend in the milk and cream. Stir until boiling, draw aside and beat in the yolks.

Slice mushrooms and sauté quickly in the butter. Add seasoning. Place half the mushrooms in the prepared soufflé case. Whip the whites stiffly and fold one large tablespoon into the spinach mixture. Then carefully fold in the remainder. Turn half at once onto the mushrooms and then top with the rest of the mushrooms. Finish with the remaining spinach mixture. Scatter the top with crumbs and grated cheese.

Place in a pre-heated oven, 190°C/380°F/ Gas Mark 5 for twenty to twenty-five minutes. Carefully peel off the paper and serve at once.

Serves 4

Oeufs au Cresson

A cold first course. Eggs are poached, then served on chopped watercress dressed with French dressing. A green mayonnaise then coats the eggs. Serve with thin brown bread and butter.

5 new laid eggs
2 bunches good watercress
½ pint (300 ml) thick mayonnaise
2–3 tablespoons (35–57 ml) French dressing
A dash of Tabasco sauce
A few drops lemon juice

French poach the eggs and when firm lift out carefully and slip into a bowl of cold water. Set aside.

Pick over watercress, take half a bunch and boil for five to six minutes in slightly salted water. Drain well and press through a wire strainer. There should be one to two teaspoons of purée. Set aside.

Lift the eggs from the water and drain well on a paper towel.

Chop rest of watercress coarsely, using stalks and leaves. Moisten with the French dressing and add a dash of Tabasco.

Arrange down the centre of a dish, and set the eggs on this. Stir the purée into the mayonnaise, add lemon juice to taste and coat eggs with the mayonnaise.

Serves 6

Oeufs Pochés aux Crevettes

A dish to be conjured up and planned for a special lunch party in summer. Choose it for a main course with, perhaps, a cream of cucumber soup (hot or iced) to precede it.

6 new laid eggs
1¾ pints (875 ml) aspic jelly made with fish stock
6 prawns split in half for decoration
½ bunch watercress

Prawn mousse :

5 oz (140 g) prawns
6 oz (170 g) fillet of whiting or haddock
2 oz (56 g) unsalted butter well creamed
¼ pint (142 ml) Béchamel sauce made with :

French poach eggs until firm. Slip them into cold water until wanted.

Prepare the mousse : allow prawns to thaw out over-night and poach fish in a covered dish. Dry prawns well, mince or pound with the white fish, adding the cold Béchamel by degrees. Add the butter, adjust seasoning and colour with a spot of carmine. Add the cream, set aside.

Prepare the chaudfroid sauce : have ready the cooled Béchamel, add the cream and the aspic in which the gelatine has been dissolved. Strain through a fine strainer into a thin saucepan.

Choose an oval serving dish and spoon the mousse down the centre, smooth and shape with a palette knife. Drain the eggs on a clean cloth, pat dry and lift them carefully onto the mousse.

Set the saucepan of chaudfroid in a bowl of ice-cold water and stir until it thickens creamily, then spoon it over the eggs and leave to set. Coat a second time and leave to set.

Cool some aspic over ice and, as it thickens, spoon a little over each egg. When set garnish

¾ oz (21 g) butter
¾ oz (21 g) flour
¼ pint (142 ml) milk
  infused with 3
  peppercorns, slice of
  onion and small
  piece mace
2 tablespoons (35 ml)
  cream lightly whipped
A drop or two carmine

Chaudfroid sauce:
Béchamel sauce made
  with:
  1 oz (30 g) butter
  1 oz (30 g) flour
  ¾ pint (425 ml) milk
  infused with 6
  peppercorns
  ½ bayleaf, slice of onion
2 tablespoons (35 ml)
  cream
1 teaspoon gelatine
  dissolved in 4 fluid oz
  (100 ml) aspic

each egg with a split prawn and coat again
with aspic. Leave to set. Have ready the
remaining aspic set, chop and use to garnish
the sides of the dish and arrange the watercress
at each end.

Aspic jelly:
1¼ pints (710 ml) well-seasoned fish stock
2 glasses white wine
1½ oz (40 g) gelatine
2 egg whites
A squeeze of lemon juice

Put the fish stock and gelatine into a scalded
pan and dissolve over gentle heat, whip the egg
whites to a froth and add to the pan with the
wine and lemon juice. Whisk over a steady
heat until boiling-point is reached and then
allow to boil to the top of the saucepan
undisturbed; draw aside without disturbing
the crust on top and leave to settle. Boil up
twice more in the same way. Stand for five
minutes and then pour through a scalded cloth.

Serves 6

Oeufs à la Tripe

Cordon Bleu's version of
an old favourite – so
called because the
shredded egg whites and
onions resemble tripe in a
creamy sauce. Use this
dish as a first or main
course.

6–8 eggs, hard boiled
½ lb (¼ kg) onions
1½ oz (42 g) butter

Béchamel sauce:
1½ oz (42 g) butter
1½ oz (42 g) flour
¾ pint (450 ml) milk,
  infused with a bay leaf
6 peppercorns
½ bay leaf
1½ oz (42 g) grated
  cheese

Halve the onions lengthways and slice thinly.
Blanch, drain and return to the pan with the
butter. Cover and cook gently for five to seven
minutes or until tender. Meantime split the
eggs in two, remove yolks and push through
a wire strainer. Slice the whites into strips.

Prepare the sauce. Melt the butter, stir in
the flour and strain on the milk. Blend and
stir until boiling. Season.

Rub a fire-proof dish with butter, layer first
with the egg whites, spoon in a third of the
sauce, then the onions and the egg yolks. Coat
with the remaining two-thirds of the sauce and
sprinkle over the cheese. Brown in a pre-heated
oven, 190°C/375°F/Gas Mark 5.

Serves 4

Oeufs Pochés Perigord

A delicious dish for a celebration lunch party.

6 new laid eggs
¾ pint (450 ml)
   demi-glace sauce
A small half of truffle,
   finely chopped
6 croûtes stale bread,
   2½ in. in diameter,
   fried in butter until
   golden brown

Vegetable Julienne:
2 good carrots
The green part of 1–2
   leeks
2–3 sticks of the white
   part of celery
½ oz (14 g) butter
1 tablespoon (18 ml)
   sherry
1–2 tablespoons
   (18–35 ml) stock

Peel and cut carrots into fine julienne shreds. Do the same with the leek and celery. Melt the butter in a shallow pan, add the vegetables and allow to cook gently for four to five minutes. Add sherry and stock. Cover and simmer gently until tender.

Meantime French poach the eggs and then slip them into luke-warm water until wanted. To serve, heat the croûtes and arrange in individual dishes. Warm eggs by adding a dash of boiling water to the bowl. Then lift them out and dry well. Set each one on a croûte and scatter the julienne on top.

Have ready the demi-glace sauce, well simmered and syrupy in consistency. Baste each egg with a little of the sauce to which has been added a pinch of chopped truffle. Pour round a little of the remaining sauce and serve at once.

Serves 6

Shellfish

Coquilles St Jacques Parisienne

Scallops in a white wine sauce with the small white button mushrooms, 'Champignons de Paris'. A classic and delicious dish which can be either a first or main course.

Serve in the deep shells or in a gratin dish. Most scallop dishes benefit by a 'ruff' of potato purée piped round the edge of the shell or dish before browning in the oven. This helps to contain the sauce, looks attractive and is pleasantly crisp.

For a main course two large scallops should be allowed per person, and one and a half for a first course, i.e. six large scallops for four people.

6 large scallops
1½ glasses (172 ml) dry
   white wine
1 wineglass (115 ml)
   court bouillon or water
A small bouquet garni

Sauce:
1½ (42 g) butter
2 shallots, finely chopped
6 oz (169 g) white
   button mushrooms
1 oz (30 g) flour
4 fluid oz (100 ml)
   double cream

To finish:
Browned crumbs
Melted butter

Potato purée (use about
   1 lb (453 g) potatoes,
   boiled, crushed to a
   purée and beaten until
   creamy with a knob of
   butter and a little milk)

Lay the scallops in a shallow pan, pour over the wine and court-bouillon or water. Add the bouquet, cover and bring slowly to the boil. Simmer very gently for four to five minutes. Turn all into a bowl and remove the bouquet.

Wipe out the pan and prepare the sauce. Melt the butter, add the shallots and after a few seconds the mushrooms. Cover and cook for three to four minutes, shaking the pan occasionally. Then draw aside, stir in the flour and strain on the liquid from the scallops. Blend, season lightly and stir until boiling. Add the cream and simmer while you cut each scallop into two or three pieces. Add to the sauce, which should be of a good coating consistency.

Spoon into the shells or gratin dishes, dust with the crumbs and sprinkle with a little melted butter. Pipe round the potato purée using a rose pipe.

When ready to serve, brown in a pre-heated oven, 190°C/375°F/Gas Mark 5 for ten to twelve minutes.

Note: Though not a classic addition, button onions or Jerusalem artichokes cut into scallop sized pieces and cooked until tender can be added to the sauce with the scallops, especially for a main dish. Scallops are expensive and this is a good way of making them go further.

The court-bouillon mentioned in this recipe for poaching the scallops gives additional flavour, and would only be used if it was a 'left over' from other fish dishes. It keeps well in the refrigerator and should never be poured down the drain after use!

Serves 4

45

Coquilles St Jacques Aurore

This dish is not finished by browning, so keep the scallops and sauce hot in a bain-marie if not dishing immediately.

If for a main course, plain boiled rice can accompany.

8–10 large scallops
1 glass (115 ml) white wine
½ glass (60 ml) water
1 shallot, sliced
½ bay leaf

Sauce Aurore:
1 oz (30 g) butter
1 oz (28 g) flour
¼ pint (150 ml) creamy milk
3½ fluid oz (115 ml) well reduced tomato pulp made with:
   ½ lb (225 g) ripe tomatoes
   1 small clove garlic, crushed
   ½ oz (15 g) butter
Salt, pepper and a pinch of sugar
4 tablespoons (70 ml) cream

Rinse scallops and pat dry with a paper towel and set aside.

Wipe tomatoes, but do not peel. Cut in half and squeeze to remove seeds. Put into a small pan with the garlic and butter. Season, cover and cook gently to a thick pulp. Rub through a strainer and measure.

Lay the scallops in a pan and pour over the wine and water. Add a pinch of salt, the shallot and bay leaf. Poach gently for five to six minutes. Draw aside and leave while preparing sauce.

Melt the butter, stir in the flour off the heat, strain on the liquor from the scallops, blend and add the milk. Stir until boiling, season lightly and add the tomato pulp by degrees. Simmer for three to four minutes, stir in the cream and continue to cook gently until a creamy consistency.

Cut scallops into two or three pieces and add to the sauce. Cover and stand the pan in a bain-marie until ready to dish. Then spoon into the deep shells and serve very hot.

Serves 4–5

Coquilles St Jacques Sauté Bercy

8 large scallops
1 oz (30 g) butter
1 tablespoon finely chopped shallot
2 glasses (230 ml) dry white wine
A squeeze of lemon juice

Sauté the scallops in the butter for two to four minutes, remove from pan, add the shallots and simmer gently until soft and golden. Pour on the wine, add lemon and reduce by about a third. Add the stock, simmer for two to three minutes then draw the pan to one side and thicken with the kneaded butter.

1 wineglass (115 ml) light
  stock
Kneaded butter made
  with ¾ oz (21 g) butter
  and ½ oz (14 g) flour
2 tablespoons (35 ml)
  thick cream
1 dessertspoon chopped
  parsley

Bring to the boil, add the cream, boil for two to three minutes, then draw aside, add the scallops cut in half and the parsley. Simmer a further minute or two. Spoon into the deep shells and serve very hot. The shells may be garnished with a fleuron of puff pastry or piped round with a border of potato purée.

Serves 4

Coquilles St Jacques Hongroise

This makes a good first course for a dinner party or as a main course for lunch. In this case increase the quantity of scallops to two per head. Scallops are at their best in March or November.

6 large scallops
A squeeze of lemon juice
5 tablespoons (88 ml)
  water
A slice of onion
6 peppercorns
½ bayleaf

Sauce:
2 oz (56 g) firm button
  mushrooms
1½ oz (45 g) butter
Scant 1 oz (28 g) flour
1 heaped teaspoon
  paprika
8 fluid oz milk
1 cap canned pimento
2 tablespoons (35 ml)
  cream
Potato purée
1 tablespoon brown
  crumbs
A little melted butter

Poach the scallops for five to six minutes with the water, lemon and flavourings. Turn into a bowl.

Trim and wash the mushrooms, slice finely and place in a pan with half the butter; cover and simmer for two minutes. Remove the pan from the heat, drop in the remaining butter and when melted stir in the flour, paprika and milk. Blend until smooth, return to the fire and stir until boiling. Strain on the liquid from the scallops, reduce for a minute or two, then add the pimento, finely sliced, and the cream. Fold in scallops cut into two or three pieces.

Spoon the mixture back into the shells and pipe round the potato purée. Sprinkle with the crumbs and melted butter. Brown in a quick oven for seven to ten minutes.

Serves 6

Coquilles St Jacques Mornay

Scallops on a mushroom duxelles, coated with rich cheese sauce and finished 'au gratin'. Serve either as a first or main course.

6–8 large scallops
1 wineglass (115 ml) water
½ bayleaf
4–6 peppercorns

Duxelles:
8–12 oz (225–339 g) flat mushrooms
1 small onion, finely chopped
1 oz (28 g) butter
1 rounded tablespoon chopped fresh herbs – parsley, thyme or marjoram

Sauce:
1 oz (30 g) butter
1 oz (28 g) flour
½ pint (300 ml) creamy milk
4 tablespoons (70 ml) cream
2 oz (56 g) dry grated Cheshire or Cheddar cheese
Salt and pepper
½ teaspoon French mustard

To finish:
Potato purée, using about 1 lb (453 g) potatoes weighed when peeled
Milk and butter

Serves 4–6

First prepare the duxelles. Wash mushrooms, do not peel but squeeze lightly to dry. Chop finely.

Melt butter in a shallow saucepan or frying pan, add onion and after one or two minutes put in the mushrooms. Cover, cook gently for two to three minutes until the juice runs. Add seasoning and herbs and continue to cook more quickly uncovered, stirring frequently, until a moist but firm purée. Draw aside.

Rinse the scallops and pat dry with a paper towel. Lay in a shallow pan, pour over the water, add the bayleaf and peppercorns. Cover and poach gently for four to five minutes. Strain off the liquid. Slice each scallop into two or three horizontally. Turn the duxelles into the bottom of deep shells or a gratin dish. Arrange the slices of scallop on the top.

Prepare the sauce: make a roux of the butter and flour, blend in the milk and stir until boiling. Add cream, reboil and draw aside. Stir in three-quarters of the cheese by degrees and add seasonings. Coat over the sauce, sprinkle with rest of cheese and pipe round the shells or dish with the prepared potato purée. Brown for seven to ten minutes in a hot oven, 190°C/375°F/Gas Mark 5.

Moules Marinière

A classic recipe, the success of which depends entirely on the quality of the mussels and scrupulous cleaning before cooking: scrubbing of the mussels is essential, as is the scraping away of any weed from the sides to remove sand or grit. After cooking, when the top shell is removed, the beard, a 'rubber ring' which encircles the mussel, may be pulled away, otherwise this can be done by the eater with a fork.

They should be served on the half shell, in soup plates, with the liquor spooned over them. Eat with a fork (or fingers!) and provide a spoon for the sauce or better still, use the shell as a scoop. When serving mussels in this way, have individual finger bowls or a bowl of warm water on the table, and, of course, napkins.

2 quarts of good mussels
2 shallots finely chopped
1 glass (115 ml) dry
    white wine
1 wine glass (115 ml) water
1 large bouquet garni
    tied to half a stick of
    celery
1 oz (30 g) butter
1 oz (28 g) flour worked
    together for kneaded
    butter
Pepper from the mill
1 rounded tablespoon
    freshly chopped parsley

Well wash and scrub mussels in two or three waters, lifting them from one bowl to another, to avoid any grit. Discard any that are half open. When thoroughly clean, lift into a roomy saucepan, add wine, water and herbs. Cover and bring slowly to the boil. Shake the pan well during this process to ensure the mussels can come in contact with the hot liquid. When boiling cook for one to two minutes by which time the mussels should be opened.

Draw aside and tip the liquid into a bowl. Strain this through a piece of muslin into a clean saucepan. Add the kneaded butter piece by piece and when dissolved, stir until boiling. Add pepper to taste and simmer to the consistency of thin cream. Add parsley.

Remove top shell of the mussel and lay in a deep dish or tureen. Pour over the sauce, then serve at once.

Serves 4

49

Scampi are popular nowadays, if expensive, and people want to know ways of cooking them other than plain fried. Scampi in Britain are usually sold frozen and are shelled Dublin Bay prawns. They can be bought in varying sizes.

Here are two of the School's favourite recipes.

Scampi Provençale

1 lb (453 g) scampi
Seasoned flour
2 oz (56 g) butter
Plainly boiled rice to
    accompany

Provençale sauce:
2 tablespoons finely
    chopped shallots
1½ glasses (172 ml) white
    wine
¾ oz (21 g) butter
3 oz (84 g) button
    mushrooms, sliced
¾ oz (21 g) flour
1 large clove garlic,
    crushed
¾ pint (450 ml) jellied
    chicken stock
1 dessertspoon tomato
    purée
Salt, and freshly ground
    pepper from the mill
2 ripe tomatoes, peeled,
    squeezed to remove
    seeds, then chopped
1 dessertspoon chopped
    herbs, parsley, thyme
    and basil

Serves 4

First make the sauce. Pour the wine into a saucepan, add the shallots. Boil gently until reduced by a third. Tip into a bowl. Melt the butter in the pan, add the mushrooms and sauté briskly until just coloured. Draw aside and stir in the flour. Add garlic, stock and purée; blend, season and stir until boiling. Simmer for ten to fifteen minutes. Add tomatoes, reduced wine and herbs, continue to simmer for a further six minutes. Adjust seasoning and draw aside.

If not using the sauce at once, pour off and reserve.

When ready to cook, have the scampi thoroughly thawed, then pat dry with a paper towel. Roll quickly in the seasoned flour. Heat a frying pan, drop in the butter and when foaming put in the scampi. Fry briskly, turning them frequently. After four to five minutes, lift out and put into an oven-proof dish.

Bring the sauce to the boil, reduce a little if necessary, then spoon over the scampi. Slip the dish into a hot oven for three to five minutes, then serve at once with the rice.

Scampi Gourmets

This recipe is very similar to Sole Gustav but the amount of asparagus, mushrooms etc., has been increased. Also the scampi are dished on a light purée of potato which goes well with the other ingredients. When asparagus is out of season, use frozen.

1 lb (453 g) scampi
1 oz (30 g) butter, melted
Salt, pepper and a few drops Tabasco sauce
¾ lb–1 lb (339–453 g) peeled potatoes

Garnish:

½ to 1 small bundle or ½–¾ lb (225–339 g) loose asparagus
3 large ripe tomatoes, blanched, skinned, squeezed to remove seeds
4 oz (113 g) button mushrooms, sliced
1 oz (28 g) butter

Sauce Vin Blanc (Butter sauce)

2 teaspoons shallot, finely chopped
1 large wine glass (115–170 ml) white wine
2 egg yolks
1½ oz (42 g) butter

Velouté sauce:

¾ oz (21 g) butter
¾ oz (21 g) flour
½ pint (300 ml) chicken stock
4 tablespoons (70 ml) cream
A squeeze of lemon juice

Prepare butter sauce: simmer shallot in the wine until reduced by half. Work yolks well together with a nut of the butter. Pour on wine, stand bowl in a bain-marie, thicken over heat, stirring well and adding the rest of butter by degrees. Remove from heat when really thick, cover and set aside.

Trim asparagus and cut off tips about two inches long. Tie in bundles and boil in salted water until just tender. Drain and lay on a warm plate. Chop the tomatoes coarsely, cook for one minute in half the butter, turn onto the same plate. Heat the rest of the butter in the pan and sauté the mushrooms for three to four minutes. Set aside also.

Prepare velouté sauce: melt butter, stir in flour, cook for a few seconds, add stock and blend. Stir until boiling, season, add cream and continue to simmer for two to three minutes. Draw aside, stir in butter sauce by degrees and finish with a squeeze of lemon. Cover pan and keep warm in a bain-marie.

Have the scampi well thawed. Pat dry with a paper towel, turn into an oven-proof dish, add butter and seasonings, cover and poach in the oven, 180°C/350°F/Gas Mark 4 for seven to eight minutes.

Meantime, boil the potatoes and when tender drain and crush well. Beat to a purée with a knob of butter and a very little milk. Season. Lay down the centre of a serving dish, lift the scampi onto this with a fish slice. Scatter over the garnish, reheat the sauce carefully and spoon over the dish. Glaze under a hot grill, then slide the dish into a warm oven for about five minutes until ready to serve.

Serves 4

51

Lobster Thermidor

A classic dish and one to choose for a celebration. Of all the hot lobster dishes this is quite the best one for the cook-hostess to tackle, and like most, must be done with a live lobster otherwise it becomes a 'rechauffé', and much of the delicious flavour is lost.

2 small live lobsters, weighing ¾–1 lb (339–453 g) each; this allows a half lobster per person
2 tablespoons (35 ml) oil
1 oz (30 g) butter
1½ oz (42 g) freshly grated Parmesan or dry Cheddar cheese
Browned crumbs

Sauce:
2 shallots finely chopped
1 glass (115 ml) dry white wine
½ pint (300 ml) Béchamel sauce made with:
　7½ fluid oz (225 ml) creamy milk
　¾ oz (21 g) butter
　¾ oz (21 g) flour
4 tablespoons (70 ml) double cream
1 teaspoon chopped fresh French tarragon
½ teaspoon French mustard
Salt and pepper

Serves 4

Dip lobsters in cold water to rinse off any weed etc., then lay flat on a chopping board. Insert the point of a sharp knife in the cross mark on the head down to the board. Carry knife on down through the tail, then turn lobster round and cut through.

Heat the oil in a large sauté pan or frying pan with a lid, add butter and put in lobsters, cut side downwards. Cover pan and sauté gently for fifteen to twenty minutes or until they are red.

Meantime make the sauce: cook shallots in the wine until reduced by a third, stir in the prepared Béchamel, cream and tarragon. When smooth, reboil and simmer for four to five minutes.

Take up lobsters, strain the juice into the sauce, reboil. When it has attained a coating consistency draw aside and stir in 1 oz (28 g) of the cheese and the seasonings.

Crack claws and remove the meat and any creamy parts from the head and lift out the tail meat. Set the half shells on a baking tray, wedging them level with a slice of potato or the small feeler claws pushed together to form a small circle.

Add one to two tablespoons of the sauce to the head and claw meat and fill into the head shells. Put a little sauce into the tail shells and lay the tail meat, cut into thick slices and rounded side up, on the top.

Reheat the remaining sauce, add a spoonful of milk or cream if necessary and coat over the lobster halves. Sprinkle with the crumbs and rest of cheese. When ready to serve brown in a quick oven, 200°C/400°F/Gas Mark 6 for seven to ten minutes. Serve on a folded napkin garnished with watercress.

Crab Mousse

This recipe is still the best of the crab mousses and the success is due to the use of both the white and dark meat which gives richness and flavour.

This mousse is ideal for the cook-hostess for a buffet as it is quick to make. Use the packs of frozen crab containing half dark and half white meat, as they are the most economical. Serve with appropriate salads.

1-lb (453-g) pack frozen crab meat, half dark, half white
1 oz (30 g) butter
1 oz (28 g) flour
½ pint (300 ml) light chicken stock
4 tablespoons (70 ml) dry white wine
¾ oz (21 g) gelatine
½ pint (300 l) mayonnaise
¼ pint (150 ml) cream
Salt, pepper, a few drops of Tabasco sauce

To garnish:
1 hard boiled egg
Freshly chopped parsley

Optional: 2–3 tablespoons extra mayonnaise
7-inch cake tin or soufflé case, lightly oiled

Serves 6–8

Thaw out the crab meat, overnight, in the fridge. Then pat white meat dry with a paper towel. Make a sauce in the usual way with the butter, flour and stock. When boiling turn into a bowl to cool.

Add gelatine to the wine, allow to swell for a few minutes, then dissolve over a gentle heat. Draw aside.

Put the dark meat into a mixing bowl, work in the cool sauce and add the mayonnaise. Stir in the dissolved gelatine with the white crab meat. Partially whip the cream and fold into the mixture. Turn into the prepared tin or case and leave to set.

Turn out and mask top and sides, if wished, with the extra mayonnaise.

Remove yolk from the white. Wash and dry the white, then shred finely and mix with about a tablespoon of the parsley. Put yolk into a bowl strainer and press the 'mimosa' through onto the centre of the mousse. Spread out a little, then cover the edge with the egg white and parsley.

Crabe au Gratin

This makes an excellent light luncheon dish; serve it with hot rolls and a mixed green salad.

1 large crab, dressed or
   1 lb (453 g) white crab
   meat
3 oz (84 g) blanched
   almonds
1 small head celery
1½ oz (42 g) butter
1½ oz (42 g) flour
¾ pint (450 ml) milk
Pinch of ground mace

Topping:
3 tablespoons fresh
   white breadcrumbs
1 oz (28 g) butter
3 tablespoons grated
   Lancashire cheese

Split and shred the almonds and toast in the oven until golden brown; slice the celery finely and mix both with the crab meat. Make a sauce with the butter, flour and milk, season well and add to the crab mixture with the mace. Turn into a buttered gratin dish.

Melt the butter for the topping and mix it into the crumbs and cheese with a fork; scatter this over the top of the crab and bake in a moderate oven, 180°C/350°F/Gas Mark 4 for about twenty to thirty minutes until brown and crisp.

Serves 6

Pilaff aux Moules

A good dish for a lunch party as the guests do not have to cope with the shells. Some fishmongers sell mussels, in season, cooked and shelled but not preserved in brine or vinegar. Otherwise buy in the shell and cook as directed here.

2 quarts large mussels
   or approx. 1 pint
   shelled cooked mussels
¾ lb (339 g) good
   tomatoes

Pilaff:
1 medium sized onion,
   thinly sliced

If using mussels in the shell, prepare and cook as for Moules Marinière. Strain through a piece of muslin, measure and make up to 1 pint (600 ml) with chicken stock. Shell mussels completely and remove beards.

Scald and peel tomatoes, quarter, flick out seeds and cut away the small piece of stalk. Set both mussels and tomatoes aside.

Prepare pilaff: melt half the butter, add the onion and celery and cook for about two to three minutes until the vegetables are soft but not coloured. Add rice and stir over heat for a further two to three minutes. Pour on the stock and saffron. Bring to the boil, cover the pan and put in a moderate oven, 180°C/350°F/Gas Mark 4 for about twenty to thirty minutes until the rice is tender.

Fork the mussels and tomatoes carefully into the rice with plenty of black pepper, dot the remaining butter on the top and if the rice is dry

54

$\frac{1}{2}$ or 1 small head celery
2 oz (60 g) butter
6 oz (170 g) long grained
  rice
1 clove garlic
About 1 pint (600 ml)
  mussel and/or chicken
  stock
1 large pinch saffron,
  soaked in 2 tablespoons
  (35 ml) hot water

Dry grated cheese (for
  preference freshly
  grated Parmesan)

add another tablespoon or so of the stock. Leave in a warm place for five to seven minutes. Turn into a hot serving dish and serve with a bowl of grated cheese.

Serves 4

Fish

Filets de Barbue aux Concombres

The good firm flesh of brill needs little to enhance it; the simple sauce in this recipe and the delicate flavour of the garnish shows off this excellent fish to perfection.

4 or 6 fillets brill, weight about 2 lb (906 g)
1½ oz (42 g) butter
¼ pint (150 ml) water
¼ lemon
1 large cucumber or 3–4 small garden ones
¾ oz (21 g) flour
¼ pint (150 ml) milk
1 teaspoon chopped dill or parsley
1 tablespoon grated cheese

Skin the brill, fold the fillets and lay in a buttered dish. Season, pour over them the water acidulated with lemon juice and grate over a little lemon rind. Cover with greaseproof paper and poach in a moderate oven 180°C/350°F/Gas Mark 4, for fifteen to twenty minutes.

Peel and cut the cucumber in four lengthways and divide in 1½-inch lengths. Melt a good ½ oz (15 g) of the butter in a stewpan, add the cucumber and seasoning, cover and simmer until barely tender. Adjust the seasoning and add the dill.

Melt the rest of the butter in a saucepan, add the flour off the fire and strain on the liquor from the fish. Blend until smooth, thicken over the heat, add the milk and stir until boiling then reduce rapidly to the consistency of cream. Adjust the seasoning. Dish the fish, coat over the sauce, sprinkle with cheese, glaze under the grill and garnish with the cucumber.

Serves 4

Darnes de Cabillaud Bretonne

The large firm flakes of a cod steak are perfectly complemented by the subtle-flavoured cider sauce and tender strips of root vegetables. Serve for lunch or supper.

4 cod steaks
½ pint (300 ml) dry cider
A squeeze of lemon juice
1 bayleaf
2 oz (56 g) each carrot, onion and celery
1¾ oz (50 g) butter
2 shallots
¾ oz (21 g) flour
1 teaspoon chopped parsley

Wash and dry the fish, place in a fire-proof dish and moisten with four tablespoons each of cider and water, add seasoning, lemon juice and bayleaf and poach in a moderate oven for about twenty minutes.

Cut vegetables into julienne strips (the size of a matchstick) and cook in a good ½ oz (15 g) of the butter in a tightly covered small shallow saucepan, until tender (about fifteen minutes). A butter wrapper pressed down on the vegetables, as well as a tightly fitting lid, will help to prevent the vegetables browning.

Melt ¼ oz (7 g) of the butter in a saucepan, add the shallot finely chopped, cover and cook until soft but not coloured. Pour the remaining cider onto the shallot and boil rapidly until reduced to half quantity; strain on the liquor from the fish.

Work the remaining 1 oz (28 g) of butter to a

paste with the flour, whisk a small piece at a time into the liquid and when absorbed stir until boiling. Add the julienne of vegetables and parsley and adjust the seasoning.

Remove the skin and bone from the fish steaks, wipe the dish with paper towelling, spoon over the sauce and serve.

Serves 4

Cabillaud à l'Indienne

An excellent lunch or supper dish; serve it with plenty of plainly boiled rice.

2 lb (906 g) cod on the bone, preferably a tail piece
2 medium onions
2 tablespoons oil
1 tablespoon curry powder
1 tablespoon flour
½ pint (300 ml) light stock
½ oz (15 g) almonds, blanched and shredded or 1 tablespoon coconut cream
1 tablespoon mango chutney
A squeeze of lemon juice
½ lb (225 g) tomatoes
Seasoned flour, about 2 oz (56 g)
Oil for frying

Garnish:
2 large onions, cut in rings
2½ fluid oz (70 ml) milk

Serves 6

Bone and skin the fish and cut in thick fillets, about twelve pieces in all. Heat the oil in a saucepan, add the onions finely chopped and fry gently until golden but not brown, add the curry powder and after two minutes the flour. Continue to fry for two to three minutes then moisten with the stock and stir until boiling. Simmer uncovered for fifteen to twenty minutes.

Soak the almonds or melt the coconut cream in four tablespoons boiling water, add to the sauce and continue simmering a further fifteen minutes. Peel and quarter the tomatoes and remove the seeds. Stir the chutney into the sauce and add salt, pepper and a little sugar to taste. Add the tomatoes, cover and set aside.

Soak the onion rings in milk for about ten minutes, then drain and roll in the seasoned flour and fry until brown and crisp in very hot oil and drain on kitchen paper.

Roll the fish in seasoned flour and shallow fry quickly in hot oil. When brown, drain and pile up in a hot serving dish. Keep warm uncovered.

Now boil up the sauce and spoon over just enough to coat the fish and pour the rest into a sauce boat. Garnish the dish with the onion rings.

Coley Florentine

The combination of spinach and cheese sauce earns any fish or egg dish the title 'Florentine' and these two flavours go particularly well with this overlooked and frequently despised fish. The grey flesh whitens on cooking and few can resist its appeal if served in a fire-proof dish of generous proportion to allow for a border of potato purée.

Try a little nutmeg in the potato and make sure the whole dish is covered with grated cheese before baking. It should come to table golden brown and bubbling – perfect for family lunch or supper.

1½ lb (678 g) coley fillet
1 lb (453 g) fresh
    spinach or 12 oz (339 g)
    frozen leaf spinach
½ oz (14 g) butter

Mornay sauce made with:
¾ oz (35 g) butter
¾ oz (35 g) flour
½ pint (300 ml) milk
2 oz (56 g) grated
    Cheddar cheese

1 lb (453 g) floury old
    potatoes
½ oz (14 g) butter
About ¼ pint (150 ml)
    boiling milk
A 'grate' of nutmeg

Serves 4

Wash and skin the fish and cut into neat portions and place in a buttered fire-proof dish. Season with salt and sprinkle over two tablespoons of milk; cover with a butter wrapper and poach in a moderate oven for about fifteen minutes. Prepare the Mornay sauce reserving one tablespoonful of the cheese for the top of the dish.

Meantime cook the potatoes until tender, drain and dry well. Crush with a potato masher until perfectly smooth with the butter or pass through a mouli sieve. Push to the bottom of the saucepan, cover with the boiling milk and put the lid on the pan. Leave at the back of the stove.

If using frozen spinach, open the packet and leave to thaw while the potatoes are cooking, then drain away any liquid and heat in the ½ oz butter until dry.

Cook fresh spinach for about five to eight minutes, drain thoroughly and beat in the ½ oz butter until all the water has been driven off – the steam should stop rising and the spinach start to stick at the bottom of the pan. Place the spinach in a fire-proof dish, drain each piece of fish on a fish slice and arrange on top. Coat the fish and spinach with the Mornay sauce.

Beat up the potatoes until light and fluffy, season carefully with the nutmeg and add extra salt and pepper if necessary. Place in a large forcing bag fitted with a vegetable rose nozzle and pipe them in a border around the dish.

Dust with the reserved cheese and bake in a hot oven until brown, 200°C/400°F/Gas Mark 6 – allow seven to eight minutes if everything is freshly cooked but twenty to thirty minutes at 180°C/350°F/Gas Mark 4 if prepared ahead of time.

Filets de Barbue Juliette

A perfect choice for a main course at a lunch or dinner party as the dish is really complete in itself. Serve it with a purée of potatoes beaten with hot milk until light and white as foam or, in season, small new potatoes tossed in butter and parsley. Large fillets of plaice can be used instead of brill for this dish – cooking time ten to fifteen minutes.

4 large fillets brill
  (2¼ lb/1 kg)
6 oz (170 g) button
  mushrooms
¼ pint (150 ml) white
  wine
A squeeze of lemon juice
2 aubergines
Butter or good oil for
  frying

Béchamel sauce made with:
½ pint (300 ml) milk
  infused with 6
  peppercorns, a small
  piece mace and a
  bayleaf
Scant 1½ oz (40 g) butter
1¼ oz (35 g) flour
1 shallot or pickling
onion
2–3 tablespoons cream

Garnish:
4 tomatoes
1 tablespoon chopped
  parsley

Serves 4

Skin the fillets, cut in half, wash and dry well and lay in a buttered fire-proof dish. Slice the mushrooms finely, scatter them over the fish, season with salt and a squeeze of lemon and pour over the wine. Cover with a thickly buttered paper and set aside.

Peel and slice the aubergines, score lightly, sprinkle with salt and leave pressed between two plates for 30 minutes. Scald and skin the tomatoes, cut in halves and season with salt, pepper and sugar.

Cook the fish for fifteen to twenty minutes in a moderate oven. Prepare the Béchamel sauce.

Rinse and dry the aubergines and fry in hot butter or oil until golden brown and tender; keep warm. Fry the tomatoes in the same pan.

Drain the liquid from the fish into a small pan, add the finely chopped shallot, reduce to about four tablespoonsful (70 ml) and add to the Béchamel sauce. Stir the sauce until boiling, add the cream and simmer gently for two to three minutes.

Arrange the aubergines down the centre of the serving dish, set the fillets on top and spoon over the sauce. Garnish with tomatoes, rounded side up, and dust with the chopped parsley.

Filets de Cabillaud Cubat

Another fish dish that will stand on its own as a main course for a luncheon or dinner party. It can be prepared early in the day if the instructions in the footnote are followed. The combination of two sauces makes the choice of accompanying vegetables easier: try French or runner beans, seakale spinach, or mange-tout peas – all delicious.

2¼ lb (1 kg) steak of cod
¼ lemon
8 oz (225 g) mushrooms
½ oz (15 g) butter
1 dessertspoon chopped
  mixed herbs

Béchamel sauce made with:
A good oz (30 g) butter
1 oz (28 g) flour
¼ pint milk infused with
  a slice of onion and
  6 peppercorns
A pinch of ground mace

Mornay sauce:
¾ oz (35 g) butter
¾ oz (35 g) flour
½ pint (300 ml) milk
2 oz (56 g) grated cheese
  (Farmhouse Cheddar is
  excellent but for a
  special party ½ Gruyère
  and ½ Parmesan gives
  perfection)

Garnish:
6–8 slices of a French roll
  fried in butter

Serves 6

Cut the fish from the bone, skin and remove any fin bones and divide each piece into four thick cutlets; place in a well buttered dish, season with salt and freshly ground white pepper and sprinkle with lemon juice.

Wash and finely chop the mushrooms without peeling and sauté them in the butter until the purée leaves the sides of the pan; add seasoning and herbs and tip into a small bowl.

Prepare the Béchamel sauce in the usual way using the same saucepan, season with the mace and when complete add the prepared mushroom duxelles and set aside.

Cover the fish with thickly buttered paper and cook in a moderate oven 180°C/350°F/Gas Mark 4 for fifteen minutes.

Meantime prepare the Mornay sauce. Melt the butter, add the flour, blend in the milk and stir continually until boiling; cook for one minute then draw aside and beat in the cheese a little at a time. Reserve about one dessertspoonful of cheese for the top of the dish. Season the sauce with salt, pepper and mustard.

Reheat the mushroom purée, spread down the centre of a serving dish and arrange the fish on top. Coat the fish with the Mornay sauce, sprinkle with the reserved cheese and glaze under the grill. Garnish with the croûtes, cut ¼-inch thick and fried golden brown in hot butter.

Note: If you are preparing the dish early in the day do not reheat the mushroom purée but spoon it carefully into the buttered fire-proof serving dish and arrange the fish on top. Mix the reserved spoonful of cheese with half the amount of browned breadcrumbs. Coat the fish with the Mornay sauce and scatter the cheese and crumbs over the top. Leave to cool.

Fry the croûtes for garnish to a pale golden brown and leave on a baking sheet ready for re-heating.

Set the oven at 180°C/350°F/Gas Mark 4, thirty-five minutes before you expect to eat. This allows fifteen minutes for the oven to reach cooking temperature and twenty minutes for the fish to heat through and brown the top. Allow ten minutes for eating the first course and during this time the croûtes of bread should be slipped into the oven and the heat reduced.

Croquettes de Poisson à la Crème

An elegant first course for a special dinner party and suitable for a main course at a luncheon. The charm of these croquettes lies in the fact they contain no potato and the chef's old trick of adding the small amount of gelatine to the mixture during preparation makes them relatively easy to handle. It is not a recipe to tackle if you are short of time!

1 lb (453 g) fresh
  haddock or whiting
  fillet
1 level teaspoon gelatine
1 tablespoon (18 ml)
  water
½ pint (300 ml) milk
1 slice onion
½ bayleaf
Small piece mace
A good 2 oz (60 g)
  butter
2 oz (56 g) flour
1 egg

For coating and frying :
3 tablespoons seasoned
  flour
1 egg
1 tablespoon (18 ml)
  salad oil
Dried white crumbs
Deep fat

Serves 4

Cook and flake the fish and soak the gelatine in the water. Heat the milk with the flavourings, cover and leave to infuse for ten minutes then strain. Melt the butter, add the flour away from the heat and blend in the milk. Stir over a gentle heat until boiling and cook for one minute; remove the pan from the fire and stir in the soaked gelatine. Beat the fish into the sauce a little at a time and work well. (This point is important and helps to prevent the croquettes splitting when immersed in the hot fat and certainly gives a mixture that is easier to handle when cold.)

Adjust the seasoning and add the beaten egg. Spread the mixture one inch deep in a gratin dish or shallow cake tin, cover with foil or a butter wrapper and leave until quite cold; chill if possible.

Divide the mixture into ten or twelve equal portions and, using two knives, roll and shape on a floured board. Beat the egg with the salad oil and pour onto a plate. Have the fine dry white crumbs on a sheet of greaseproof paper. Coat each croquette with the egg and crumbs: avoid using your fingers.

Heat the deep fat to haze point, 190°C/ 380°F, checking first that you have sufficient fat to cover the croquettes completely. Fry in two batches until golden brown; drain well.

Serve garnished with fried parsley. For this the parsley must be in prime condition, well washed and thoroughly dried.

After frying the croquettes turn the heat out under the deep fat bath and draw the pan away from any other boiling ring. Place the parsley in the frying basket and ease it gently into the fat. Remove it as soon as the spluttering stops and while the parsley is still bright green; drain and use.

For a dinner party where wine is served, it is better to accompany the croquettes with Hollandaise sauce rather than Tartare sauce; but if this is too difficult try a mayonnaise made with lemon juice and finished with a little soft tomato purée, a trace of grated orange rind and juice, and a tablespoon of whipped cream.

For a main course luncheon party dish serve with Pommes Allumettes, potatoes cut twice as thick and twice as long as a regular sized match, fried in the same way as chips. The following tomato sauce, delicately flavoured with cloves and quite thick with small pink shrimps, would complete the picture.

Tomato and shrimp sauce:
½ lb (225 g) tomatoes
1 oz (28 g) butter
1 tablespoon each finely diced onion and carrot
½ oz (14 g) flour
1 tablespoon (18 ml) tomato purée
¼ pint (150 ml) light stock
1 bay leaf
2 cloves
4 tablespoons (70 ml) thick cream
½ lb picked pink shrimps

Wipe the tomatoes, cut in half and squeeze out the seeds; rub these in a nylon strainer to extract all the juice and add this to the stock. Discard the seeds.

Melt the butter, add the vegetables, cook slowly until soft but not coloured, blend in the flour, cook a few minutes to a pale straw colour then add the tomatoes and bruise well with a wooden spoon.

Stir in the tomato purée and stock and bring to the boil. Season with salt and pepper from the mill, add the bay leaf and cloves, half cover the pan and simmer gently for thirty minutes. Strain.

Return the sauce to the rinsed pan, adjust the seasoning and reduce if necessary to improve the texture, thickness and flavour, add the cream, reboil, then add the shrimps. Keep warm until ready to serve, but do not boil.

Haddock Bercy

Another simple but excellent sauce and just the recipe to choose when there is a little wine left in a bottle after a dinner party; if none is at hand, a dry cider is just as good. Use this for cod steaks, fillets of plaice, lemon sole and haddock.

1½ lb (680 g) fresh
    haddock fillets, plaice
    or lemon sole
Juice ¼ lemon
¼ pint (150 ml) water
Salt
6 peppercorns
2 tomatoes
1 shallot
1 glass (115 ml) dry
    white wine or cider
1 oz (28 g) butter
Good ½ oz (15 g) flour
2 teaspoons chopped
    parsley
1 tablespoon (18 ml)
    cream or 'top of the
    milk'

Garnish:
1–2 slices of light white
    bread
1 oz (28 g) butter
A small piece of garlic

Serves 4

Wash and dry the fish and remove the skin; place in a fire-proof dish, sprinkle with salt, add the lemon juice and water and place the peppercorns to one side away from the fish. Cover with foil or buttered paper and poach in a moderate oven, 180°C/350°F/Gas Mark 4 for ten to fifteen minutes depending on the thickness of the fish fillets or steaks. Meanwhile scald and peel the tomatoes, cut in four, remove the seeds and cut again in two or three pieces, set aside.

Chop the shallot finely, put in a saucepan with the white wine or cider and boil until reduced to half quantity. Work the butter and flour to a paste with a palette knife. Strain the liquid from the fish onto the shallot and wine and thicken with the 'kneaded butter' by whisking in a small piece at a time. Allow each piece to melt before adding the next. Simmer for two to three minutes, adjust the seasoning, add the parsley, cream and tomatoes and reheat carefully.

Remove the crusts from the bread and cut it into triangles. Soften the butter and work in the garlic crushed to a paste with a pinch of salt. Spread the bread with the garlic butter and toast until golden brown.

Place the fish in a hot gratin dish, spoon over the sauce, arrange the garlic croûtes around and serve.

Petits Pains de Poisson

There was a time when no one who was both cook and hostess would entertain the idea of

Remove skin and bone from the fish and use to make the stock for the sauce, flavouring it with a squeeze of lemon, vegetables and herbs; season with salt and six peppercorns and

making fish creams because the mincing and pounding of raw fish was messy and time consuming, but the Magimix has changed all that. So if you are the lucky owner of one of these marvellous machines there is no need to reserve this recipe for a special invalid! Sophisticated guests and children alike will love them. Any thick fillet or cutlet of white fish can be used, coley, fresh haddock, plaice and hake being particularly suitable.

1 lb (453 g) coley or
    fresh haddock fillet
A good 1½ oz (45 g)
    butter
Scant 1½ oz (40 g) flour
½ pint (300 ml) milk
1 egg
1 yolk
Salt and white pepper
A pinch ground mace

Filling (optional):
4 oz (113 g) button
    mushrooms
½ oz (14 g) butter
1 teaspoon finely
    chopped shallot

Sauce for finishing:
1 oz (28 g) butter
1 oz (28 g) flour
½ pint (300 ml) fish stock
    made from the skin
    and bone of the fish
4 tablespoons (70 ml)
    milk
2 tablespoons (35 ml)
    cream

Serves 6

simmer very gently about twenty minutes.

Make the white sauce in the usual way and allow to cool completely.

Prepare the filling. Wipe and trim the mushrooms and slice finely. Cook the shallot in the butter until soft but not coloured, add the mushrooms, season and sauté briskly for one minute. Turn onto a plate to cool.

Place the fish, cut in chunks, and the cold sauce in the Magimix and blend until smooth. (This can be done a little at a time in a blender.) Add the eggs, seasoning and spice to taste.

Butter twelve dariole moulds and fill to within ¼ inch of the top, tap each mould firmly on the table to settle the mixture into the bottom of the tin and then make a hole down the centre with the wet handle of a wooden spoon. Fill with the mushrooms, spread over a little more fish mixture and cover the top of each mould with foil or buttered greaseproof paper.

Cook *au bain marie* in a moderate oven, 180°C/350°F/Gas Mark 4 for fifteen to twenty minutes.

Prepare the sauce. Melt the butter, add the flour and cook carefully to a pale straw colour. Draw the pan to one side and blend in the stock, stir until the sauce begins to thicken, add the milk and bring to the boil. Simmer for five minutes, adjust the seasoning and add the cream.

Turn the fish creams into a gratin dish and coat with the sauce.

If entertaining do not remove the moulds but leave the gratin dish in a very low oven or warming cabinet and the sauce in a double saucepan, both creams and sauce can be kept warm successfully for fifteen to twenty minutes. Lift off the moulds and coat the 'creams' with the sauce as your guests are seated.

Harengs Moutardé

Now that herrings are in short supply and relatively expensive, they are finding their place where they rightly belong, among the gourmet dishes. We have always considered this recipe the most delicious lunch dish and plain boiled potatoes, old or new, are the best accompaniment.

4 filleted herrings
2 medium onions, weight 4 oz (113 g)
2 oz (56 g) butter
Salt and black pepper
½ oz (14 g) flour
1 rounded teaspoon French mustard
A pinch of sugar
½ pint (300 ml) water
4 tablespoons (70 ml) cream or 'top of the milk'
1 oz (28 g) grated cheese

Slice the onions finely, place in a shallow pan with just over half the butter, press a butter wrapper, greaseproof paper or foil on the onions, cover with lid and simmer gently until soft and golden.

Lay the herrings flat, skin side down in a buttered dish, season well and cover with a piece of butter paper and cook in a moderate oven for fifteen to twenty minutes. Melt the remaining butter in a saucepan, draw aside and blend in the flour, mustard, seasoning and sugar. Pour on the water, stir until boiling, simmer for five minutes, add the cream and reboil; remove from the heat and stir in half the cheese.

Remove the paper from the herrings, scatter the onions over the top and coat with the sauce; sprinkle with the rest of the cheese and glaze under the grill.

Serves 4

Merlans Alsacienne

Whiting is held in the highest esteem by chefs who find its delicate flesh particularly suitable for quenelles and stuffings for other fish. However, the very friable nature of the flesh means it does not travel well, but if you live not far from the sea and can buy fillets of whiting and hard white cabbage, this is the recipe to choose.

Cut the cabbage in quarters, remove the hard core and shred finely. Slice the onion and put in a shallow casserole with half the butter. Cook slowly over gentle heat until soft and yellow, then add the cabbage and stir well; season and moisten with the cider. Cover closely with a buttered paper and lid and cook slowly until tender. Allow about thirty minutes and stir from time to time.

Skin the fish if not done by the fishmonger, fold and lay in a fire-proof dish; season, add the peppercorns and bay leaf and stock or water. Poach in a moderate oven for about fifteen minutes.

The succulent vegetable, delicate fish without bones and the cheesy sauce combine to make the perfect family luncheon dish.

4 large fillets whiting, approx. 1½ lb (650 g)
1 small hard white cabbage 1–2 lb (650–900 g)
1 medium onion
2 oz (56 g) butter
4 tablespoons (70 ml) cider
½ bay leaf
6 peppercorns
6 tablespoons (108 ml) fish, vegetable stock or water
¾ oz (21 g) flour
8 fluid oz (225 ml) milk
1 oz (28 g) grated Cheddar cheese

Melt the rest of the butter in a saucepan, draw aside and blend in the flour and milk, return to the heat and stir until boiling. Strain the liquor from the fish, add to the sauce and simmer for three to four minutes until creamy. Remove the sauce from the heat, adjust the seasoning, add a little ready mixed English mustard and beat in half the cheese a little at a time.

Turn the cabbage into a fire-proof serving dish, place the fish across the top and mask with the sauce. Scatter the reserved cheese over the top and brown under the grill or in a quick oven.

Serves 4

Haddock Hongroise

The sauce in this recipe makes it one of the most popular fish dishes with the students at the cookery school; it is quick and easy to prepare and we generally serve it with freshly boiled nouilles tossed in butter.

Halibut, a fine firm fish which can be a little dry to eat is excellent cooked the same way.

1½ lb (680 g) haddock, block fillets or 2 lb (1 kg) steak halibut
Juice ¼ lemon
(Continued overleaf)

Wash, dry and skin the haddock fillets; if using halibut just trim the fins with scissors. Place the fish in a fire-proof dish, season with salt, pour over the lemon juice and water and place the peppercorns to one side. Cover with foil or buttered paper and poach in a very moderate oven for ten to fifteen minutes for haddock, and fifteen to twenty minutes for halibut.

Trim and wipe the mushrooms, slice finely and place in a saucepan with half the butter, cover and simmer for two minutes. Draw the pan aside, drop in the remaining butter and when melted blend in the flour, paprika and milk. Return to the heat and stir until boiling. Strain on the liquid from the fish and boil for one to two minutes; add the pimento, finely sliced.

4 tablespoons (70 ml)
water
6 peppercorns

Sauce :
2 oz (60 g) mushrooms
A good 1 oz (30 g)
butter
1 oz (28 g) flour
1 teaspoon Hungarian
paprika
½ pint (300 ml) milk
1 cap canned pimento

Place the fish in a serving dish, removing skin and bone from the halibut and spoon over the sauce.

Serves 4

Filets de Maquereaux Mireille

Rich in natural oil this handsome fish must be eaten fresh and when you tire of them soused and eaten very cold with freshly baked bread, try this recipe. With a subtle combination of flavours, it is perfect self-catering holiday food! If you catch your own fish, remember to gut them on the shore. You can always ask your fishmonger to do this for you.

4 mackerel or 2 if very
large
2 tablespoons seasoned
flour
2 oz (56 g) butter or
bacon fat
2 oz (56 g) flat
mushrooms
1 small onion
1 clove garlic
1 tablespoon (18 ml)
wine vinegar
Salt and pepper

Garnish :
4 tomatoes
1 tablespoon chopped
parsley

Fillet the fish, which is quite easy to do if you split them down the back and cut the flesh off the back bone on either side. Wipe and chop the mushrooms, do not remove stalk or peel. Chop the onion and garlic together very finely. Skin and slice the tomatoes for garnish, season and set aside ready for cooking.

Coat the fillets with the seasoned flour and fry them in the hot butter or bacon fat until brown and crisp. Lift carefully into a serving dish and keep hot.

Pour off the butter in the pan and wipe it with a paper towel. Reheat the pan, add the rest of the butter and when foaming add the mushrooms, onion and garlic. Cook well, about five minutes, to drive off all the moisture from the mushrooms and to soften the onion, sprinkle with the wine vinegar and seasoning and pour over the fish.

Wipe out the pan again and sauté the tomatoes or grill them if preferred and arrange around the fish. Dust the fish with the chopped parsley and serve piping hot.

Serves 4

Choose either of the following recipes when the fishmonger has large fat fillets of fresh plaice on sale and you are looking for a main course suitable for a dinner or luncheon party.

Danish Plaice

7 fillets plaice
Salt and pepper
4 tablespoons (70 ml) water
Juice ½ lemon *or* 4 tablespoons (70 ml) white wine

For coating and frying fish:
2 tablespoons seasoned flour
Beaten egg and dry white crumbs
Deep fat

1–1½ lb (½ kg) potatoes
8 small spears asparagus, fresh or frozen
2 oz (56 g) button mushrooms

Sauce:
1 oz (28 g) butter
A good ¾ oz (23 g) flour
7½ fluid oz (225 ml) creamy milk

Serves 4

Skin the fillets, wash and dry. Take four of them, tuck the ends under, making each fillet the same size and lay them in a buttered dish. Season with salt and white pepper and pour over the water and lemon juice. Cover with a butter wrapper or foil and set on one side. Cut the remaining three fillets into four lengthwise; flour and egg and crumb them.

Cook the potatoes, drain and dry and pass through a mouli sieve or work to a purée in a Magimix and beat well with a 'nut' of butter and one tablespoon of hot milk, add a grating of nutmeg or a pinch of ground mace.

Poach the four fillets in a moderate oven for ten to fifteen minutes.

Cook the asparagus; slice the mushrooms and cook for one minute in a tablespoon of water and a little lemon juice.

Pipe the potato purée in a thick rope at each end of a large sole dish and place the drained fillets of fish in the middle. Cover carefully and return to the oven turned to its lowest setting.

Fry the crumbed strips of fish in deep fat until golden brown, drain well and place on crumpled kitchen paper or a wire rack on a baking sheet and keep warm while preparing the sauce.

Melt the butter, add the flour and pour on the cooking liquor from the fish, stir until thickening then add the milk. Stir until boiling and simmer to a creamy consistency. Adjust the seasoning, add the asparagus and mushrooms and reheat carefully if necessary. Coat the sauce over the poached fillets and arrange the fried fillets at each side of the dish.

Plaice Durand

A perfect choice for those who grow their own vegetables as they can be sure to have a young medium-sized turnip and fresh carrots! The white wine may be replaced with dry cider.

4 large fillets plaice, 6–7 oz (200 g) each
1 glass (115 ml) white wine
A squeeze of lemon
Seasoning

Vegetable Paysanne:
3 medium carrots (approx. 6 oz/170 g)
1 turnip
2 medium onions (approx. 6 oz/170 g)
½ oz (14 g) butter
1 glass white wine (115 ml)
Bouquet garni
4 tomatoes

To finish:
½ pint (300 ml) double cream
1 tablespoon chopped parsley

Serves 4

Set the oven at 180°C/350°F/Gas Mark 4.

Wash and skin the fish, trim, fold and place in a buttered dish. Season with salt and white pepper and pour over the wine and lemon juice; cover with buttered paper or foil and set aside while preparing the garnish.

Slice the carrots and onions into thin rounds. Peel the turnip thickly, cut in four and trim away the sharp cut edges with a potato peeler, then cut each piece in rounds to match the carrots.

Melt the butter in a small flame-proof casserole, add the root vegetables, stir well, cover and cook very gently for two to three minutes. Pour the wine over the vegetables, add seasoning and herbs; cover tightly, bring to the boil and place in the pre-set oven for fifteen to twenty minutes.

Skin the tomatoes, cut out the small core at the stalk end, squeeze the tomatoes carefully to remove the seed and chop the flesh roughly.

Poach the fish for ten to fifteen minutes.

Check the vegetables at the end of fifteen minutes and if tender and dry, remove the bouquet of herbs and add the tomatoes; return to the oven to heat through.

Strain the liquor from the fish into a saucepan and reduce to half quantity, pour in the cream, season well and simmer until thick. Add the parsley. Place the vegetables in a hot dish, lay the fish on the top and coat over with the sauce.

Dover or lemon sole can be used for the following recipe but keep it for a special occasion in late spring or early summer when fresh English asparagus is as its best. The method of preparing the wine sauce means the dish can be glazed under the grill and consequently kept warm without spoiling the appearance.

Filets de Sole aux Asperges

8 fillets of sole total
    weight 1½ lb (approx.
    800 g)
Salt and white pepper
Juice ¼ lemon
8 fluid oz (240 ml) water
8 spears asparagus
4 oz (113 g) picked
    shrimps or small
    prawns

Wine sauce:
1 glass (115 ml) white
    wine
1 shallot or pickling
    onion
6 peppercorns
½ bay leaf
1 egg yolk
2 oz (56 g) butter

Roux:
1¼ oz (35 g) butter
1 oz (28 g) flour

Garnish:
Fleurons of puff pastry

Serves 4

Skin the fillets, then wash and dry them. Should they be cross fillets taken right off one side of the fish, fold in half lengthways, if single fillets just tuck under each end making each fillet look the same size. Lay in a dish, season, pour over the lemon juice and water, cover with buttered paper and leave ready for poaching.

Cook the asparagus and place shrimps in a small dish with a nut of butter.

Prepare the wine sauce. Chop the shallot finely and place in a small pan with the wine and flavourings and boil rapidly until reduced to a teaspoonful. Should the pan boil dry add one teaspoonful of water, not more wine. Work the egg yolk in a small basin with a small piece of the butter and strain on the reduced wine. Whisk or beat in a bain-marie until thick, adding the remaining butter piece by piece. Put on one side.

Poach the fish in a moderate oven, 180°C/350°F/Gas Mark 4 for ten to twelve minutes.

Meantime prepare the roux. Melt the butter, blend in the flour and cook slowly to a pale straw colour and draw the pan aside.

Tip the liquid from the fish into a measure – you need ½ pint (300 ml) – return the fish with the dish of prawns to the oven turned to its lowest setting. Trim the asparagus.

Pour the fish stock on to the roux, blend until smooth and whisk over heat until boiling. Draw the pan aside, season and beat in the butter sauce. Cover and keep warm in a bain-marie.

Lay the fish in a hot serving dish, scatter over the shrimps and aparagus and coat with the sauce. Glaze lightly under grill and surround with the fleurons just before serving.

Filets de Sole Dugléré

Named after a famous chef and prepared originally with Dover or lemon sole this dish has a delicious and simple sauce. We think it makes the very best family dish, not with sole but with the freshest and cheapest white fish of the day. Try cod, haddock, hake, ling or grey mullet.

If you have no chives add a sliced shallot when poaching the fish and add parsley to the sauce. The sauce should look creamy, quite green with chives or parsley and the strips of tomato easily identified.

4 large fillets Dover or
    lemon sole; total
    weight 1½ lb (approx.
    800 g)
Salt and 6 white
    peppercorns
Juice ½ lemon
¼ pint (150 ml) water
½ bay leaf
1 sliced shallot or
    pickling onion

Sauce:
¾ oz (21 g) butter
¾ oz (21 g) flour
5 tablespoons (75 ml)
    creamy milk
2 teaspoons snipped
    chives or chopped
    parsley
2 ripe tomatoes

Serves 4

Wash, dry and skin the fish, place in a buttered dish, season with salt, pour over the lemon juice and water and place the peppercorns, bay leaf and shallot to one side. Cover with a butter wrapper or foil and poach in a moderate oven, 180°C/350°F/Gas Mark 4 for ten to twelve minutes.

Peel, quarter and de-seed the tomatoes and cut in coarse shreds. Prepare the sauce. Melt the butter, blend in the flour and cook carefully until the roux 'marbles' and is a pale straw colour; draw the pan off the heat.

Hold the fish in place with the paper and strain off the liquid into a measure; check the quantity, you need 7½ fluid oz (220 ml), blend this into the roux.

Return the pan to the fire and stir until the sauce begins to thicken, then add the creamy milk and continue to stir until boiling. Reduce for one to two minutes, draw aside and add the chives or parsley and tomatoes; adjust the seasoning.

Remove bay leaf, peppercorns and onion from the fish and wipe away any excess liquid with a paper towel.

Reheat the sauce to boiling point, coat it over the fish and serve at once.

Soles Fourées aux Crevettes Roses

There is no doubt in our minds that this is the best sole dish for the cook hostess to choose when she wants fish as a main course for a luncheon or dinner party. All the preparation can be done well ahead of time and there is no last minute sauce making or finishing to do.

For this recipe black or Dover sole is essential, and you allow one slip sole, weighing between $\frac{1}{2}$–$\frac{3}{4}$ lb (approx. 300 g), per person. A sharp knife with a thin blade is a 'must' for lifting the fillets off the bone.

4 slip soles
2–3 oz (80 g) butter
8 tablespoons fresh white
   crumbs

Filling:
$\frac{1}{2}$ oz (14 g) butter
$\frac{1}{2}$ oz (14 g) flour
$\frac{1}{4}$ pint (150 ml) milk
$\frac{1}{2}$ lb (225 g) fresh pink
   shrimps *or* 4 oz (113 g)
   small frozen prawns
4 oz (113 g) mushrooms
1 tablespoon (18 ml)
   cream
Seasoning
A pinch of ground mace

Garnish:
1 bunch watercress

Serves 4

Wash and dry the fish. Do not remove the head or tail as these help to keep the fish in shape. Remove the white skin; the black skin is, as a general rule, removed by the fishmonger.

Trim the fins with scissors. With a sharp knife lift the top two fillets as far as the fin bone starting from the centre back bone but do not detach them. Turn the fish over and do the same on the other side; cut out the backbone with scissors.

Prepare the filling. First shell the shrimps – this is really worthwhile; if using frozen prawns allow to thaw completely in the refrigerator.

Make a sauce with the butter, flour and milk, season to taste and add the prawns; run the cream over the top and set aside. Trim, wipe and quarter the mushrooms and sauté quickly in $\frac{1}{2}$ oz (14 g) butter, mix carefully into the sauce, add the mace and adjust the seasoning.

Lay the fish in a buttered fire-proof dish, fill with prawn mixture, reshape, brush with melted butter and scatter over the breadcrumbs. Sprinkle again with melted butter.

Bake in a moderate oven 180°C/350°F/Gas Mark 4 for twenty to thirty minutes. Pass under a hot grill to finish browning. Serve with bouquets of crisp watercress.

We have frozen this dish with great success. Cool the fish as quickly as possible, lift carefully onto foil, pack in a shallow container and freeze quickly.

Thaw for four to five hours at room temperature, lift the foil on to a baking tray and bake uncovered for thirty minutes in a moderate oven, 180°C/350°F/Gas Mark 4.

Filets de Sole Gustave

A main course dish for a very special occasion – probably best kept for when you are dining *à deux*.

1 sole, weighing approx. 2 lb (1 kg), filleted
1 glass (115 ml) white wine
Salt and 6 peppercorns
2 tablespoons (35 ml) thick cream
½ lb (225 g) potatoes
½ small vegetable marrow or 2 courgettes

Hollandaise sauce:
3 tablespoons (50 ml) white wine vinegar
6 peppercorns
A slice of onion
A blade of mace or ½ bay leaf
2 egg yolks
3 oz (75 g) unsalted butter

Garnish:
6 asparagus spears, fresh or frozen, cooked
3 large firm mushrooms
2 ripe tomatoes

Lay the fillets, quite flat, in a dish; pour over the wine, add salt and peppercorns, cover with buttered paper and leave ready for poaching.

Prepare the Hollandaise sauce, cover and set aside.

Cook the potatoes in salted water and after fifteen minutes add the peeled and sliced marrow or courgettes and continue to cook for about five minutes until tender. Drain well, add a nut of butter and return to gentle heat to drive off any residual water. Crush with a potato masher and season well. Cover and keep warm.

Poach the fish in a moderate oven for eight to ten minutes.

Slice the mushrooms, scald and peel the tomatoes, cut in four, scoop out the seeds and cut again in shreds. Cook the mushrooms in a tablespoon of water for one minute.

Spoon the vegetable purée into a buttered gratin dish and place the fillets of fish on top. Boil the liquor from the fish until reduced to half quantity and add it to the Hollandaise sauce with the cream. Add the asparagus, mushrooms and tomato to the sauce. Coat the sauce over the fish and glaze lightly under the grill.

Serves 2

Filets de Sole Gratinées Valentino

For the cook hostess this dish will score on many points. It can be prepared well ahead of time, it needs no last minute touches and it is served in the cooking dish – all splendid reasons for choosing it for a main course for dinner when

Skin, wash and dry the fillets. Make a Béchamel sauce with the butter, flour and milk infused with onion, peppercorns and bay leaf and season well. Stir in the prawns and mace and run the cream over the surface of the sauce; cover and allow to cool.

Cook the asparagus, refresh with cold water and drain thoroughly. Lay the thinner fillets, i.e. those with the white skin, in a buttered fire-proof dish. Stir the cream into the prawn

guests arrive for the week-end on Friday evening.

2 × 1¼ lb (556 g) lemon or Dover sole, filleted
1¼ oz (35 g) butter
Good 1 oz (30 g) flour
½ pint (300 ml) milk
A slice of onion
6 peppercorns
½ bay leaf
4 oz (113 g) picked shrimps or frozen prawns
Pinch of mace
1 tablespoon (18 ml) cream
12 spears asparagus

Topping:
2 oz (56 g) butter
2 oz (56 g) fresh white breadcrumbs
1 oz (28 g) grated Parmesan or dry Cheddar cheese

mixture, spread it over the fillets and lay the asparagus on top. Cover with the remaining fillets, placing them skinned side down.

Melt the butter, stir in the crumbs and cheese and sprinkle over the fish. Bake in a moderately hot oven, 190°C/375°F/Gas Mark 5 for about twenty to twenty-five minutes, when the crumbs should be brown and crisp. Serve hot.

Serves 4

Rainbow trout, a small round fish with delicate white flesh, is bred in specially conditioned tanks; always in season and weighing from 6–10 oz (170–285 g) it is a reliable choice when planning menus.

The following two recipes give the colour and strength of flavour that perhaps the fish alone lacks and make excellent main course dishes.

Truites Meunière à la Niçoise

Serve this for a luncheon with new potatoes tossed in butter and parsley to accompany and a side salad.

If you possibly can, buy the black ripe olives from a delicatessen; these will be soft, sweet and juicy, avoid those stoned and canned in brine.

4 trout
2 tablespoons seasoned flour
3 oz (84 g) butter
4 oz (113 g) mushrooms
4 tomatoes
12 black olives
Juice ½ lemon
Seasoning
1 tablespoon mixed chopped herbs

Wash and dry the trout, trim the fins and tails but do not remove the heads. Roll in seasoned flour. Wipe and trim the mushrooms and cut in thick slices; skin and quarter the tomatoes and remove the seeds.

Heat a large frying pan, drop in 1½ oz (42 g) butter and when foaming put in the trout and fry for five minutes on either side until golden brown. Lift carefully onto a hot serving dish.

Meantime, prepare the garnish, melt ½ oz (14 g) butter, add the mushrooms and sauté briskly for one minute, then add the tomatoes and olives. Season to taste and heat thoroughly; spoon over the trout.

Wipe out the frying pan, add the remaining butter and heat to a nut brown. Pour in the seasoned lemon juice and herbs and pour over the fish while still foaming. Serve at once.

Serves 4

Truites Farçis Aurore

This dish is well suited as a main course for lunch or dinner. Serve with plain boiled new potatoes tossed in butter with parsley.

Split the trout down the back and carefully remove the backbone and head. Set aside while preparing the farce. Skin the whiting, pass through the mincer or work in the blender. Break whites with a fork and beat into the fish gradually, either by hand or in the blender. Pass through a wire sieve.

5 even sized trout
1 oz (30 g) butter

Farce :
¾ lb (375 g) whiting,
   pike or fresh haddock
   fillet
2 small egg whites
2 caps canned pimento
½ medium onion
¼ pint (150 ml) thick
   cream

To finish :
3 fluid oz cream
½ teaspoon paprika
1 tablespoon (18 ml)
   canned pimento juice

Chop the pimento and rub through a nylon strainer and grate the onion to obtain about one dessertspoonful of juice. Work the pimento purée and onion juice into the fish, then beat in the cream by degrees. Season with salt and white pepper.

Fill this farce into the trout, reshape and lift carefully into a well buttered fire-proof dish. Pour over a little melted butter and cook in a moderate oven for fifteen to twenty minutes. Slide under the hot grill for a few minutes to crisp the skin.

Boil the cream with the parika and pimento juice until it thickens a little, season and pour round the fish.

Serves 5

The colour of the flesh of trout depends on its habitat and feeding, and when bred for the table in tanks or in cages in sea-water lochs they invariably have pink flesh. When these are available the idea of the Truites Farçis Aurore recipe can be used but the white fish used for the farce. This would be the main course of a very memorable meal.

Truites Farçies Ecossaise

4 pink fleshed trout each
   weighing approx. 12 oz
   (350 g)
1 oz (28 g) butter

Farce :
1 lb (453 g) whiting
   fillets
2 egg whites
¼ pint (150 ml) cream
Salt and pepper

Garnish :
1 large or 2 medium
   cucumber
1½ oz (42 g) butter
Fresh dill

Serves 8

Have the fish filleted and divided into two separate fillets. Set aside while preparing the farce as described in the previous recipe, replacing the salmon with the whiting.

Spread the farce on the top half of each fillet, draw the tail section over and smooth the sides. Place the fillets in a buttered fire-proof dish, pour over a little melted butter and cook as before.

Meantime prepare the garnish. Peel the cucumber, cut in four lengthways and cut again into 1½-inch pieces; trim to an olive shape with a speedy-peeler. Blanch in boiling salted water, drain and simmer in the butter for seven to eight minutes until tender. Adjust the seasoning and add the dill.

Serve the fish garnished with the cucumber and serve small new potatoes and Hollandaise sauce separately.

Truites Farçis au Saumon

An impressive dish for a dinner party. See if your fishmonger has a salmon head for sale, this can be an excellent 'buy' and let him know that you hope to get about 6 oz (170 g) raw flesh from it.

All the preparation can be done in the morning and the fish left in a cool larder in the dish ready for cooking. Remember to wash and pick over the watercress and leave up-side down in a small bowl of cold water.

With the oven pre-set any unskilled help can cope with cooking if supplied with a minute-minder.

Although the recipe is written for four trout, the filling would be adequate for five. Double ingredients of farce are necessary if the dinner party is for ten to twelve people.

4 even sized trout
½ oz (14 g) butter

Farce:
½ lb (225 g) steak salmon
   (to give approximately
   6 oz /170 g when
   skinned, boned and
   minced)
1 large egg white
3 fluid oz (75 ml) cream
Salt and pepper

Serves 4

Split the trout down the back and carefully remove the backbone and head. Set aside while preparing the farce. Break the egg white with a fork and add gradually to the minced raw salmon, working well with a wooden spoon. (This whole process of mincing and adding the egg white can be done to perfection in a Magimix.)

Place the mixture in a small bowl on ice, beat in the cream and season with salt and ground white pepper. Fill this farce into the trout, re-shape and lift carefully into a buttered fire-proof dish. Pour over a little melted butter and cook in a moderate oven, 170°C/325°F/Gas Mark 3 for about fifteen to twenty minutes. Slide under the hot grill for a few minutes to crisp the skin. Serve garnished with watercress and whipped butter delicately flavoured with orange handed separately.

Whipped butter sauce:
6 oz (170 g) unsalted butter
Salt
A squeeze of lemon
4 tablespoons (70 ml) white wine
Juice and rind ¼ small orange
Freshly ground white pepper
2 tablespoons whipped cream

Rinse a small basin with boiling water and dry well; put in the butter, cut into small pieces, and whisk until very soft and almost liquid; add the salt. Whisk in, a little at a time, the lemon juice, wine and orange; season with pepper.

If this part of the sauce is prepared early in the day, warm the basin carefully by dipping it in and out of hot water and whisk the butter again until soft and any liquid that might have separated from the butter has been absorbed. At the last moment fold in the whipped cream.

Sea trout, a fish similar in shape to salmon but with softer and more delicately flavoured flesh, would always be our choice for a special party during May through to July. While it would be hard to better it served cold and accompanied with cucumber salad and a green mayonnaise, if you want a hot dish or you are faced with a frozen fish to cook, the following recipe would be perfect. The sauce is similar to the 'beurre blanc' served with fish in the Loire district.

Truite Saumonée Savennières

2½–3 lb (1¼ kg) salmon trout
2 glasses (230 ml) white wine
4 tablespoons (70 ml) water
Squeeze of lemon juice
Salt
6 white peppercorns
½ bay leaf
1 shallot
4–6 oz (150 g) unsalted butter
2 tablespoons whipped cream

Garnish:
1 large cucumber
½ oz (14 g) butter
Sprays of fresh dill

Serves 6

Trim the fins and tail of the trout, wash, paying particular attention to the cavity that held the guts and scraping away any blood adhering to the back bone. Dry the fish well and cut out the gills if not removed by the fishmonger.

Place the fish in a shallow pan or fish kettle with the wine, water and seasonings, add the bay leaf, cover and bring *very slowly* to simmering point. Draw the pan to the side of the stove and leave fish to poach for twenty minutes.

Meantime chop the shallot and cook in ½ oz (14 g) of the butter until golden, set aside. Trim and cook the cucumber as described in the recipe for Truites Farçies Ecossaise and keep warm.

Tip the liquor from the fish onto the shallot and boil until reduced to half quantity; strain. Whisk the rest of the butter in a hot basin until very soft, indeed almost liquid, but it must not melt to an oil. Add the reduced liquor from the fish a little at a time and, when completely absorbed, adjust the seasoning, fold in the whipped cream and serve in a small bowl.

Lift the fish carefully onto a hot dish, remove the skin but leave on the head and tail. Surround the fish with the cucumber and dill and serve very hot with small new potatoes. The butter sauce will start melting as soon as it touches the hot fish.

Filets de Sole Andalouse

An excellent choice if you are looking for a cold dish without mayonnaise, suitable for a buffet or a summer luncheon dish when tomatoes are large and ripe. Serves eight at a buffet when other dishes are available or four as a main course for lunch.

2 × 1¼ lb (approx. 680 g) lemon or Dover sole, filleted
4 large ripe tomatoes
Olive oil

Dressing:
6 tablespoons (105 ml) olive oil
2 tablespoons (35 ml) wine vinegar
¼ pint (150 ml) fresh tomato sauce made with:
  ¾ lb (339 g) tomatoes
  1–2 teaspoons tomato purée
  ½ clove garlic
  Pared rind and juice ½ lemon
  Salt, pepper and sugar to taste
1 tablespoon mixed chopped fresh herbs (parsley, chives and thyme)

Skin and trim the fillets, fold and poach in lemon and water as in the recipe on p. 84. Meantime scald and skin the tomatoes, cut in half and flick out the seeds. Heat two to three tablespoons olive oil in a frying pan and pass the tomatoes quickly through the oil starting them cut side down in the pan; season and lift onto a plate to cool.

Wipe and slice the tomatoes for the sauce and cook with all the other ingredients until thick and pulpy. Strain. Split the anchovy fillets in two and soak in a little milk to remove the excess salt. Wash and pick over the watercress.

Whisk the oil, vinegar and tomato sauce together, adjust the seasoning and add the herbs. Place the tomato halves on a serving dish, lay a fillet of fish on top and coat with the dressing. Drain the anchovy fillets and arrange on the fish. Garnish with bouquets of watercress.

Garnish:
8 fillets anchovy
Watercress

Serves 4 as a main course

Mousse de Saumon Nantua

The firm, rich flesh of this luxury fish can be 'stretched' with sauce and mayonnaise to make a superb mousse. This

Lay the salmon in a shallow pan with the sliced vegetables, herbs, vinegar and seasoning and pour over just sufficient water to cover. Put a lid on the pan, bring very slowly to the boil then turn off the heat and leave the salmon

recipe, with prawns or shrimps to give extra bulk and a delicious accompanying sauce, makes a perfect main course dish for a lunch or dinner party. Well garnished, it looks handsome on a buffet and is easy to serve and eat at a supper party when 'forks only' is the rule.

1 lb (453 g) steak of salmon
1 onion
1 carrot
Bouquet garni
1 tablespoon (18 ml) white wine vinegar
1 teaspoon salt
6 peppercorns
½ pint (300 ml) cold white sauce made with 1 oz (28 g) butter and 1 oz (28 g) flour
½ pint (300 ml) thick mayonnaise
¾ oz (21 g) gelatine
2 tablespoons (35 ml) water
4 tablespoons (75 ml) white wine or tomato juice
¼ pint (150 ml) double cream
½ lb (225 g) fresh prawns or 1 pint pink shrimps
2 egg whites

Sauce:
½ pint (300 ml) thick mayonnaise
1 cap canned pimento and 2 tablespoons (35 ml) of the juice
4 tablespoons (70 ml) tomato juice
Tabasco
2 tablespoons lightly whipped cream

to cool in the liquid. Meantime shell the prawns or shrimps and set aside.

Prepare the tin or soufflé case. Lightly oil a 7-inch cake tin or soufflé case with a disc of waxed paper or foil at the bottom.

Drain the fish, flake and pound with the sauce until smooth; add the mayonnaise.

Soak the gelatine in the water, add the tomato juice, dissolve over a gentle heat and stir into the salmon mixture. Lightly whip the cream and fold into the mixture with the prawns.

Whisk the egg whites until firm and fold quickly into the mousse. Turn at once into the prepared mould. Cover with foil and leave in the refrigerator to set.

Chop and rub the pimento and juice through a nylon strainer or work in a blender with the mayonnaise. Stir in the tomato juice, adjust the seasoning using salt, sugar and Tabasco to taste. Fold in the cream.

Shell the prawns and, if large, split the tail like a butterfly. Slice the cucumber leaving on the skin and season with salt, sugar and black pepper from the mill. Sprinkle with one tea-spoon white wine vinegar mixed with one teaspoon water.

Turn the mousse onto a serving platter and mask with a little of the sauce. Garnish the top with a few of the split prawns and dust with paprika pepper. Surround with the cucumber and dill or watercress and the remaining prawns.

Garnish:
1 cucumber
Sprays of fresh dill or watercress
½ lb (225 g) fresh prawns

Serves 6–8

Filets de Sole à l'Indienne

A super dish for a summer supper or a cold buffet at any time of the year. The delicate sauce should have only a suggestion of curry flavour.

2 lemon or Dover sole, each weighing approx. 2 lb (1 kg) filleted
Juice ¼ lemon
4 tablespoons (70 ml) water
Seasoning

Curry cream sauce:
2 tablespoons (35 ml) oil
1 tablespoon chopped onion
1 clove garlic
2 teaspoons curry powder
¼ pint (150 ml) tomato juice
2 slices lemon
1 tablespoon (18 ml) apricot jam
½ pint (300 ml) mayonnaise

Rice salad:
6 oz (170 g) long grain rice
½ lb (225 g) fresh prawns or 4 oz (113 g) frozen
4 oz (113 g) firm white mushrooms
About ¼ pint (150 ml) French dressing

Garnish:
8 thin slices lemon
Paprika pepper
Watercress (optional)

Serves 8

Skin and trim the fillets of sole, fold and lay in a fire-proof dish, season with salt and white pepper and pour over the lemon juice and water. Cover with a buttered paper and poach in a very moderate oven. Allow to cool in the liquid.

Cook the rice and, even though it is to be eaten cold, rinse with hot water, then drain thoroughly. Prepare the sauce. Cook the onion and chopped garlic in the oil without colouring, add the curry powder, cook for one to two minutes then add the tomato juice and lemon. Simmer for about five minutes, stir in the jam and, when melted, strain and allow to cool.

Shell the prawns; wipe, trim and cut the mushrooms in thick slices. Mix the French dressing into the rice using a fork, season well and add the prawns and mushrooms.

Spoon the rice salad into a serving dish and lay the fillets of fish on top. Add the curry foundation to the mayonnaise a little at a time, tasting as you go and adjust the seasoning. Soften the flavour if necessary with a spoonful of cream or if the sauce is *very* thick try one or two teaspoons of boiling water.

Coat each fillet with a tablespoon of the sauce, place a slice of lemon on top and dust with paprika. Garnish the dish with watercress and serve the rest of the sauce in a small bowl or sauce boat.

Beef

Bitkis à la Russe

This recipe is *not* just another 'meat ball' and to be perfect the instructions must be followed implicitly. The result will then be light in texture, delicious in flavour and in good contrast to whichever sauce is chosen.

Bitkis are Russian in origin and the quantity of meat needed will serve four to six people and so can be considered economical. They freeze well when cooked. Freeze some of the chosen sauce in a separate carton for addition to the dish on re-heating.

1¼ lb (556 g) good beef
  mince, that freshly
  minced from the
  shoulder steak is the
  best, as it contains a
  modicum of fat
1 small onion (2 oz/56 g)
  finely chopped
1 cup (10 fluid oz/300 ml)
  fresh white
  breadcrumbs, made
  from stale bread
1 tablespoon chopped
  parsley
1 teaspoon chopped
  thyme
¼ pint to 7½ fluid oz
  (225 ml) cold water
1 small carton (5 fluid oz
  or 150 ml) sour cream
  or plain yoghurt
Seasoned flour
¾ pint (450 ml) well
  flavoured brown or
  tomato sauce

Serves 4–6

Turn the mince into a bowl, add onion, crumbs and herbs. Mix thoroughly. Do this in the mixer using 'the paddle' or with your hand, kneading as for bread. Once mixed, season very well and work in the water gradually. This must be added slowly and the mixture worked continuously until light in texture. To judge when enough water has been added, throw a small cake of the mixture onto a wetted board and if it will keep its shape the mixture is ready for use.

Divide out into ten or twelve good tablespoons. With a wet palette knife shape into moderately thick cakes (like a fish cake) taking care that there are no cracks. Have ready a plate of seasoned flour, dip the bitkis in this and fry briskly in a small quantity of hot dripping until golden brown on both sides.

Lift into an oven-proof dish. Heat the chosen sauce, stir yoghurt or cream until smooth then streak into the sauce. Spoon over the bitkis until well coated, then put into a pre-heated moderate oven, 180°C/350°F/Gas Mark 4 for thirty to thirty-five minutes. Turn the bitkis over once during this cooking.

Serve very hot with the accompanying vegetable. For brown sauce have minced or finely chopped 'sweet and sour' cooked beetroot, heated with salt, sugar and a dash of vinegar. For a tomato sauce serve Carrots Vichy. Either sauté or creamed potatoes should accompany.

Filet de Bœuf Braisé aux Champignons

The perfect way for the cook hostess to prepare and serve a fillet of beef. With the sauce prepared the day before a party, or even taken from the freezer, work and pans are cut to the minimum. The suggested cooking time will give a joint that is medium rare.

2 lb (1 kg) fillet of beef
1 oz (28 g) butter
1 onion, sliced
1 carrot, sliced
1 glass (115 ml) red wine

Demi-glace sauce:
3 tablespoons (54 ml) oil
2 tablespoons finely diced onion
2 tablespoons finely diced carrot
1 tablespoon finely diced celery
1½ tablespoons (25 g) flour
1 pint (600 ml) jellied brown stock
1 tablespoon tomato purée
A few mushroom peelings
A bouquet garni

Garnish:
½ lb (225 g) mushrooms
1–2 tablespoons (30 ml) oil or 1 oz (28 g) butter

Serves 6

Prepare the sauce. Heat the oil gently, add the diced vegetables and cook slowly until the onion is transparent and the carrot and celery begin to shrink and are all about to start browning. Stir in the flour with a metal spoon or small wire whisk and cook very slowly to a good russet brown. Draw the pan off the heat, allow to cool a little, then pour on three-quarters of the stock and add the remaining ingredients. Season very lightly, return to the heat and, stirring constantly, bring slowly to the boil. Half cover the pan with the lid and simmer very gently for about thirty minutes.

Skim off any scum that rises to the surface. Add half the reserved stock, bring to the boil, skim and simmer for five minutes. Repeat this process with the remaining stock, then strain through a conical strainer, pressing the vegetables gently to extract any juice. Rinse and wipe the pan and return the sauce to it; partly cover and continue to simmer the sauce until it is very glossy and the consistency of syrup.

Set the oven at 180°C/350°F/Gas Mark 4. Tie the meat with fine string at 1-inch intervals – this will prevent the meat curling when it is browned and so make it easier and quicker to carve. Heat a flame-proof casserole, drop in the butter and when foaming put in the beef and brown it on all sides; remove from the pan, lower the heat under the pan, add the sliced onion and carrot, cover and cook slowly for five minutes.

Pour off any surplus fat from the vegetables, replace the meat, add the wine, bring to the boil and allow to reduce to half quantity. Replace the meat, pour over the sauce and bring to the boil; cover and cook in the pre-set oven for thirty minutes.

Sauté the mushrooms briskly in hot oil or butter for one minute only, season with salt and freshly ground black pepper.

Take up the meat, remove the string and keep warm. Boil up the sauce well, strain into a saucepan and keep over very low heat.

Carve the meat in ¼-inch slices and arrange on a hot serving dish; any juices that run from the meat while carving must be tipped quickly back over the meat and not be added to the sauce. The meat will absorb the juice at once but the appearance of the sauce would be spoilt.

Spoon a little of the hot sauce over the meat and garnish with the mushrooms. Pour the rest of the sauce into a gravy boat and serve separately.

Note for the cook-hostess:
When the meat is cooked, remove the string as directed above but strain the sauce and return it to the casserole; replace the meat in the sauce, cover the pan and keep it in the warming oven with the mushroom garnish in a separate dish. Keep a flat dish and sauce boat in the oven as well so the meat can be carved and served with ease in the dining room.

This dish takes its name from the garnish and has many variations. The following method of preparing a cauliflower is particularly suitable for a dinner party as the vegetable can be prepared in the morning.

'Dubarry' always denotes the use of cauliflower and so the dish becomes Filet de Bœuf Braisé Dubarry.

Dubarry garnish:
1 large cauliflower

Mornay sauce:
  1 good oz (30 g) butter
  1 oz (28 g) flour
  ½ pint (300 ml) milk
  2 oz (56 g) cheese, grated

Sprig the cauliflower and boil until just tender. Drain and refresh by pouring a cup of cold water over. Take about two sprigs at a time and squeeze lightly together in a piece of muslin. Set these bouquets on a greased baking sheet.

Prepare the mornay sauce. With this recipe, reserve a little cheese for sprinkling over the cauliflower after coating each sprig with the sauce. Twenty minutes re-heating in oven is enough to make the cauliflower hot and golden-brown.

Minute Steaks Montpensier

Serve this dish in early summer when small new potatoes can be cooked with fresh garden mint, and asparagus is in season.

Followers of the classic cuisine would expect to find in this recipe a good slice of truffle on each steak, but we think the tinned variety has little to recommend it save the colour, so we use mushroom instead and find it combines perfectly with the asparagus garnish.

4 thinly cut sirloin steaks
1¾ oz–2 oz (55 g) butter
1 tablespoon (18 ml) brandy
4 tablespoons (70 ml) jellied brown stock

Garnish:
1 bunch asparagus (allow 4–5 spears per head)
4 button mushrooms

Serves 4

First prepare the garnish. Trim and tie the asparagus in four small bundles, cook in boiling salted water until tender. Drain and refresh.

Wipe the mushrooms and trim the stalks level with the caps. Lift the asparagus into a shallow pan, heat gently in ¼ oz (7 g) butter until the steam stops rising and season with salt and pepper from the mill. Add an extra ½ oz (14 g) butter in small pieces to the pan, shake gently to blend it in and keep on one side. Sauté the mushrooms in ¼ oz (7 g) butter and keep warm.

Heat a heavy frying pan, drop in ½ oz (14 g) butter and fry the steaks over a fierce heat for one minute on one side, turn and cook only half a minute on the other side. Lift immediately and lay flat on the serving dish. Add the brandy to the frying pan and when it has all but disappeared add the stock and simmer until well reduced. Draw the pan aside and add the remaining butter a small piece at a time. Season with pepper from the mill.

Put a mushroom on each steak and spoon over the 'glaze' from the pan. Place a 'bundle' of asparagus by each steak, cut and pull away the string.

Bœuf Braisé Mâconnaise

Less expensive cuts of beef benefit greatly by being marinaded, a process which makes the meat more succulent and with a fuller flavour. Within reason, the longer the meat is left in the marinade, even up to three of four days in a

Prepare the marinade: Slice carrot, onion and garlic thinly. Put into a pan with the rest of the ingredients, bring to the boil, pour off and cool.

If using brisket, roll and tie up firmly. Tie aitchbone if necessary to make a neat joint. Set in a bowl, pour over the marinade, cover and set in a cool place or refrigerator for two to three days.

To braise, take up meat and pat dry. Heat a

refrigerator, the better.

In this recipe brisket, aitchbone or silverside can be used. The first has more fat than the other two but does contribute to the richness of the gravy, and is a less expensive cut.

Marinade:
1 large carrot
1 medium sized onion
1 large clove garlic
A bouquet of herbs
8 peppercorns
2 tablespoons (35 ml) oil
2 wineglasses (230 ml) red Mâcon

2½–3 lb (1½ kg) brisket of beef

For braising:
2 tablespoons (35 ml) oil or dripping
1 large carrot, sliced
1 large onion, sliced
1 clove garlic, chopped
1 bouquet of herbs
1 wineglass (115 ml) Macon
¼ pint (150 ml) jellied brown stock

Sauce:
1 small onion, finely chopped
1 tablespoon (18 ml) oil or dripping
1 tablespoon flour
½ pint (300 ml) jellied brown stock

Garnish:
¾ lb (339 g) button onions
½ oz (15 g) butter
1 rounded teaspoon sugar
6 oz (169 g) button mushrooms

thick iron cocotte, put in the oil and when hot, the meat. Brown fairly quickly on all sides. Take out, lower heat, put in the vegetables, cover and allow to sweat gently for five to seven minutes. Set meat on top, tuck in the bouquet and pour round wine and stock. Season lightly. Put cocotte into a slow to moderate oven, 170°C–175°C/325°F–335°F/Gas Mark 3 for 2–2½ hours or until really tender. Baste and turn occasionally.

Meantime prepare sauce. Heat oil, brown onion gently without scorching, stir in flour and allow to colour well. Strain the marinade and add with the stock. Bring to the boil skimming well, simmer for seven to ten minutes.

Meantime prepare the garnish. Blanch onions, strain and return to the pan with the butter and sugar. Cover and cook gently for five to seven minutes, shaking pan occasionally or until tender and well glazed. Draw aside.

Wash and trim the mushrooms, then add them whole to the sauce. Take up the meat, keep warm while straining the gravy. Add this to the sauce and boil gently until syrupy in consistency. Adjust seasoning.

Slice the meat, lay overlapping on a serving dish. Spoon over a little of the sauce and serve the rest separately. Arrange onions at each end of the dish.

Serves 6

Paupiettes de Bœuf

Known in Britain as beef olives, these have been popular for many years. This is a good winter dish, usually served on a purée of potatoes or chestnuts. Alternatively glazed chestnuts, button onions or braised celery can accompany.

8–10 thin slices topside of beef – about 3 in × 5 in. (8 cm × 13 cm) – the butcher will cut them for you.

For braising :
1–2 tablespoons good dripping
A plateful of sliced root vegetables, carrots, onions and celery
1 glass (115 ml) red wine *or* 1 glass (70 ml) sherry
½–¾ pint (300–450 ml) jellied brown stock
1 bouquet garni
Kneaded butter or arrowroot

Stuffing :
1 cup (3 oz/84 g) fresh crumbs
1 small onion, finely chopped
Scant 1 oz (28 g) butter
2 rashers streaky bacon, shredded
1 tablespoon mixed chopped thyme and parsley
1 teaspoon grated orange rind
A little beaten egg to bind

Trim the beef slices to neaten if necessary. Chop or shred any trimmings and put them into a bowl with the crumbs. Soften the onion in the butter without colouring and add to the bowl with the bacon, herbs and grated rind. Season well and moisten with a little of the egg. Spread this stuffing on the meat, fold over the sides and roll up. Tie with thread.

Brown the paupiettes in the dripping. Take out and replace with the vegetables, cover and allow to sweat for seven to eight minutes. Then lay paupiettes on top, pour over wine or sherry and ½ pint (300 ml) of the stock. Tuck in bouquet and cover tightly. Bring to the boil and braise in a moderate oven, 170°C–180°C/ 325°F–350°F/Gas Mark 3–4 for 1–1½ hours or until very tender. Add remaining stock during the cooking to keep the paupiettes well moistened.

Meantime prepare a good potato or chestnut purée and the chosen garnish.

To dish : spoon the purée down the centre of the serving dish. Take up the paupiettes, remove thread and arrange them on the purée. Strain the gravy into a pan, make up if necessary with stock to a good half pint. Thicken a little with kneaded butter or arrowroot. Season. Spoon some of the gravy over the paupiettes and serve the rest separately.

Garnish :
Glazed chestnuts, glazed onions or braised celery
Potato purée or chestnut purée
For glazed onions see Bœuf Mâconnaise.

Serves 4–5

Chestnut purée :
Dried chestnuts or the tinned purée are convenient to use. For dried, soak overnight and simmer for thirty to forty minutes in a well flavoured stock, before draining and mashing as for potatoes. The tinned purée can be turned out into a pan with a good knob of butter and plenty of seasoning. The addition of a little chopped celery is an improvement. Heat gently, stirring well, until very hot.

Glazed chestnuts:
1–1½ lb (453–478 g)
    sound chestnuts

For these, fresh chestnuts are a 'must' and provided one has the best Italian, well worth the trouble of peeling.

Blanch the chestnuts and leave in the boiling water off the heat. Take nuts out one at a time and peel off both outer and inner skins.

For glazing take:
1 onion, sliced
1 stick of celery, sliced
½–¾ pint (300–450 ml)
    brown jellied stock
A good nut of butter

Put nuts into a shallow saucepan or casserole. Add the rest of the ingredients, salt and pepper, cover pan and simmer until nuts are tender. Take off lid and continue to cook gently until liquid has reduced and the chestnuts glazed in appearance.

Do not stir but tip gently into a basting spoon for dishing.

Sauté de Bœuf Vin Rouge

Beef 'skirt' makes an excellent sauté, of which this recipe is an example. The meat has a 'quick' marinade in red wine, vegetables and spices before cooking.

Choose the 'skirt' that lies beneath the fillet, though a thin-looking cut it can be tender and is full of flavour.

1½ lb (678 g) skirt
1 medium sized onion,
    finely chopped
2 cloves garlic, finely
    chopped
1 teaspoon chopped
    thyme
2 glasses (230 ml) red
    wine
1 oz (28 g) butter
1 level tablespoon flour
½ pint (300 ml) good
    brown stock
½ lb (225 g) even sized
    flat mushrooms

Cut the skirt into six diagonal pieces. Put the onion, garlic, thyme and wine into a pan, bring to the boil and reduce by about a quarter. Draw aside and cool slightly.

Heat a sauté pan, drop in the butter and brown the pieces of beef quickly in this. Take out, lay in a dish and pour over the marinade. Leave for thirty minutes.

Add flour to the sauté pan, reduce heat and allow to colour. Pour on the stock, stir until boiling, season and simmer for five to ten minutes. Add the beef and marinade, cover and cook very gently for thirty to thirty-five minutes.

Trim mushrooms and lay on top of the steak. Cover again and continue to cook until the meat is tender, shaking the pan occasionally.

Serves 4–5

93

Sauté de Bœuf aux Piments Verts

If preparing this dish for a party we might choose the tail end of the fillet, but if you can order your meat well in advance try skirt – if well hung this can be very tender. This thin cut of meat, a continuation of the undercut of sirloin, needs to be cut in much larger pieces than usual for a sauté.

1½ lb (678 g) skirt
1 oz (28 g) butter or good beef dripping
1 tablespoon brandy
¾ pint (450 ml) demi-glace sauce (see recipe for *Filet de Bœuf Braisé aux Champignons*)
4 tablespoons (70 ml) double cream
2 teaspoons green peppercorns

Serves 4–5

Cut the meat into 2½-inch (6-cm)) squares and brown quickly in the hot butter or dripping. Flame with the brandy – this will burn up the excess fat and develop a very fine flavour. When the flames subside pour in the demi-glace sauce, cover and simmer gently until the meat is tender, about forty-five minutes. The time depends on the quality of the meat so be prepared to cook it longer if necessary.

Adjust the seasoning, add the cream and peppercorns, and reheat to boiling point.

Serve with a purée of potatoes, adding two tablespoons of grated celery when you beat in the hot milk. French beans would make an excellent choice for a second vegetable or chicory for those who enjoy its rather special flavour.

Endive au Four
4–6 heads of chicory, depending on size – these should be firm and white
1 oz (28 g) butter
A good pinch salt dissolved in 1 tablespoon water
Juice ¼ lemon

Wipe and trim the chicory, cut out the core at the base of each piece and place in a well buttered casserole. Pour over the water and lemon juice and grind over some black pepper. Spread the rest of the butter on a piece of grease-proof paper and press this down on the chicory; cover tightly and bake in a very moderate oven 170°C/325°F/Gas Mark 3 for 1½–2 hours.

Garrick Steak

In the 1930s this dish was a speciality of the Garrick Club. Then it was done with prime rump steak and may still be served there. Here in the School the recipe has been adapted

Prepare stuffing. Wash, dry and chop mushrooms. Cook onion gently in the butter, without colouring, for two to three minutes. Add mushrooms and continue to cook for four to five minutes. Increase heat to drive off excess moisture, draw aside, add herbs and ham or bacon. Stir in crumbs and seasoning. Leave to cool.

nowadays to a less expensive cut and is braised in place of grilling.

Stuffing:
1 small onion, finely chopped
4–6 oz (113–169 g) 'flat' mushrooms
1 oz (28 g) butter
2 teaspoons freshly chopped herbs–parsley and thyme
1 slice (approx. 1 oz/ 30 g) cooked ham or 1 rasher streaky bacon, chopped
2 tablespoons fresh white breadcrumbs
Salt, and pepper from the mill

1½–2 lb (453 g–1 kg) slice buttock steak
1 tablespoon beef dripping or oil
3 rashers streaky bacon
2 medium sized onions, sliced
2 medium sized carrots, sliced
2 stalks of celery, sliced
½ pint (300 ml) strong brown stock

To finish:
1 rounded tablespoon freshly chopped parsley
1 oz (28 g) butter
2–3 tablespoons mushroom ketchup or Worcester sauce

Serves 4–6

Trim steak and with a sharp knife make a slit in the side without the fat, to form a deep pocket. Fill the stuffing into this and sew up with a trussing needle and fine string.

Heat dripping in a large stewpan or casserole, put in the steak and cook quickly until brown on both sides. Take out, cool pan and line bottom with the bacon rashers, put the vegetables on top, cover and cook gently for five to seven minutes. Lay the steak on the top, season and pour round the stock. Cover pan tightly and braise in the oven at 170°C–230°C/ 325°F–450°F/Gas Mark 3–4 for 1½ hours or until very tender.

Take out the steak, remove strings and lay in a hot dish for serving.

Strain liquid into a pan, skim to remove any fat, reduce a little and thicken slightly if necessary with a teaspoon of slaked arrowroot. Pour a little round the steak and serve the rest separately.

Just before serving: brown the butter in a small pan, add the parsley and Worcester sauce and at once pour over the steak.

Lamb

Breast of Lamb Soubise

A good, satisfying and economical dish for lunch on a bleak day. Preparation should be started the day before.

2 lean breasts of lamb, weighing 2½–3 lb (1–1½ kg) in all
1 carrot
1 onion
1 stick celery
4–6 peppercorns
Large bouquet of herbs

Topping:
6 medium sized onions, about 1 lb (453 g)
2 oz (56 g) butter
1 cup (3 oz/84 g) fresh white crumbs
2 oz (56 g) grated Cheddar cheese

½–¾ pint (300–450 ml) piquant tomato salpicon or sauce

Serves 4–5

Soak the meat in plenty of cold water with salt for two to three hours before cooking. Drain and put into a large pan with cold water to cover and the rest of the ingredients. Add a little salt, cover and simmer for 1½–2 hours, skimming occasionally, or until a bone can be easily pulled out.

Take up, remove all the bones and lay meat on a flat dish. Cover with another and put a weight on top. Leave until the next day, then trim and lay in a shallow oven-proof dish.

Meantime prepare the topping. Slice onions, melt butter in a shallow pan, add onions and fry gently, stirring occasionally until golden. Draw aside, cool, then stir in crumbs and about two-thirds of the cheese. Season. Cover the meat with this mixture, pressing it on lightly. Scatter over the remaining cheese.

Add two to three basting spoonfuls of the lamb stock round the dish to keep the meat moist and put into a pre-heated oven, 180°C–190°C/350°F–375°F/Gas Mark 4–5 for twenty-five to thirty minutes until the top is nicely brown and crisp. Pour round a little of the tomato salpicon or sauce and serve very hot.

Note: To make for easy serving, cut the meat into six or seven diagonal slices when cold and pressed. Reshape on the dish before covering with the topping.

Tomato salpicon or sauce:
This may be frozen in small cartons; make it when there is a glut of tomatoes.

½ oz (14 g) butter
1 small onion, finely chopped
1 large clove garlic, crushed with salt
1 medium sized can (8 oz/225 g) Italian tomatoes or 6 oz (169 g) ripe tomatoes in season, peeled, quartered and seeded
2½ fluid oz (70 ml) stock
1 teaspoon chopped fresh or dried basil
Salt, pepper, a pinch of sugar

Soften the onion in butter without colouring. Add garlic, canned or fresh tomatoes, and the seasoning, stock and herbs. Simmer for six or seven minutes until thick. If necessary strengthen flavour with a little tomato purée. If a sauce is required, rub through a strainer.

Cotelettes d'Agneau aux Pointes d'Asperges

A delicious dish for a midsummer party – serve with potato mayonnaise or a hot potato vinaigrette.

2 lb (approx. 1 kg) small boned best end neck lamb, chined

Root vegetables to flavour

1 bunch asparagus

Aspic:

1¾ pints (1 l) chicken stock well seasoned and free from grease

¼ pint (150 ml) dry white wine

2 oz (56 g) gelatine

2 egg whites

1 × 8-inch moule à manqué

Serves 4–5

Trim the meat by removing the chine bone and shortening the cutlet bones to 3½ inches (9 cm), if this has not been done by the butcher. Simmer the meat with the flavouring vegetables and seasoning, barely covered by water, until tender (about forty to forty-five minutes). Leave to cool in the liquid.

Prepare the aspic jelly. Turn the stock into a large scalded pan. Add the gelatine to the wine and leave to soak for about five minutes; whip the egg whites to a froth. Dissolve the gelatine carefully in the stock, add the egg whites to the pan and whisk steadily to boiling point. Draw the pan aside and allow to settle. Reboil without whisking, remove the pan from heat and after five minutes pour the contents of the pan through a scalded cloth. If at this point the aspic is not crystal clear, place a clean bowl under the cloth and pour the contents of the first bowl very gently over the 'filter' that is the egg white on the cloth.

Cook the asparagus, refresh with a little ice cold water to preserve its colour and drain well. Take up the lamb and divide into cutlets; drain on kitchen paper.

Pour enough cool jelly into the mould to cover the mould by about ½ inch. When set arrange the asparagus tips on this and set with a little more jelly. Arrange the cutlets on top and fill the mould to the top with cold aspic just on the point of jelling. Leave to set.

Dip the mould quickly in and out of hot water, wipe with a clean dry cloth and turn at once onto a cold serving dish. Surround with chopped jelly to garnish.

Hot potato vinaigrette:

1 lb (453 g) small new potatoes

3–4 sprigs fresh mint

½ teaspoon salt

4 tablespoons (70 ml) white wine

2 tablespoons good salad oil

Black pepper from the mill

1 teaspoon white wine vinegar

1 tablespoon snipped chives

Scrub the potatoes, just cover with boiling water, add the mint and salt and cook until almost tender, tip into a colander and rinse the pan. Skin the potatoes while still hot, return to the saucepan with the wine and place over very gentle heat, cover and complete their cooking. Pour the oil over the potatoes, season with pepper, sprinkle in the vinegar and add the chives.Rotate the pan to blend the ingredients and keep on the side of the stove for five minutes to mellow and for the potatoes to absorb the flavour of the wine and chives.

Epaule d'Agneau aux Fines Herbes

Another good luncheon party dish especially suitable when fresh herbs are available. Make sure the stuffing is really green with herbs.

3–3¼ lb (1½ kg) shoulder of lamb
1 oz (30 g) butter
Pepper, ground from the mill
1 wineglass white wine or juice from 1 orange, for roasting

Stuffing:
2 oz (60 g) butter
2 tablespoons chopped parsley
1 tablespoon chopped mint
1 tablespoon snipped chives
1 teaspoon chopped thyme or marjoram
Pepper, ground from the mill
1 teacupful fresh breadcrumbs
1 beaten egg

Serves 6

Bone out the shoulder of lamb. Boil bones with vegetables, bouquet garni and seasoning to make ½ pint (283 ml) stock.

To prepare stuffing: pound the butter with the herbs, seasoning and breadcrumbs until smooth, then add the beaten egg, a little at a time. Open out the joint, spread with stuffing, roll up and tie.

Set oven at 200°C/400°F/Gas Mark 6. Spread the joint with 1 oz (30 g) butter, grind over a little pepper, pour on the wine or orange juice and roast in the pre-set oven for 1–1¼ hours, basting well. Turn joint after forty minutes and add a little stock (one to two tablespoons) to the pan if the wine or juice has evaporated.

Take up joint, remove string and place on a hot serving dish. Deglaze the tin with the rest of the stock, boil up well and strain. Serve with a good plain gravy.

Carré d'Agneau à la Grecque

Good for entertaining as it keeps hot satisfactorily without spoiling, and for those who like a garlicky spicy dish. The neck can either be boned out and rolled or, as given here, 'on the bone'.

2 lb (1 kg) best end neck of lamb, chined only
1 tablespoon (18 ml) oil
½ oz (15 g) butter
1 medium sized onion, chopped
2 large cloves garlic, chopped
1 oz (28 g) butter
1 level tablespoon flour
½ pint (300 ml) chicken or bone stock
1 × 15-oz (445-g) can Italian tomatoes or, when in season, 1 lb (453 g) ripe tomatoes, concassed
1 rounded teaspoon tomato purée
1 teaspoon sugar
Salt, black pepper from the mill and a pinch of ground allspice

Garnish:
4 even-sized ripe tomatoes
1–2 oz (28–56 g/ 12–18) black olives, halved and stoned
1 large tablespoon mixed chopped fresh herbs
1–2 teaspoons arrowroot to bind

Serves 4–5

Remove chine bone and skin the neck if the butcher has not already done so. Cut away about an inch or so of fat from the cutlet bones and trim end bones into 'battlements'. Heat oil in a thick cocotte or casserole, add butter and put in the lamb. Brown on a moderate heat. Take out and pour off all but one tablespoon of the fat. Add onion and garlic, and allow to soften. Draw aside, stir in flour, stock and tomatoes. Bring to boil, replace lamb, cover and place in the oven, 180°C/350°F/Gas Mark 4 for forty-five to fifty minutes. Baste and turn joint over once or twice.

Take up meat and keep warm. Rub gravy through a strainer into a saucepan, skim well. Slake arrowroot with one or two tablespoons of stock and stir enough into the sauce to thicken lightly. Bring to boiling point.

Add garnish. Scald and skin tomatoes. Quarter and remove seeds, add to the sauce with the olives and herbs. Adjust seasoning. Divide lamb into cutlets and arrange 'en couronne' in a serving dish. Spoon the garnish in the centre and a little of the sauce over the cutlets. Serve the rest separately.

Cotelettes d'Agneau Doria

Very good for a spring luncheon party. Though a good brown sauce can accompany, a mousseline or light Hollandaise (p. 76) is perhaps more in keeping with the garnish. For entertaining the Hollandaise will keep warm more satisfactorily.

A best end should give five good cutlets though one may have a 'double bone' which should be taken out. If the dish is for more than four or five people a second piece of best end is required for six.

2 lb (1 kg) best end of lamb, chined only and with the cutlet bones sawn through to within about 2½ inches (6 cm) of the meat
Seasoned flour
1 beaten egg with a large pinch of salt added
2–3 cups (6–9 oz/ 170–253 g) dried white crumbs
3–4 tablespoons (50–70 ml) salad oil
1 oz (30 g) butter, preferably clarified

Garnish :
1 large cucumber
1–2 bunches spring onions, according to size
2 teaspoons freshly chopped mint
1 oz (28 g) butter

Remove chine bone and divide the neck into plump cutlets. Trim, scraping bones clear of fat. Brush with flour, dip into the beaten egg, brushing off any surplus. Put crumbs on a large sheet of paper, lift cutlets onto this, one at a time and press on the crumbs well using a palette knife. Lift onto a rack and leave until ready to fry.

Cook cucumber before doing so. Peel and split into four lengthways, then cut across into one-inch pieces. Blanch for two to three minutes in boiling water, strain, refresh and drain well.

Heat oil in a large frying pan, add butter and at once put in cutlets. Fry *gently*, turning once only, until golden brown, four or five minutes. Lift out onto rack, set on a tray and slip into a warm oven, 150°C–170°C/300°F–325°F/Gas Mark 2–3 for three to four minutes.

Melt butter in a shallow pan, add onions trimmed but with about one inch of green left on. Cover and gently cook for four to five minutes, then add cucumber, season and replace cover. Simmer for five minutes or until just tender, shaking the pan occasionally. Then add the mint.

Arrange cutlets 'en couronne' on a serving dish and if wished, garnish each bone with a cutlet frill. Set the garnish at side or in the centre. Serve at once with the chosen sauce.

Serves 4–5

Navarin de Mouton

When well made this can be delicious and is certainly not just 'another stew'.

A navarin traditionally indicates that it is made with mutton which gives the good flavour. In the recipe given here middle neck is used, though in Scotland this tends to become part of another joint. A pound piece of 'runner' (from the middle neck and shoulder) makes an excellent navarin.

2–2½ lb (1–1¼ kg) middle
   neck mutton or lamb
2 medium sized onions,
   split and each half cut
   into three downwards
2 medium sized carrots,
   cut in half and across
1 large tablespoon
   dripping
1 tablespoon flour
1½ pints (900 ml) good
   stock
1 bouquet garni
1 teaspoon tomato purée
Salt, and pepper from
   the mill

Serves 4

Cut the meat into convenient sized pieces. Soak in slightly salted water over-night. Drain and dry the pieces well.

Heat the dripping and brown the meat thoroughly on all sides, using moderate heat, in a casserole. Take out and put in the vegetables. Continue to fry gently until well coloured. Draw aside, and sprinkle with flour. Return to the heat; allow to brown for a few minutes then add the stock, herbs, tomato purée and seasoning. Bring to the boil, put in the meat, cover and cook gently in the oven, 170°C–180°C/325°F–350°F/Gas Mark 3–4 or on the cooker top, whichever is convenient, for 1–1½ hours until the meat is tender and the gravy well reduced. Serve in the casserole with creamed potatoes to accompany.

Gigot d'Agneau Bordelaise

This really *is* a 'party piece', delicious to eat with its rich wine sauce, good to look at, and not uneconomical. It is easy,

Bone out the leg starting at the thigh end and cutting away the meat down and around the bone. Avoid slitting the skin on the side and work with short sharp strokes of the knife down to the shank, folding back the flesh.

too, to carve as the leg is boned before stuffing; it may be prepared and cooked ahead of time.

Serve with small new potatoes plainly boiled and tossed in butter and parsley, or 'pommes fondants'. For a green vegetable serve French beans or baby sprouts.

1 leg of lamb, about
   3½–4 lb (1½–2 kg)

Farce:
6 oz (169 g) flat
   mushrooms
1 oz (28 g) butter
1 shallot, finely chopped
2 teaspoons finely
   chopped fresh herbs
8 oz (225 g) sliced cooked
   gammon

Braising:
2–3 tablespoons
   (35–50 ml) oil
A plateful of sliced root
   vegetables, carrot,
   onion and celery
2 cloves garlic
A bouquet garni
½ pint (300 ml) jellied
   stock
½ bottle red Bordeaux
Salt and black pepper
   from the mill

Sauce:
½ oz (14 g) butter
½ oz (14 g) flour
Red wine reserved from
   the braised lamb
2 teaspoons tomato purée
½ pint demi-glace sauce
   (this can come from
   the freezer)
A nut of butter

Serves 6

Wash and chop the mushrooms finely, cook in the butter with the shallot for four or five minutes or until most of the moisture has been driven off. Season and add the herbs. Cool.

Separate the ham slices, spread each with the mushroom duxelles and arrange them overlapping on a flat surface. Roll up and insert inside the leg. Sew up the openings and tie if necessary to neaten.

Heat oil in a thick cocotte or casserole, brown lamb in this, take out and add the vegetables. There should be enough to cover the bottom well. Put on the lid and cook gently for seven to ten minutes until the fat is absorbed and the vegetables nicely coloured.

Place the lamb on top, add garlic and bouquet. Turn wine into a pan, bring to the boil, reduce for two to three minutes or allow it to catch alight. Pour half over the lamb and reserve remainder for the sauce. Add stock and seasoning. Cover and put into a pre-heated oven, 170°C–180°C/325°F–350°F/Gas Mark 3–4 for approximately 1¾ hours or until tender when pierced with the trussing needle.

Take up, set on a dish and keep warm. Strain the gravy from the vegetables, skim and set aside.

Prepare the sauce. Brown the flour lightly in the butter, add the remaining red wine, the gravy, tomato purée and demi-glace. Stir well and boil gently for five or six minutes until syrupy. Finish with the nut of butter.

To serve, remove the string from the lamb and spoon a little of the sauce over. Serve the rest separately.

Côte d'Agneau Bretonne

An old favourite of the Cordon Bleu, and an ideal dish for a lunch party.

Care should be taken that the meat is not over-roasted but remains delicately pink when carved. The farce should be a good green and well flavoured. Take care not to add too much egg as this tends to make it hard instead of succulent.

2 lb (1 kg) loin or best end neck of lamb
2–3 tablespoons oil or dripping
Dried white or browned crumbs (raspings)

Farce:
1 medium sized onion, chopped
2 oz (56 g) butter
1 cup (3 oz/84 g) fresh white breadcrumbs
2 large tablespoons freshly chopped parsley
Grated rind of ½ orange and the juice
Seasoning
A little beaten egg to bind

Gravy:
½ onion, sliced
½ pint (300 ml) strong stock made from the bones
1 tablespoon redcurrant jelly
Juice of half an orange

Garnish:
Glazed onions, carrots or button sprouts

Bone out the lamb and prepare the farce. Soften onion in butter, add to the crumbs, with the parsley, orange rind and seasoning; bind with the orange juice and a very little beaten egg. Spread this over the inside of the meat, roll up and tie, or pin, securely. Roll in seasoned flour, brush with beaten egg and roll in the dried crumbs. Heat the fat in a roasting tin and, when it is smoking, put in the meat, set on a grid. Baste and roast for forty-five minutes to one hour.

Take up the meat, remove the string and keep warm while preparing the gravy. Tip off fat from the roasting tin, add the sliced onion and cook gently until brown. Dust in one teaspoon flour, add stock and redcurrant jelly; boil up well, season, sharpen with the orange juice, then strain.

Slice the meat, arrange overlapping down a serving dish. Garnish with the glazed onions, carrots or sprouts. Spoon over a little of the gravy and serve the rest separately.

Glazed onions: Blanch onions, drain, return to pan, add a large nut of butter and a teaspoon of caster sugar. Cover and cook gently until golden brown, shaking frequently.

Carrots: Quarter carrots, put in a pan with salted water to cover, a nut of butter and a teaspoon of sugar. Cook until the water has evaporated and the carrots covered with a glaze. Season with black pepper, chopped parsley and mint.

Sprouts: Trim. Cook in fast boiling salted water for four to five minutes, drain and return to pan with a good nut of butter, salt and pepper from the mill.

Shake up over heat before dishing.

Serves 4–5

Carré d'Agneau Rôti

A choice meat course for a lunch party. Not original but to our mind better than a crown roast. Serve with home-made redcurrant jelly or, in Spring, with the freshest of mint sauces.

2 × 1½ lb (680 g) best end neck of lamb, chined only
1½ oz (42 g) butter
Juice of 1 orange
Pepper from the mill
About ½–¾ pint (283–425 ml) strong stock made from the chine bones
Cutlet frills

Remove chine bones and prepare stock. Saw through neck bones to shorten them slightly. Trim away fat and gristle from the bones and score necks with the point of a sharp knife. Spread with the butter and grind over some pepper.

Set the necks together, upright, interlacing the bones. Tie round with fine string. Pour round the juice of the orange and three to four tablespoons stock. Roast in a pre-heated oven, 190°C/375°F/Gas Mark 5 for approximately forty to forty-five minutes, basting frequently. Add more of the stock as the liquid reduces. Take up and dish meat, remove string, and top bones with the cutlet frills.

Deglaze pan with rest of stock, season and strain. Pour round a little of the gravy and serve the remainder in a gravy boat.

Serves 6

Topinambours (Jerusalem Artichokes) Velouté

One of the best ways to serve these artichokes. They are excellent with plain roast lamb and are at their best from October to February.

1½–2 lb (680 g–1 kg) artichokes
12 button or pickling onions
½ pint (283 ml) water
¾ pint (425 ml) milk
1¼ oz (35 g) butter
1¼ oz (35 g) flour
2 tablespoons cream
2 large ripe tomatoes
1 rounded dessertspoon freshly chopped parsley

Serves 6

Peel and trim artichokes. Cut into walnut sized pieces. Put into a pan with the water and half the milk, salt lightly and bring to the boil. Simmer until barely tender, for ten to fifteen minutes.

Meantime, blanch onions for five to seven minutes until barely tender. Drain. Scald, quarter and seed tomatoes. Cut each quarter in half lengthways. Drain artichokes reserving ½ pint (283 ml) of the liquid. Turn artichokes into a casserole for serving. Add onions and keep warm. Rinse out pan.

Melt butter, stir in flour, cook for a second or two, then blend in the reserved artichoke stock and the rest of the milk. Stir until boiling, cook for a minute or two, season and add cream. Stir in the tomatoes and lastly the parsley. Pour this sauce over the artichokes and onions, cover casserole and heat in a slow oven for six to ten minutes.

Pork
and
Ham

Pork

The majority of the recipes given here are for pork fillet or tenderloin. This is really the best and most economical cut for entertaining, having little or no waste.

Pork meat is dense and requires slow and thorough cooking, and, for example in a sauté where a sauce is used, keeps hot without spoiling. It will be noticed that most of the dishes are finished with cream or the addition of butter to the sauce. This is to give succulence and tenderness to the fillet which has very little or no fat.

When clarified butter is used remember to take a little more than called for in the recipe before clarifying, i.e. for 1 oz (28 g) clarified butter take 1½ oz (42 g) salted or fresh butter. The advantage of clarified butter is that it can be taken to a higher temperature without burning and so is valuable in frying or sautéing.

For those who either do not like or cannot eat pork, try lamb fillets. Some butchers in the larger towns have these or will cut them for you. They come from either side of the top of the neck and are not so large as the pork fillet. They also cost less.

With the exception of the paupiettes, the fillet of pork Calvados and 'en croute' the recipes given here are also suitable for the lamb.

Sauté de Porc à la Façon de Meaux

1¼–1½ lb (approx. 650 g)
  pork fillet or tenderloin
1 medium sized onion
1½ oz (42 g) butter
1 oz (28 g) flour
¾–1 pint (450–600 ml)
  jellied veal or chicken
  stock
Seasoning
½ lb (225 g) button
  mushrooms
5 tablespoons (75 ml)
  thick cream
A pinch sugar
1 tablespoon 'Moutarde
  de Meaux' (important
  to use the true French
  variety of Meaux
  mustard)

Serves 4–5

Cut the pork in ½-inch (1-cm) diagonal slices, chop onion finely, wipe and trim the mushrooms. Melt the butter in a sauté pan, add the meat a few pieces at a time, and fry briskly until brown. Add the onion, lower the heat and continue to cook for two or three minutes.

Draw aside, stir in the flour and add the stock. Blend until smooth, season and bring to the boil, cover and simmer until the pork is tender, about thirty to forty minutes, then add the mushrooms and cook for a further five minutes.

Add the cream, reboil, check the seasoning, add the sugar and bind if necessary with one teaspoon arrowroot slaked with one tablespoon stock or water. Draw the pan to one side, mix a large spoonful of the sauce with the mustard, return this to the sauté pan and blend it in carefully. Reheat but do not reboil after the mustard has been added. Serve with plain boiled rice or new or puréed potatoes.

Filet de Porc Calvados

Like all dishes made with pork fillet (or tenderloin of pork as some butchers call it) this one will keep hot very well or can be prepared early in the day for a dinner party and reheated. Calvados (apple brandy) can be replaced with a small glass of dry sherry.

2 pork fillets, 1¾–2 lb approx. (800–900 g)
2 shallots or pickling onions
1 oz (28 g) butter
1 large dessert apple (Cox's pippin)
1½ oz (42 g) walnut kernels ground
2 oz (56 g) seeded raisins, split in half
2 oz (56 g) fresh white breadcrumbs
1 tablespoon chopped parsley
1 small egg

For pot roasting:
1 oz (28 g) butter
1 glass (35 ml) Calvados
½ pint (300 ml) dry cider
Bouquet garni
Kneaded butter made with:
   1 oz (28 g) butter and ¾ oz (20 g) flour
4 tablespoons (70 ml) double cream

Garnish:
1 head of celery cut in batons and tied in 6 small bundles
2 dessert apples

Serves 6

Split each pork fillet open, not quite in half, lay flat and bat out lightly. Cut the fillets almost in half, so the two tapered pieces will make a good middle layer.

Chop the shallot finely, peel and core the apple and cut in small dice. Cook the shallot in the butter until soft, increase the heat under the pan, add the diced apple and cook for one or two minutes. Add the raisins, fry for another minute, then add the walnuts, crumbs and parsley. Season well and bind with the beaten egg. Sandwich the three layers of meat with this mixture, reshape and tie up.

Heat a shallow casserole, drop in the butter and while still foaming, put in pork and brown on all sides. Cover tightly and cook gently for ten to fifteen minutes. Flame with the Calvados and moisten with about half the cider, season and add the bouquet garni. Cover again, bring to the boil and continue to cook on top of the stove or in a moderate oven, 180°C/350°F/Gas Mark 4 for forty-five minutes or until the pork is tender.

Meantime boil the celery in water with a tablespoonful of milk and a little salt, drain well when tender and moisten with a very little butter. Cut the apples in slices ½-inch (1-cm) thick, stamp out the core and fry quickly in hot butter until brown.

Take out the pork, strain off the liquor, skim and add the remaining cider to bring the liquid to ½ pint (300 ml). Thicken with a little kneaded butter, reboil and add the cream. Adjust the seasoning and boil again. Reduce a little if necessary to give a good syrupy texture.

Slice the meat, lay on a dish, spoon over the sauce and garnish with the celery and apple. Scatter over the chopped parsley.

This dish freezes well. Wrap the meat unsliced, with sauce and garnish packed separately.

After thawing the meat, stir the sauce in a casserole over a gentle heat until smooth and bring to the boil. Put in the meat, baste well with the sauce, cover with foil and the lid of the pan and place in a moderate oven, 190°C/375°F/Gas Mark 5 for thirty minutes. Heat the garnish separately. Slice and garnish meat as described in the recipe.

Filet de Porc 'En Cocotte' Duxelles

A particularly good way of serving this lean cut of pork. As a close textured meat it benefits from the creamy and delicately flavoured sauce.

Pork fillet is available all the year round and makes a 'good buy' as there is little or no waste. For those who prefer another meat, a cut from the 'oyster' (shoulder) of veal is ideal, though not so easily obtainable.

Serve for a lunch or dinner party with a potato and celeriac purée and/or a green vegetable to accompany. This dish keeps hot without spoiling if guests are late. It also freezes well.

2 pork tenderloins or
   fillet, 1¾–2 lb
   (339–453 g)
1 medium sized onion
1½ oz (45 g) butter
1 oz (30 g) flour
¾–1 pint (450–600 ml)
   jellied veal or chicken
   stock
2½ fluid oz (75 ml)
   double cream

Duxelles:
½ lb (226 g) flat
   mushrooms
½ oz (15 g) butter
1 dessertspoon mixed
   chopped fresh herbs
   and parsley
Salt, and pepper from
   the mill

Serves 4–6

Prepare duxelles. Wash and chop mushrooms finely. Melt butter in a sauté pan, add mushrooms. Cook gently until the juice runs, then add herbs and seasoning. Increase heat, stir frequently for four or five minutes, by which time much of the moisture should have evaporated. Draw aside.

Cut pork into ½-inch–¾-inch (1–2-cm) diagonal slices. Melt butter in a casserole, add meat and sauté briskly over moderate heat until it is nicely coloured. Finely chop onion, lower heat and add. Continue to cook for two or three minutes.

Draw aside, stir in the flour and add stock. Blend, season and bring to a gentle boil. Add duxelles, cover and put into a pre-heated oven, 180°C/350°F/Gas Mark 4 until the pork is really tender, about forty-five to fifty minutes.

Take up, adjust seasoning and add cream. Bring to boiling point. Blend a teaspoon of arrowroot with two to three tablespoons of water. Draw aside casserole and add arrowroot when off the boil. Bring to simmering point and serve, if wished, in the casserole.

For freezing omit the arrowroot and allow to get quite cold. Turn into a container. Wrap and freeze. To thaw, allow twenty-four hours in a refrigerator. Turn into a casserole and heat gently, shaking the casserole from time to time. When nearing boiling point, add the slaked arrowroot, off the heat. Shake gently to mix well. Reboil and serve.

Purée de Celeri-Rave:
1 celeriac (weight ½ lb/226 g)
1 lb (453 g) potatoes
1 oz (30 g) butter

Peel and cut the celeriac in wedges and place in a pan with cold water and salt to taste. Boil gently for twenty minutes then add the potatoes and continue to cook until both vegetables are tender.

Drain off the water and put back on low heat to dry. Crush the vegetables with a potato masher, add the butter and pepper from the mill and a little sugar to taste. Beat in a little hot milk, keeping the pan over gentle heat. Serve.

Filet de Porc Genoise

A delicious spicy dish. For real success special care should be given to the sauce, which must be rich and not too sharp in flavour. Cream is not added but the sauce is finished with the addition of butter which gives the necessary fat mentioned earlier, and also helps to thicken it without too much reduction.

Tomato sauce:
- 1 oz (30 g) butter
- 1 medium sized onion, chopped
- 1 medium sized carrot, grated
- 1 lb (453 g) ripe tomatoes *or* 1 × 8-oz (226-g) can Italian tomatoes
- 1 large clove garlic, chopped
- 1 bay leaf
- 1 teaspoon chopped fresh or dried basil
- ½ pint (300 ml) jellied chicken stock
- Tomato purée if necessary
- Butter to finish, about 1 tablespoon

- 1¼–1½ lb (566–678 g) pork fillet
- 1 oz (30 g) clarified butter or 2 tablespoons (35 ml) oil
- 1 glass (70 ml) sherry

Serves 4–5

Soften the onion in the butter for the sauce. Add the carrot and the tomatoes cut in half and squeezed to remove seeds. Cover and cook gently for five to six minutes. Then add herbs and stock. Season well. Bring to boil and simmer for ten to fifteen minutes. Rub through a strainer and return to the pan. Simmer very gently while preparing the pork.

Remove any gristle from the fillets and sauté over moderate heat in the clarified butter until just coloured, turning frequently. Flame with the sherry, cover at once and simmer on cooker top or put into a moderate oven, 170°C–180°C/325°F–350°F/Gas Mark 3–4 for fifteen minutes. Now pour over the sauce, cover tightly and continue to cook in the oven for twenty to twenty-five minutes until tender. Take out the pork and keep warm.

Strain sauce into a clean pan, adjust seasoning and strengthen flavour if necessary with a little tomato purée. Boil up well, draw aside and add the butter in small pieces, stirring it well in.

Slice the fillets diagonally and arrange in a serving dish. Spoon over the sauce and serve with tagliatelle or a saffron rissoto.

Paupiettes de Porc Normande

The stuffing for these uses belly pork which contains a good amount of fat to make the finished dish succulent and the meat tender. The 'topping' of apple and sour cream is especially good.

1–2 pork fillets,
  tenderloin, weight
  1¼–1½ lb (678 g)

Stuffing:
6–8 oz (170–225 g) fresh
  belly pork
3 oz (84 g) fresh
  breadcrumbs
1 onion, chopped and
  blanched
1 tablespoon chopped
  sage and parsley
Grated rind and juice of
  ½ lemon
Beaten egg to bind

For braising:
2 tablespoons (35 ml)
  dripping
1 onion
1 carrot
2 sticks celery
½ pint (300 ml) jellied
  brown stock
¼ pint (150 ml) dry cider
Bouquet garni
Seasoning

To finish:
1 crisp dessert apple,
  Cox's for preference
½ oz (15 g) butter
4 tablespoons (70 ml)
  sour cream

Serves 4–5

Split the pork fillets, bat out between waxed or oiled paper and cut into eight pieces – very thin and about 4 × 5 inches (10 × 12 cm).

Prepare the stuffing: coarsely chop or mince the belly pork, mix with all the other ingredients and season well; spread on the slices of pork, roll up and tie with thread or very fine string.

Heat the dripping in a shallow casserole and brown the paupiettes well, lift from the pan, lower the heat and add the vegetables, cut into dice. Cover the pan and cook gently until the vegetables begin to colour.

Spoon or tip off any excess dripping and replace the paupiettes in the casserole, season and add the bouquet of herbs and pour over the stock and cider. Bring to the boil, cover and place in a moderate oven at 180°C/350°F/Gas Mark 4 for about fifty to sixty minutes.

Take up, lift the paupiettes from the casserole and skim off any fat. Strain the stock and thicken slightly with arrowroot or potato flour. Peel and dice the apple, brown in the hot butter and pour on the sour cream and allow to bubble for two or three minutes.

Remove string from the paupiettes, place in a deep entrée dish, pour over the thickened gravy and spoon the apple and sour cream on top.

Sauté de Porc Hongroise

This recipe is a particular favourite of the Cordon Bleu, quick and easy to make and one that has stood the test of time. It freezes well.

1¼-1½ lb (566–678 g) pork fillet
1¼ oz (36 g) clarified butter
1 small onion, finely chopped
1 glass (70 ml) sherry
1 tablespoon paprika
1 tablespoon flour
7½ fluid oz to ½ pint (225–300 ml) jellied stock
Salt and pepper
4 oz (113 g) button mushrooms, trimmed and washed
4 tablespoons (70 ml) double cream

Cabbage Alsacienne:
1 small to medium size white cabbage
2–3 sticks celery, sliced
1 large onion, thinly sliced
1 oz (30 g) butter
1 wine glass (115 ml) each white wine and stock
1 tablespoon chopped parsley

Remove any skin or gristle from the fillets and cut diagonally across into 1½-inch (2–3-cm) pieces. Heat the butter in a sauté or shallow pan, put in the pork and sauté briskly turning frequently until barely coloured.

Add chopped onion and after one or wo minutes the sherry. Allow to reduce for thirty seconds than stir in the paprika and then the flour. Pour in the stock, season and bring to the boil. Cover and simmer gently for thirty-five to forty-five minutes or until the pork is tender. After half an hour put in the mushrooms whole. When pork is cooked, add the cream and continue to simmer for one or two minutes before serving.

Cabbage Alsacienne:
Meantime prepare the cabbage. Cook onion and celery in the butter in a casserole for two to three minutes. Shred cabbage finely, pack into the casserole, layer with salt and pepper from the mill.

Pour over the wine and stock, press a piece of foil or greaseproof paper on the top. Cover with the lid and cook gently for about fifteen to twenty minutes. Stir occasionally with a fork. When just tender add parsley and serve with the pork.

Serves 4–5

Filets de Porc aux Abricots

This delectable dish *must* be prepared with fresh apricots, neither tinned nor dried will do. Happily for those planning menus the recipe can be chosen

Halve the apricots, remove the stones and poach lightly in four tablespoons (70 ml) water and two teaspoons sugar. Roll the pork in the seasoned flour. Heat the oil in a flame-proof casserole, drop in the butter, add the pork and brown well on all sides; reduce the heat, add the shallots and cook for two to three minutes;

during two periods of the year when apricots arrive from the Southern and Northern hemispheres.

1–2 pork fillets (weight about 1½–2 lb approx./ 780 g–1 kg)
¼ lb (113 g) apricots
1 tablespoon seasoned flour
1 tablespoon (18 ml) oil
½ oz (14 g) butter
2 shallots
2 tablespoons (35 ml) brandy
½ pint (300 ml) jellied brown stock
2 fluid oz (65 ml) cream

flame with the brandy. Surround the pork with the apricots, season well, cover tightly and cook in a moderate oven, 180°C/350°F/Gas Mark 4 for about forty-five to fifty minutes.

Take up the pork, slice and place in a casserole for serving. Add the stock to the cooking pan, boil up well and rub the contents through a nylon strainer or whirl in a blender. Reduce the sauce a little, adjust the seasoning, add the cream and pour it over the pork. Return the pork to a slow oven, 170°C/325°F/ Gas Mark 3 for about twenty minutes or until the meat becomes well impregnated with the apricot sauce.

When in season serve with new Jersey potatoes tossed in butter and chives and spinach 'en branche' or French beans as a second vegetable.

Serves 6

Filets de Porc 'En Croûte'

This is essentially a dinner party dish and can be prepared well in advance. It can be frozen before cooking but allow twelve hours or more in the refrigerator before baking.

8 oz (225 g) puff pastry
2–2½ lb (approx. 1 kg) pork fillets
Oil for roasting

Duxelles Farce:
1 × 2 oz (56 g) onion, finely chopped (size of a golf ball)
6 oz (169 g) flat mushrooms, chopped
1 oz (30 g) butter
1 tablespoon chopped mixed herbs
Salt and pepper
2 large tablespoons fresh white crumbs
Beaten egg to bind

Have ready the puff pastry; if it is bought choose a type that is made with butter.

Trim the fillets, first removing any skin. Split lengthways, bat out between waxed paper or foil. Trim again to neaten.

Prepare the farce. Cook the onion a few minutes in the butter, then add the mushrooms. Continue to cook rapidly for five minutes, stirring occasionally. Draw aside, add herbs, seasoning and the crumbs. Add a little beaten egg to bind, then turn onto a plate to cool.

Shred any trimmings there may be and add to the farce. Spread this on the fillets, place one on top of the other, and tie or skewer neatly. Set on a grid in a roasting tin, pour over two or three tablespoons (35–50 ml) oil and roast in a hot oven, 190°C–200°C/375°F–400°F/Gas Mark 5–6 for about 1–1¼ hours. Baste well.

Take up and leave until quite cold. Remove any strings, then wrap the sliced ham round the meat. Roll out the pastry fairly thinly to a large rectangle. Brush edges lightly with water. Set meat in centre and wrap over the edges, press down firmly and trim off surplus pastry. Turn over onto a damped thick baking sheet to bring the smooth side of the pastry uppermost. Roll out trimmings and cut into

4–6 oz (113–169 g) sliced cooked gammon

¾ pint (450 ml) demi-glace or sauce Italienne (p. 88) to accompany

A little watercress to garnish

fleurons. Brush roll with beaten egg and decorate with the fleurons.

Bake in a pre-heated oven 220°C/425°F/Gas Mark 7 for about forty-five minutes and until well browned. Lift onto a serving dish, garnish with the cress and serve with the accompanying sauce.

Serves 6

Mousse au Jambon

Serve this for a supper party with a side salad of pineapple or orange combined with tomatoes, chives and French dressing and a casserole of new potatoes in a creamy curry sauce.

1 lb (453 g) ham
3 oz (84 g) butter
1 teaspoon tomato purée
½ pint (300 ml) demi-glace sauce (see recipe for *Filet de Boeuf Braisé aux Champignons*) from the freezer, thawed and beaten well
2 tablespoons (35 ml) cream
2 tablespoons (35 ml) sherry

To finish:
½ pint (300 ml) aspic jelly
12 small flat mushrooms cooked

Serves 4

Mince the ham; cream the butter until quite soft and partially whip the cream. Pound or work the ham with the tomato purée in a food processer and add the sauce by degrees. Fold in the butter, cream and sherry. Turn into a 7-inch soufflé case, smooth the top and set in a cool place for about ten minutes to firm.

Run a thin layer of aspic over the mousse and, when set, arrange the garnish on the top, dipping the mushrooms first in a little aspic. Set the garnish in another layer of aspic and then fill to the top of the dish with the rest.

Pommes à l'Indienne:

1–1½ lb (678 g) baby new potatoes
1½ oz (42 g) butter
1 shallot
1 dessertspoon curry powder
1 oz (28 g) flour
1 pint (600 ml) milk
Seasoning
1 bay leaf

Scrub the potatoes and cook in boiling water for five minutes, then drain and peel.

Chop the shallot finely and cook in the butter with the curry powder for one or two minutes then blend in the flour and milk. Stir until boiling, season and simmer gently for three to four minutes.

Place the potatoes in a casserole, add the bay leaf and pour over the sauce; cover and cook in a moderate oven, 180°C/350°F/Gas Mark 4 for about eight to ten minutes or until tender.

Jambon au Blanc

4–5 lb (2 kg) piece of
  green gammon from
  the top part of the leg
A large bouquet garni
  containing 2 sticks of
  celery
1 large onion, stuck with
  a clove
About 12 peppercorns

Sauce:
½ pint (300 ml) Alsatian
  wine
5 oz (140 g) unsalted
  butter
1½ oz (42 g) flour
3 egg yolks
4 tablespoons (70 ml)
  cream

*Garnish and accompanying
vegetables:*
1 lb (½ kg) small new
  carrots
2 lb (1 kg) very small
  young broad beans
3 bunches spring onions
1½ lb (675 g) *small* new
  potatoes
2 tablespoons chopped
  parsley

Serves 6–8

Soak the gammon overnight in cold water.

Rinse the meat well, place in a saucepan covered with fresh water, add the herbs and set on a low heat. Over a span of one hour bring to simmering point. Add the onion and peppercorns, maintain a very gentle heat and check frequently that only tiny bubbles rise to the surface and cook at this speed for two hours. *The liquid should never boil hard.*

Cook the carrots and broad beans separately in the usual way. Trim the onions and tie in about six small bundles; these and the potatoes can be cooked until tender in the pan with the gammon. Allow thirty minutes for the potatoes and ten minutes for the onions.

Make a start on the sauce. Boil the wine in a 2-pint saucepan until reduced to half quantity, pour into a small jug or basin and set aside. Melt 1½ oz (42 g) of the butter in the same pan and blend in the flour.

Work the egg yolks with a small wooden spoon and add the cream. Measure off 1 pint (600 ml) of the ham liquid and while still hot whisk into the roux of butter and flour and bring to the boil; add the reduced wine, season and simmer for five minutes. Add 2 tablespoons (35 ml) of the hot sauce to the egg yolk and pour this liaison slowly into the sauce. Reheat, stirring all the time until the sauce thickens creamily, but do not boil. Draw the pan to one side and beat in the rest of the butter a small piece at a time. Adjust the seasoning and keep warm in a bain-marie.

Take up the gammon, remove the skin and set on a large dish; surround the meat with the bundles of spring onions and arrange a few carrots and broad beans between – enough to garnish the dish but not to impede the carver.

Moisten the meat and garnish with a little of the sauce. Serve the rest of the carrots and broad beans, mixed with potatoes, in a vegetable dish and dust well with chopped parsley. Pour the sauce into a large gravy boat and serve separately.

After serving this dish for a dinner party it is more than likely there would be enough over to mince 1 lb (453 g) and freeze it ready to make a mousse for a lunch or supper dish.

Jambon Véronique

Make this dish in the early autumn when really good green grapes are plentiful. The combination of the delicate flavour of the grapes in the butter sauce with the slight saltiness of the ham, makes it a dish for a really special occasion.

It should be made with a freshly cooked piece of gammon; this is a lean cut which contrasts well with the butter sauce and can be taken from the middle or corner. If possible have a fair sized piece. Once boiled slice off what is required, and the remainder makes a useful cold joint.

A piece of middle cut or
  gammon bacon 3½–4 lb
  (1½–2 kg) – choose
  unsmoked for a more
  delicate flavour
1 large onion, sliced
1 large carrot, sliced
Bouquet garni
A few peppercorns

Butter sauce :
2 shallots, finely chopped
1 generous glass
  (115–120 ml) white
  wine
3–4 oz (84–113 g) butter
2 egg yolks

Soak the gammon for two to three hours in cold water. Drain, put into a pan with cold water to cover. Add the vegetables, bouquet and peppercorns. Bring slowly to the boil, skimming well. Simmer, allowing twenty minutes to the pound and fifteen minutes over. Draw aside and leave to cool.

Prepare the sauce: cook the shallots in the wine until the liquid is reduced to about half, strain onto the yolks beaten with a nut of the butter. Stand in a bain-marie and, stirring continually, add the remaining butter piece by piece until the sauce thickens. Set aside.

For the flour sauce: melt the butter, stir in the flour, cook for a few seconds, then pour on the stock, blend and bring to the boil. Cook for a few minutes, beat in the butter sauce and add the cream.

Leave in a bain-marie while reheating the ham. Take up, skin and slice what is required. Lay on a hot dish. Moisten with a spoonful of the ham stock. Add the grapes to the sauce. Gently reheat, then spoon over the sauce. Serve with plainly boiled new potatoes.

Serves 4–6

1 oz (30 g) butter
1 oz (28 g) flour
¾ pint (375 ml) white
  bone stock (chicken or
  veal)
4 fluid oz (125 ml) cream
½–¾ lb (225–339 g) green
  grapes, peeled, pipped
  and sprinkled with
  lemon juice

Veal

Rôti de Veau à l'Orange

The following recipe is perfect for a dinner party – it satisfies guests who like 'a roast' but the addition of stock and cream keeps the meat very succulent even if kept warm after dishing.

2–3 lb (1–1¼ kg) shoulder of fillet of veal, boned and suitable for stuffing
8 anchovy fillets, chopped
2 cloves garlic, crushed
2 oz (56 g) butter
2 bay leaves
2 shallots
8 fluid oz (240 ml) stock
1 orange, peeled and thinly sliced

Stuffing:
5 tablespoons fresh white crumbs
2 tablespoons chopped parsley
3 oz (84 g) raisins, stoned and split
Grated rind and juice of 1 orange
Seasoning
1 oz (30 g) butter
2 shallots finely chopped
2 tablespoons shelled walnuts, coarsely chopped
Beaten egg

To finish:
1 teaspoon arrowroot
3 tablespoons (50 ml) cream
Slices of orange fried
Chopped parsley

Serves 6

Crush the anchovy with the garlic to a paste, then with a sharp pointed knife make 12-16 incisions all over the surface of the joint. Work the paste well into these.

Prepare the stuffing: put the crumbs, parsley, raisins and orange rind together and season well. Heat the butter in a small pan, add the shallots, soften slightly, add the walnuts and allow to colour. Cool a little and then add to the crumbs. Bind with beaten egg and enough orange juice to make a good moist mixture. Stuff into the joint and sew up with a coarse thread or string. Heat the butter for roasting, put in the meat, baste, add the shallots, bay leaves, liquid and sliced orange. Put into a moderate oven and cook, basting fairly frequently, for about two hours. If the liquid in the pan reduces too much add a little extra water or stock to keep the quantity to about ¼ pint (150 ml).

Serve the meat on a hot dish, then draw out the threads with care. Strain the gravy into a small saucepan, deglaze the tin with a little stock or water and add to the gravy. Thicken very slightly with arrowroot mixed with a little water; reboil, add the cream, boil hard for a minute or two. Spoon a little of the gravy over the meat and pour the rest into a sauce boat. Garnish the dish with slices of fried orange, and finish with a sprinkling of chopped parsley.

Escalopes de Veau Maintenon

A recipe of many years' standing. Apart from being delicious it is ideal for entertaining as the escalopes can be completed and left ready for the final browning without spoiling.

5 large veal escalopes
1½ oz (45 g) butter
1 shallot
1 teaspoon flour
1 teaspoon tomato purée
2½ fluid oz (75 ml) sherry
¼ pint (150 ml) stock

Salpicon:
4 oz (113 g) mushrooms
1 shallot, finely chopped
1 oz (30 g) butter
Scant ½ oz (14 g) flour
A little good stock
1 tablespoon (18 ml) sherry
4 oz (113 g)) shredded ham

Mornay sauce:
1 oz (30 g) butter
1 oz (30 g) flour
½ pint (300 ml) milk
2 oz (60 g) dry grated cheese

Sauté the escalopes in half the butter until golden brown on both sides, allowing about seven or eight minutes. Remove from the pan and press flat.

Chop the shallot finely, add to the pan and cook until golden. Stir in the flour, allow to colour, then blend in the tomato purée, sherry and stock. Bring to the boil, season and simmer for one minute. Strain and keep hot.

Prepare the salpicon: sauté the sliced mushrooms and shallot in half the butter. Season, add flour and about 2½ fluid oz (70 ml) stock. Reboil, add the sherry and ham. Prepare the mornay sauce and set aside.

Take up the escalopes, lay on a baking tin, cover each with the salpicon. Coat with the mornay sauce, dust with cheese and brown under the grill or in a quick oven to allow them to heat through as well as brown. Arrange the veal on a serving dish and pour round the gravy.

Serves 5

Noix de Veau Braisé au Piments Doux

A dish to put on the menu for a celebration lunch. It freezes well and so is ideal to have ready for an important occasion.

Brown the meat slowly on all sides in the oil and butter, pour over the wine, add the tomato purée, herbs and seasoning. Cover the pan tightly and cook for one hour in a very moderate oven, 170°C/325°F/Gas Mark 3.

Meantime grill the red pepper until the skin is charred and easy to scrape away, then rinse

2 lb (907 g) oyster of veal
or a piece cut from
the topside of the leg
1 tablespoon (18 ml)
salad oil
½–1 oz (14–28 g) butter
1 glass (115 ml) white
wine
1 dessertspoon tomato
purée
Bouquet garni
¾ pint (450 ml)
demi-glace sauce
1 fresh red pepper
¼ lb (113 g) button
mushrooms

in cold water. Remove the core and seeds, slice
the flesh and keep on one side. Trim and wash
the mushrooms.

Have the demi-glace, freshly made or from the
freezer thawed, add to the veal and continue to
cook for forty to fifty minutes. Take up the meat
and place in an oven-proof casserole; add the
pepper and mushrooms and return to the oven
for ten to fifteen minutes before serving. Serve
with 'nouilles au beurre' or small new potatoes
and a second vegetable such as spinach,
courgettes or French beans.

Serves 6

Cotelettes de Veau Coupole

Choose small veal chops
or, if not available,
escalopes.

This dish is very good
for a party, but the port
is a necessary ingredient;
it adds the spicy
sweetness of flavour
which is essential. The
recipe is quick to make.

5–6 small veal chops
(as for the Marengo)
2 oz (56 g) butter
½ lb (225 g) button
onions, blanched
6 oz (169 g) button
mushrooms
2 glasses (100 ml) port
7½ fluid oz (225 ml)
jellied stock
Kneaded butter made
with rest of butter and
½ oz (15 g) flour
worked together
1 small carton, 4 fluid oz
(100 ml) double cream
Salt and pepper

Sauté chops until barely coloured in two-thirds
of the butter. Take out, add onions well drained,
sauté a few minutes, put in the mushrooms.
After a minute or two add the port, allow to
reduce a little. Replace chops, pour over stock,
shake pan gently and bring to boil. Season,
cover and simmer for six to eight minutes.

Dish the chops, draw pan off heat and add
the kneaded butter piece by piece. Reboil
when melted and add cream. Boil up well,
adjust seasoning and spoon over the meat.
Serve very hot.

Serves 5–6

Scallopini à la Crème

One of the quickest and simplest of dishes to make and, to our mind, more attractive than the large escalope. Veal of the first quality must be used for this.

1–1¼ lb (453–566 g) fillet of veal, cut into slices and batted out thinly
1½ oz (42 g) butter
1 glass (70 ml) sherry
1 medium sized onion, finely chopped
4 oz (113 g) button mushrooms, thinly sliced
1 level tablespoon flour
7½ fluid oz (225 ml) good chicken stock
Salt and pepper
1 small carton (4 fluid oz/125 ml) double cream

Cut the veal slices into two to three pieces. Heat a large sauté pan, drop in 1 oz (30 g) of the butter and when foaming sauté the pieces of veal, quickly turning once only.

Flame with the sherry, take out the veal, add remaining butter, onion and mushrooms, lower heat and sauté for three or four minutes, draw aside and stir in the flour. Blend in the stock, season and replace the veal.

Cover and simmer for five or six minutes. Remove lid and add cream. Shake pan gently and continue to cook for a few minutes until thick and creamy. Serve very hot with potatoes or rice, and a green vegetable.

Serves 4–5

Fricadelles à la Grecque

A somewhat similar method to that of the beef bitkis. The dish is Polish in origin and like bitkis the meat must be thoroughly worked with the liquid, in this case milk to give fat.

The sauce given here is tomato which gives piquancy to the bland flavour of the veal.

1¼ lb (556 g) finely minced veal
2 shallots, finely chopped

Put the veal and shallots into a bowl, add half the milk to the crumbs and allow to soak for a few minutes. Add to the meat by degrees, working well. As the mixture thickens pour in just enough of the rest of the milk to make it light and spongy. Taste for seasoning.

Divide mixture into pieces the size of a large walnut. When ready to fry, heat oil in a frying pan, add butter. Roll the fricadelles in the flour and fry quickly until just coloured. Lift out straight into a shallow fire-proof dish. Reheat the tomato sauce and spoon over the dish. Put into a moderately hot oven, 170°C–180°C/325°F–350°F/Gas Mark 3–4, for twenty-five to thirty minutes.

Half way through the cooking, turn the

4 oz (113 g) white
　　breadcrumbs
8–10 fluid oz (250 ml)
　　milk
Salt and pepper
Seasoned flour
3–4 tablespoons oil
1 oz (28 g) butter
¾ pint (450 ml) well
　　seasoned tomato sauce
4 tablespoons (70 ml)
　　sour cream

fricadelles in the sauce and spoon over the sour
cream. Return to the oven. Serve very hot with
boiled rice to accompany.

Serves 4–5

Escalopes de Veau Créole

One of the best of the
escalope recipes. The
light spiciness of the
sauce goes well with the
bland flavour of the veal,
as does the fresh
pineapple and rice.

　The addition of the
yolks to the sauce can
be omitted, especially if
the dish is to be kept
warm. In this case, add
the cream to the sauce
and boil gently for three
or four minutes.

5–6 veal escalopes
1½–2 oz (42–56 g)
　　unsalted butter

Velouté sauce :
1 oz (30 g) butter
1 rounded teaspoon curry
　　powder
½ teaspoon paprika
¾ oz (21 g) flour
¾ pint (450 ml) jellied
　　chicken stock
¾ gill (125 ml) double
　　cream
2 egg yolks (optional)

Serves 5–6

Trim and bat out the veal. Cut each escalope
into three. Gently heat a thick frying pan, drop
in the butter and when melted lay in the veal.
Sauté gently for four to six minutes without
allowing them to take colour. Lift veal into the
serving dish.

　Prepare the sauce : melt butter and add curry
powder and paprika off the heat. Gently cook
for a second or two, then stir in the flour.
Draw aside and blend in the stock. Season
lightly and stir over a moderate heat until
boiling. Boil gently for three or four minutes.

　Blend the cream with the yolks (if used) and
add this liaison by degrees to the sauce. Adjust
the seasoning. Reheat the veal and pour over
the sauce. Serve with boiled rice into which
fresh pineapple and split almonds have been
forked.

Rice :
½ lb (225 g) long-grained
　　rice
1 small pineapple, peeled,
　　sliced and shredded*
2 oz (56 g) almonds,
　　blanched and split

*If fresh pineapple is unobtainable, use
pineapple slices or spears canned in unsweetened pineapple juice.

Ragoût de Veau Créole

This dish has charm and is always appreciated by those who eat it. The ragoût should be rich in colour and flavour, and the veal cut from a thick slice so that the pieces are not too small.

1½–2 lb (678 g–1 kg) oyster of veal, without bone
1 × 4-oz (113 g) gammon rasher bacon, unsmoked
1 tablespoon (18 ml) oil
1½ oz (42 g) butter
1 medium sized onion, chopped
1 large clove garlic, chopped
1 level tablespoon flour
1 large glass (115–130 ml) dry white wine
½–¾ pint (300–450 ml) veal or chicken stock
2 rounded teaspoons tomato purée
1 small bay leaf
Salt, and pepper from the mill

Saffron rice:
1 medium sized onion, sliced
1 oz (28 g) butter
4–6 oz (113–169 g) mushrooms, sliced
6 oz (169 g) ripe tomatoes, peeled and thickly sliced
1 green pepper, shredded and blanched
4 oz (113 g) long grained rice
A large pinch saffron soaked in 1–2 tablespoons (18–35 ml) water
¾ pint (450 ml) chicken or veal stock

First prepare the ragoût. Cut the meat into ¾-inch to 1-inch squares and the gammon into thick strips. Heat oil in a flame-proof casserole, add butter and when foaming put in the veal. Sauté briskly until just coloured. Lift out with a draining spoon and put in the onion and garlic. Sauté gently for three or four minutes until just brown. Meantime blanch the bacon, drain and add to the casserole. Sauté for one or two minutes, draw aside and stir in the flour. Add wine, stock and tomato purée, bring to the boil, add bay leaf and the veal, season, cover and put into a moderate oven, 180°C/350°F/Gas Mark 4 for forty-five to fifty minutes or until the veal is tender.

Meantime make the pilaff: melt the butter in a casserole, add the onion and mushrooms, sauté gently for three of four minutes. Then add the rest of the ingredients, season and bring to the boil. Cover and put into the oven with the ragoût. Cook until rice is just tender and the stock absorbed, about fifteen to twenty minutes.

Turn the pilaff into a serving dish, and serve the ragoût in the casserole in which it was cooked.

Serves 4–5

Côtes de Veau Sauté Marengo

At certain times small veal chops can be bought in the shops weighing not more than 3½ oz (95 g) each, and these are ideal for this dish. Failing these, use a piece cut from the oyster, about 1½–2 lb (680–907 g). Cut into 1-inch squares and cook in the same way.

The characteristic of a 'Marengo' is a sauce of fresh tomatoes, white wine and mushrooms.

5–6 small veal chops
2 oz (56 g) clarified
  butter
1 × 2-oz (56 g) onion
  (the size of a golf ball)
  finely chopped
4 oz (113 g) 'cup'
  mushrooms, quartered
1 level tablespoon flour
½ lb (225 g) ripe
  tomatoes, peeled and
  concassed
2 cloves garlic, crushed
  to a cream with salt
1 glass (115 ml) dry
  white wine
1 teaspoon tomato purée
¼ pint (150 ml) jellied
  veal or chicken stock
Salt, pepper from the mill
  and a pinch of sugar
  sugar

Cut heart shaped or
  triangular croûtes of
  stale bread
Chopped fresh parsley

Serves 4–5

Fry the chops in the butter until just coloured, turning once only. Take them out and add the onion and mushrooms. Lower heat and cook gently for four or five minutes.

Draw aside, stir in the flour, add tomatoes, garlic, wine and purée. Blend in the stock, season and bring to the boil. Tip into a bowl and replace the chops in the pan. Pour over the sauce and simmer for eight to ten minutes. Meantime fry the croûtes in clarified butter or oil.

Arrange chops in serving dish, boil up the sauce and spoon over the dish. Garnish with the croûtes and sprinkle with the chopped parsley.

Veau Braisé Doria

A good example of one of the best ways to cook a less expensive cut of veal. You can bone out the meat yourself but it saves time if the butcher does it for you.

The dish is named 'Doria' because of the cucumber garnish, the delicate flavour of which goes well with the veal. But other vegetables such as young carrots or baby broad beans can replace it.

If wished, the stuffed breast can be served cold with appropriate salads. In this case press overnight after cooking; the gravy can have the addition of a little gelatine to set it when brushing over the cold joint.

3 lb (1½ kg) boned
  breast of veal

Farce:
8 oz (225 g) cooked
  shoulder ham, finely
  chopped or minced
1 medium sized onion,
  chopped
1 oz (30 g) butter
2 oz (1 cup/60 g) fresh
  breadcrumbs
1 large tablespoon freshly
  chopped parsley
1 teaspoon chopped
  thyme
1 small beaten egg

First prepare farce. Soften onion in butter without colouring. Combine with the other ingredients adding enough of the egg to bind. Season well.

Flatten the meat out on a board and cut in half. Spread one half with the farce and place the other half on top. Sew round the edges with a trussing needle and fine string.

Rub the butter round the bottom and sides of a thick casserole. Spread the rashers on the bottom and add the vegetables. Cover and allow to sweat for seven or eight minutes. Place the veal on top, pour round the sherry and add the bouquet and stock. Grind over some pepper and cover tightly. Braise in a slow to moderate oven, 170°C–180°C/325°F–350°F/ Gas Mark 3–4 for about an hour. Then remove lid, baste well and continue to cook for another forty to forty-five minutes until tender and the meat is coloured. Baste occasionally.

Take up, remove string, slice and arrange on a serving dish. Strain gravy and thicken slightly with a little kneaded butter or arrowroot. Spoon a little over the dish and serve the rest separately. Garnish with cooked cucumber: peel, cut into chunks and blanch. Drain well. Return to pan with a knob of butter, shake up over heat for two or three minutes. Season, add a good sprinkling of chopped parsley and serve.

Serves 6–8

For braising:
1 oz (28 g) butter
3–4 rashers streaky bacon
2 large carrots, sliced
2 large onions, sliced
2 sticks celery, sliced
1 glass (70 ml) sherry
1 bouquet garni
½–¾ pint (300–450 ml)
  jellied stock

Poultry

Poulet Farçi à la Crème

One of the best and more unusual recipes for a stuffed chicken. The light curry flavoured cream sauce, together with 'olives' of cucumber, go well with the rice farce.

As the breastbone is left in, this helps the carver. Slice as for a turkey from each side of the breast and continue down the sides of the bird including the thigh meat.

3½ lb (1¾ kg) roasting chicken
1 medium sized onion, sliced
1 oz (28 g) butter
A bouquet garni
6 peppercorns
7½ fluid oz (225 ml) jellied stock made from the carcass bones
Juice of ½ lemon

Farce:
4 oz (113 g) thick grained rice, previously cooked
1 oz (28 g) butter
1 medium sized onion, finely chopped
4 oz (113 g) cooked ham, shoulder cut, finely chopped or minced
2 tablespoons freshly chopped parsley
2 teaspoons chopped thyme
1 small beaten egg
Salt and pepper

1 large cucumber
½ oz (15 g) butter
1 tablespoon chopped parsley

First bone out the chicken, slitting the skin down the back and cutting away the flesh, remove the backbone, rib cage and thigh bones only. Refrigerate chicken while making a good stock from the bones. Simmer for two or three hours, then strain and cool. When cold, remove all fat. Measure the amount required.

Prepare farce: soften onion in the butter, turn into a bowl with the rice and ham. Add herbs, bind with the egg and season well. Spread over the cut surface of the chicken, pushing the farce well down into the thigh cavities. Fold over the skin and sew up.

Reshape the chicken and truss.

Melt the butter in a thick cocotte or casserole, add the onion and cook for a few minutes without colouring. Set chicken on the top, pour over lemon juice, add bouquet, peppercorns and stock. Cover tightly and simmer for thirty-five to forty minutes on gentle heat.

Meantime prepare cucumber and sauce. Peel cucumber, quarter lengthways and cut across into ¾-inch–1-inch (2-cm) lengths. Shape with a potato peeler into 'olives'. Blanch, drain and refresh. Return to the pan with the butter, season.

For the sauce: melt butter, add curry paste, cook for two or three seconds, then stir in flour. Blend in the milk. Lift chicken onto a plate and keep warm. Strain off the stock.

Add to the sauce, stirring well and bring to the boil. Adjust seasoning and add cream. Allow to boil gently while carving the chicken as described. Lay on the serving dish and spoon over the sauce. Add parsley to cucumber and reheat. Arrange at each end of the serving dish.

Sauce:
1 oz (30 g) butter
2 teaspoons curry paste or mild curry powder
Scant 1 oz (28 g) flour
½ pint (300 ml) creamy milk
2½ fluid oz (70 ml) thick cream

Serves 6

Poulet au Citron

A good dish for spring or early summer when the herbs are at their best.

2 × 2½ lb (1¼ kg) spring chicken
2 oz (56 g) butter
Pared rind and juice of half a lemon
Salt and freshly ground pepper
2 glasses (230 ml) sweet white wine
1 glass (115 ml) jellied chicken stock
1 rounded tablespoon freshly chopped herbs, parsley, thyme and marjoram
Kneaded butter skimmed from the gravy
Chives

Serves 4–6

Choose a large thick cocotte or casserole. Place on a moderate heat, drop in butter and when foaming put in the chickens, breast side downwards. Turn down heat and cook very gently for ten to fifteen minutes, turning the birds frequently until nicely coloured. Draw aside, add lemon rind and juice, seasoning, wine and stock. Bring to the boil, scatter over the herbs, cover and cook gently in a pre-heated oven, 180°C/350°F/Gas Mark 4 for thirty minutes.

Take up the chickens, skim off any surplus butter from the gravy and mix with one tablespoon flour to a smooth paste. It may be necessary to add a small knob of butter to this. Take out lemon rind and add the kneaded butter in small pieces. When dissolved, reboil, adjust seasoning and set aside.

Carve the chickens by detaching the legs and cutting the wing and breast from each side of the carcass in one piece. If wished the legs can be cut in half and a small piece of the breast sliced off to go with the drumstick.

Slip the chicken into the oven for a few minutes to heat thoroughly. Boil up the gravy and spoon over the dish. Snip over the chives and serve with Château potatoes.

Poulet en Cocotte Bonne Femme

A simple classic recipe, the excellence of which depends on the slow and careful browning of the chicken. This dish freezes well, but it is advisable to omit the potatoes and to add them, blanched, to the cocotte on reheating. Simmer until they are tender before serving.

1 × 3½–4 lb (1¾–2 kg) roasting chicken
4 oz (113 g) unsmoked streaky bacon
1 tablespoon (18 ml) oil

Remove rind from bacon, cut into lardons, blanch, drain and set aside.

Heat oil in a large oval cocotte or flame-proof casserole. Add butter and while still foaming put in the chicken. Lower heat and allow to brown slowly. Turn the bird from time to time so that all sides are browned evenly. This process may take twenty minutes and must not be hurried.

Take up chicken and set on a board. Meantime add the bacon to the cocotte with the mushrooms whole or, if 'cups', quartered, and the onions. Allow to brown slowly.

Joint the chicken; this size bird should cut into six to seven pieces. Stir the flour into the cocotte, pour on ¾ pint (450 ml) of the stock, bring to the boil and season. Put in the chicken

1 oz (28–30 g) butter
4 oz (113 g) button or
  'cup' mushrooms
18 pickling onions
1 oz (28 g) flour
1 pint (600 ml) chicken
  stock
1 bouquet garni
3 medium to small sized
  potatoes *or* 10–12 baby
  new potatoes
Chopped parsley

Serves 5–6

joints and tuck the bouquet down the side. Cover and set cocotte in a pre-heated oven, 180°C/360°F/Gas Mark 4. Leave for thirty-five minutes.

Have the potatoes cut in four lengthways. Trim off the sharp edges with a potato peeler and then blanch. If using new potaotes, leave whole. Add to the cocotte with the remaining stock. Continue to cook for a further twenty to twenty-five minutes or until tender.

To serve, remove bouquet and if the gravy is too thin, skim off a tablespoon of the butter and mix with a level tablespoon of flour. Add to the gravy off the heat, shaking the cocotte gently. When dissolved bring to the boil, adjust seasoning, sprinkle the top with chopped parsley and serve in the cocotte.

Poulet Napolitana

A partly braised and roasted chicken and a dish that not only needs little attention, but keeps hot satisfactorily if guests are late. If wished the sauce can come from the deep freeze.

3½ lb (1¾ kg) roasting
  chicken
1½ oz (35 g) butter
2 rashers bacon
1 onion
1 carrot
Bouquet garni
2 glasses white wine
½ lb (226 g) spaghetti or
  tagliatelle

Mornay sauce:
1 oz (25 g) butter
1 oz (25 g) flour
½–¾ pint (283–425 ml)
  milk
2–3 oz (56–84 g) grated
  cheese, (½ Gruyère, ½
  Parmesan or a dry
  Cheddar)
½ gill (75 ml) cream

Spread half the butter on the breast of the chicken. Lay the bacon on the bottom of a casserole, cover with the sliced vegetables, set chicken on top, add bouquet, cover and set on a slow heat for ten minutes. Remove lid, add wine, season and put into a moderately hot oven, 180°C/360°F/Gas Mark 4 for fifty minutes to one hour, basting occasionally.

Meantime cook the pasta, drain and refresh; toss in the remaining butter with salt and pepper to taste.

Make the sauce in the usual way. Stir in two-thirds of the cheese. Strain on liquid from the chicken and add to the sauce with the cream.

Carve the chicken, arrange in a hot gratin dish and spoon over the sauce. Sprinkle with the rest of the cheese and brown lightly under the grill or in a quick oven. Serve the pasta separately.

Serves 4–6

Poulet Sauté Paulette

An entrée for early summer when fresh asparagus can be had. The cream sauce contains finely diced vegetables and is made lightly piquante with French mustard.

To sauté :

1 × 3 lb (1¼ kg) roasting chicken, jointed
2 tablespoons (35 ml) oil
1 oz (28 g) butter
A good pinch of saffron soaked ½ hour in 1 tablespoon (18 ml) water
A good pinch each of ground mace and ginger
Black pepper and salt
1 glass (70 ml) sherry
¼ pint (150 ml) jellied chicken stock

Sauce :

1 oz (28 g) butter
1 small onion, finely chopped
1 × 2 oz (60 g) carrot, finely diced
3–4 button or white mushrooms, finely chopped
1 level tablespoon flour
4 large tablespoons (100 ml) thick cream
1 level tablespoon (18 ml) Dijon mustard

Garnish :

1 bundle asparagus or sprue, trimmed, tied in bundles and boiled 7–8 minutes, then drained

Serves 4

Heat oil and butter in a large sauté pan. Put in the chicken joints, skin side down, and sauté gently until golden brown and the skin is crisp.

Draw aside, sprinkle over saffron and spices, a little salt and a good grinding of pepper. Turn the pieces of chicken over and flame with the sherry. Pour over the stock, cover and simmer for fifteen to twenty minutes. Turn pieces over after about five minutes.

Meantime prepare the sauce. Melt the butter, add onion, carrot and mushrooms, cover and cook very gently for five or six minutes or until carrot is tender. Draw aside and stir in flour. Tip on the liquid from the chicken (straining it first if necessary), blend and stir until boiling. Adjust seasoning and add cream.

Take up chicken and trim away any pieces of bone and arrange chicken in an entrée dish. Boil up the sauce and spoon over the dish.

Dip asparagus in boiling water or heat in a little melted butter. Arrange at each end of the dish.

Poulet Farçi – Sauce Madère

This is an example of a chicken completely boned out with the exception of the wing bones, which help to keep its shape. The bird is then stuffed with the farce, pushed well down into the thigh cavities. After sewing up the back, the bird is reshaped and trussed.

This dish is ideal for a dinner party as it 'stretches'.

3–3½ lb (1½–1¾ kg) roasting chicken
2 oz (56 g) butter
¼–½ pint (150–300 ml) good chicken stock
1 glass (70 ml) brown sherry

Farce:

1 oz (30 g) butter
1 medium sized onion, finely chopped
1 lb (453 g) minced veal
2 oz (56 g) fresh breadcrumbs
1 tablespoon mixed chopped fresh herbs
Salt and pepper
1 small egg

¾–1 pint (450–600 ml) demi-glace sauce
1½ glasses (105 ml) Madeira

Serves 6

Bone out the chicken completely, first splitting the skin down the back and cutting away the flesh from the carcass and leg bones, but leaving in the wing bones and pinions.

Prepare farce. Soften onion in the butter, turn into a bowl with the veal, crumbs, herbs and seasoning. Bind with the egg and work well to mix thoroughly. Lay chicken flat on a board, spread with the farce, pushing it down well into the thigh and drumstick cavities. Fold over the skin, sew up and reshape chicken. Truss.

Set in a roasting tin, pour round ¼ pint (150 ml) of the stock. Spread butter onto a piece of greaseproof paper and cover the bird with this. Put into a pre-heated oven, 190°C–200°C/375°F–400°F/Gas Mark 5–6 and roast for half an hour.

Remove paper, pour over sherry and add the remaining stock. Baste well and continue to roast for a further thirty to forty minutes, basting occasionally or until the bird is a good brown. Then remove trussing strings, carve and arrange on serving dish. Keep warm.

Reduce Madeira to half, add the demi-glace and boil up well. Spoon a little over the chicken and serve the rest separately.

Chicken and Peach Curry

A lovely dish for a dinner party on a warm summer's evening. Make it in July or early August when peaches are at their best.

1 × 3½–4 (1½–2 kg) roasting chicken
1 small bunch French tarragon
4 tablespoons (70 ml) olive oil or a good quality oil
¼–½ pint (150–300 ml) chicken stock, well seasoned
4 ripe peaches, medium size

Sauce:
3 tablespoons (53 ml) oil
1 medium size onion, chopped
1 dessertspoon curry powder
1 teaspoon curry paste
½ teaspoon ground cumin
1 dessertspoon grated green ginger
1 tablespoon coconut cream
1 glass (70 ml) port
1 teaspoon tomato purée
¼ pint (150 ml) chicken stock
Salt, pepper from the mill
1 tablespoon redcurrant jelly
½ pint (300 ml) double cream
Lemon juice

Serves 4

Put the tarragon inside the chicken and rub the outside skin well with the olive oil. Pour round ¼ pint (150 ml) of the stock and place chicken in a pre-heated oven, 190°C/375°F/Gas Mark 5. Roast, basting well and turning the chicken from time to time. Allow 1–1¼ hours and add more stock if the liquid in the tin reduces too much. The chicken should be well glazed and browned. When cooked, take up and allow to get quite cold.

Meantime prepare the sauce: lightly brown the onion in the oil, add the spices, cook for one minute then add the coconut cream, port, tomato purée and stock. Season and add the jelly. Stir until boiling, then simmer for fifteen to twenty minutes. Strain, rinse out the pan, pour in the cream and add the curry sauce. Allow to boil gently uncovered for twelve to fifteen minutes, until syrupy. Pour into a bowl, cover and leave until cold.

Rub the back of a knife over the skin of the peaches, then peel and cut into thick wedges against the stone. Lever the slices off gently. Stir the sauce well, then add the peaches and a squeeze of lemon juice.

Carve chicken, dish. Spoon the sauce and peaches over and around. Serve with a paprika rice salad, i.e. plainly boiled rice into which a French dressing flavoured with paprika has been forked.

Poulet en Cocotte

Chicken is pot roasted in a wine sauce with courgettes and mushrooms to accompany.

1 × 3½ lb (1¾ kg) roasting chicken
1½ oz (42 g) butter
1 medium sized onion, thinly sliced
1 medium sized carrot, thinly sliced
Mushroom trimmings
3 tablespoons (53 ml) sherry
1 level tablespoon flour
1 glass (115 ml) red wine
½ pint (300 ml) jellied stock
1 teaspoon tomato purée
A bouquet garni

Garnish:
¾ lb (339 g) courgettes
½ lb (225 g) 'cup' mushrooms
1 oz (28 g) butter
2 shallots, chopped
4 tablespoons (70 ml) thick cream

Serves 4–6

First prepare garnish: trim courgettes and cut into diagonal slices. Peel mushrooms and cut stalks level with the caps. Set both courgettes and mushrooms aside, but reserve stalks and peelings for the chicken.

Now brown the chicken slowly in a cocotte in the butter, turning it frequently. Take out, add onion, carrot and the mushroom trimmings; sauté for three or four minutes until the vegetables are just coloured.

Replace chicken and flame with the sherry. Reduce to almost nothing (one to two minutes) then draw aside, stir in the flour and add wine, stock and purée. Bring to the boil, shaking pan gently, season and add bouquet. Cover tightly and set in a pre-heated oven, 180°C/350°F/Gas Mark 4 for forty-five to fifty minutes. Turn the bird once or twice during this time.

Meanwhile plunge the courgettes into boiling salted water, boil for one minute only, then strain and rinse quickly with cold water. Drain well.

Melt the butter in the pan, add the shallots and mushrooms. Cover and cook for three or four minutes, then turn onto a plate, put in the courgettes and lay the mushrooms on top. Pour over the cream, season, cover and cook in the oven for six or seven minutes or until the courgettes are just tender. Remove lid and cook briskly to reduce a little.

Take up the chicken and strain the sauce into a clean pan. Adjust seasoning and leave to simmer to a syrupy consistency while carving the chicken. Dish and spoon over the sauce. Gently fork up the courgettes and mushrooms and arrange at each end of the dish or serve separately if wished.

Salmagundy

A dish for a buffet lunch or supper. The recipe is adapted from an eighteenth-century recipe meaning 'a mixed salad' and should be well decorated with 'primroses and violets'! This is a modern version.

3½ lb (1¾ kg) roasting chicken
½ lb (226 g) cooked ham
1 lb (453 g) Dutch white cabbage
2 dessert apples
6 eggs, hard boiled
4 oz (113 g) Philadelphia cream cheese
6 sweet cocktail gherkins
1 tablespoon relish or chutney
1 tablespoon chopped parsley

Cole Slaw dressing:
1 tablespoon sugar
1 dessertspoon flour
1 teaspoon salt
1 dessertspoon made mustard
1 tablespoon water
¼ pint (142 ml) each vinegar and water
1 egg, beaten
½ oz (15 g) butter
Cream

Serves 6–8

Mix the dry ingredients together, add the mustard and about one tablespoon of water. Add to the mixture of vinegar and water and cook thoroughly.

Add the butter in small pieces to the egg, pour on the hot vinegar mixture and beat well. When cold dilute with cream.

Poach the chicken in sufficient water to cover it, together with pot herbs and seasoning to flavour; leave to cool in the stock. Remove all skin and bone and shred the meat. Cut the ham in julienne strips.

Shred the cabbage and mix it with just enough of the cream dressing to moisten and bind together. Add the chicken, ham and sliced apple.

Cut the eggs in two lengthways, take half the yolks and pound with the cream cheese, season and add the finely chopped gherkin and relish or chutney to bind. Fill the egg whites with this mixture. Make a pyramid of the chicken, ham and cabbage salad in an entrée dish and surround with the stuffed eggs. Sieve the remaining egg yolks over the top of the salad and sprinkle with chopped parsley.

Poussins Farçis Mâconnais

The poussins are partially boned, stuffed and cooked 'en cocotte' with red wine, sautéd mushrooms and glazed onions as a garnish.

3 double poussins
1½ oz (42 g) butter
2 glasses (230 ml) red Mâcon
½–¾ pint (300–450 ml) jellied stock
1 large bouquet herbs

Kneaded butter to thicken made with:
  1 oz (28 g) butter and 1 oz (30 g) flour

Farce:
½ lb (225 g) minced pork
2 shallots, finely chopped
1 oz (30 g) butter
3 oz (84 g) fresh white breadcrumbs
1 teaspoon chopped thyme
1 small beaten egg
Pinch allspice
Salt and pepper

Garnish:
6 oz (169 g) button mushrooms
8–12 oz (225–339 g) 'pickling' onions
1 oz (28 g) butter
1 teaspoon sugar

Serves 6

Split the skin of the poussins down the back, and bone out the carcass and rib cage, but leave in the leg and wing bones. Spread out the birds and season the cut surface.

Prepare the farce: turn pork into a bowl. Soften shallots in the butter, add to the pork with the crumbs, thyme, beaten egg and seasoning. Work well. Spread this evenly on the poussins, sew up the cut skins and truss into shape.

Heat a large casserole or cocotte, put in the butter and while still foaming lay in the poussins. Brown them slowly on all sides, then add the Mâcon, bring to the boil and cook gently until reduced by about a quarter. Season and add ½ pint (300 ml) of the stock and the herb bouquet.

Cover tightly and cook in a moderate oven, 170°C–180°C/325°F–350°F/Gas Mark 3–4 for forty-five minutes.

Meantime prepare the garnish: sauté the whole mushrooms quickly in half the butter and set aside. Blanch onions, drain and return to the pan with rest of butter, the sugar, salt and pepper from the mill. Cover pan and cook on low heat for six to seven minutes or until tender and the onions brown and sticky. Shake pan frequently without removing the lid.

Take up poussins, remove trussing strings and split in half. Snip off the knuckle bones and the pinions. Arrange them, slightly overlapping, on a serving dish and keep warm.

Strain the cooking liquid into a saucepan. Skim off a tablespoon of the butter from the surface and add to the kneaded butter. Whisk into the liquid and stir until boiling. Adjust seasoning and boil rapidly to a syrupy consistency, adding a little of the remaining stock if necessary.

Put in the mushrooms and spoon sauce over the poussins. Arrange the onions at each end of the dish.

Caneton en Gelée aux Cerises

One of the best of cold duck dishes and suitable for a buffet. Small ducks or duckling about 2½–3 lb (1¼–1½ kg) in weight are the best to use.

Carve each bird into four portions, taking about a third of the breast with the leg and thigh and the remaining breast with the wing.

2 × 2½–3 lb (1¼–1½ kg) duckling, dressed weight
¼ pint (150 ml) good stock
1 glass (115 ml) Burgundy or red wine

Liver paté:
8 oz (225 g) chicken liver and the liver from the ducks
4 oz (113 g) butter
1 medium onion
1 small bouquet garni
1 clove garlic
Seasoning
1 tablespoon (18 ml) brandy

Accompaniment:
1 lb (453 g) cherries (red) preferably Morellos
4 fluid oz (125 ml) port
2 tablespoons caster sugar
1 orange
4 tablespoons redcurrant jelly

To finish:
1 pint (600 ml) aspic jelly
1 bunch watercress

Serves 8

Set the ducks in a roasting tin with the giblets, stock and wine. Roast in a hot oven, 190°C–200°C/375°F–400°F/Gas Mark 5–6 for forty to sixty minutes, according to size. Baste and turn occasionally.

Meantime, prepare the pâté. Chop the onion and garlic finely and soften in 1 oz (30 g) of the butter until just turning colour. Add the liver, herbs and seasoning and fry together for about three minutes. Cool, then mince and pound until smooth or work in a Magimix. Work in the remaining butter and when smooth add the brandy. Spoon the pâté onto a serving dish to make a platform for the duck.

Stone the cherries and place in a casserole with the sugar and a pinch of powdered cinnamon. Cover and cook slowly for five minutes. Remove from the heat and allow to cool. In another pan, reduce the wine by half, adding the grated rind and juice of the orange, also the juice from the cherries. Then add the redcurrant jelly and when melted add to the cherries.

When the duck is quite cold, carve and arrange on the pâté. Brush with aspic jelly on the point of setting, and garnish the dish with watercress. Hand the cold cherry compote separately.

Caneton aux Cerises

This is a hot version of the cold duck served on a liver pâté. Here the pâté is omitted and the duck served as a salmis, i.e. roasted and then finished in a rich demi-glace sauce.

This is a good dish for a dinner party as the duck will keep hot satifactorily without spoiling and no last-minute carving is involved. The cherry compote, one of the best accompaniments to duck, is served separately. This can be made when cherries are in season and kept in the deep freeze.

2 × 2½–3 lb (1–1½ kg) duckling, dressed weight
Giblets and livers of the ducks
About ½ pint (300 ml) brown jellied stock
2 tablespoons (35 ml) oil

Sauce:
1 oz (30 g) butter
1 medium sized onion, finely chopped
1 medium sized carrot, finely diced
½ stick celery, chopped
1 oz (28 g) flour
1 pint (600 ml) jellied brown stock
1 bouquet garni
2 glasses (230 ml) Burgundy

Serves 6

Set ducks on a grid in a roasting tin, add the giblets but reserve the livers. Pour round stock and set tin in a pre-heated oven, 190°C/375°F/Gas Mark 5 and roast for forty to forty-five minutes, turning and basting occasionally until a good brown.

Meantime prepare the sauce: melt butter in a saucepan, add vegetables and allow barely to colour. Stir in flour and cook slowly to a russet brown. Pour on three-quarters of the stock, blend, add the herb bouquet and season lightly. Simmer with the pan partially covered for twenty to twenty-five minutes. Draw aside, add half the remaining stock, reboil and skim well. Repeat this process with rest of stock and skim again. Strain into a clean pan, reserving the vegetables and set aside.

Take up ducks, pour off any fat and deglaze the tin with a little of the wine. Cut the ducks into four, and trim away any carcass bones. Add these to the tin with vegetables from the sauce, pour in the remaining wine and add the livers, chopped and crushed.

Set on a low heat and bring slowly to the boil, stirring frequently. Turn into a large strainer and press well to extract all juice. Add this to the sauce and boil gently while arranging the duck in a deep dish.

Adjust seasoning of the sauce and bind if necessary with a very little arrowroot. Spoon over the duck, slip into a warm oven for five or six minutes, then serve with a cherry compote.

Ballotine de Canard

The only way to serve duck for a dinner party at home. Boned, stuffed and roasted it will give the crisp delicious skin which makes duck so good. There are no problems over carving or trying to make one duck serve more than three.

Bone and stuff the duck the previous day, if wished, ready for roasting. The demi-glace sauce may be made well ahead of time, and frozen.

1 × 4–5 lb (2–2½ kg) duck
2–3 tablespoons (30–45 ml) oil
3 oz (85 g) button mushrooms, halved
1 glass (2½ fluid oz or 70 ml) dry sherry

Farce:
12 oz (339 g) minced veal or pork
2 oz (56 g) fresh breadcrumbs
3 oz (84 g) shredded lean ham
1 medium sized onion, finely chopped
1 oz (28 g) butter
1 dessertspoon mixed chopped herbs – sage, thyme and parsley
6–8 pistachios, blanched and shredded (optional)
2 tablespoons (30 ml) sherry
1 beaten egg to bind
Salt and pepper

½–¾ pint (300–450 ml) demi-glace sauce

Bone out the duck.

Prepare farce. Put minced meat into a bowl with the crumbs and shredded ham. Soften onion in the butter without colouring. Cool and add to the bowl with the herbs and pistachios. Add sherry, egg and seasoning; work until smooth.

Fill into the duck, roll and sew up neatly. Tie at 2–3-inch intervals with fine string. Heat oil in a roasting tin, place duck on a grid or rack in the tin and baste with the hot oil. Set in a pre-heated oven, 190°C–200°C/375°F–400°F/ Gas Mark 5–6, and roast basting well, for 1–1¼ hours.

Have ready the demi-glace, thawed out if frozen. Take up the duck and remove strings. Pour off fat and deglaze tin with the sherry. Sauté the mushrooms in a tablespoon (15 ml) of the duck fat for 1–2 minutes. Add demi-glace and strain on the juices from the tin. Bring to the boil, skim if necessary.

Slice duck or leave whole, if wished. Dish onto a hot serving dish, spoon a little of the sauce over and round. Serve the rest separately with a cherry compote.

Demi-glace sauce:
2 tablespoons (30 ml) oil
Mirepoix of 1 tablespoon each carrot and onion and ½ tablespoon celery
1 tablespoon flour
Good ¾ pint (450 ml) brown stock
1 tablespoon chopped mushroom stalks and peelings
1 teaspoon tomato purée
Bouquet garni
Salt and pepper

Cook the vegetables in the oil until soft, then add the flour; continue cooking very slowly to a good russet brown, allow to cool a little, then pour on ½ pint (283 ml) of the stock; return to the fire, stir until boiling, add the remaining ingredients and leave to simmer very gently for about thirty to forty minutes.

Add half the remaining stock. Reboil and skim well. Repeat this process, then strain. Adjust seasoning.

Serves 6–8

Canard Farçi a l'Orange

Another recipe to solve the problem of serving duck for a dinner party. A certain amount of preparation is necessary beforehand, but once done the duck is easy to serve. The spicy stuffing is delicious with the duck and the Bigarade Sauce.

4–5 lb (2–2¼ kg) duckling
2 tablespoons (35 ml) oil
1 orange
2½ fluid oz (70 ml) stock

Stuffing:
½ lb (225 g) good
   quality pork sausages
1 oz (28 g) butter
1 small onion
4 sticks celery
2 tablespoons walnuts
Rind and juice of 1
   orange
1 tablespoon chopped
   parsley
1 teaspoon chopped sage
4 oz (113 g) fresh white
   breadcrumbs
1 beaten egg

Sauce demi-glace:
3 tablespoons (50 ml) oil
1 small carrot
1 small or half onion
1 small stick celery
1 tablespoon flour
1 pint (600 ml) brown
   bone stock
A few mushroom peelings
1 teaspoon tomato purée
Bouquet garni

Sauce Bigarade:
1 shallot
½ oz (14 g) butter
1½ wineglasses (172 ml)
   red wine

Set oven to 220°C/425°F/Gas Mark 7.

First prepare the stuffing: place the sausages in a pan, cover with cold salted water, bring to the boil and simmer for ten minutes. Allow to cool in the liquid. Melt the butter in a pan, add the chopped onion and cook until soft but not coloured. Add the chopped celery and cook for one to two minutes. Drain the sausages, remove the skins and cut into small dice. Place in a bowl with the celery and onion, roughly chopped walnuts, orange rind and juice, chopped parsley and sage, breadcrumbs and enough beaten egg to bind. Season with a little salt and pepper.

Prepare the duck for stuffing by removing the back bone. Fill the duck with the stuffing, sew up with thread or fine string, leaving long pieces of string at either end, and truss. Rub the skin of the duck with the oil, sprinkle with a little salt and set on a grid in a roasting tin. Pour round the orange juice and stock. Roast in the pre-set oven, basting and turning the bird from time to time, for 1¼-1½ hours or until tender.

In the meantime, prepare the sauce demi-glace: cut the vegetables in fine dice, heat a shallow saucepan, put in the oil and add the vegetables. Cook on a low heat until the vegetables are barely coloured, then stir in the flour and continue to cook, slowly stirring occasionally with a metal spoon until they are a good russet brown. Draw aside, add ¾ pint (450 ml) of the stock and the rest of the ingredients. Bring to the boil, half cover with the lid and simmer for twenty-five minutes. Then dépouillé the sauce with the reserved stock, strain, season lightly.

Prepare the sauce Bigarade: put the finely chopped shallot and butter into a small pan, cover and cook gently for one minute. Add wine, bay leaf and pared rind of half the Seville orange. Simmer to reduce by about one-quarter. Strain into the prepared demi-glace sauce, add redcurrant jelly and dissolve over a low heat.

Pare and cut the rest of the orange rind into needle-like shreds. Blanch in boiling water for five minutes, then drain. Add to the sauce. Cut skin and pith from the orange, cut out segments.

1 small bay leaf
1 Seville orange
2 teaspoons redcurrant
jelly
Squeeze of lemon juice

Serves 4

Squeeze the white membranes to extract any juice for adding to the sauce with the lemon juice. Simmer for four to five minutes, then add orange segments. Reheat but do not boil.

Note : Use extra lemon juice if you are unable to get Seville oranges.

When duck is cooked, remove from the tin and set on one side in a warm place. Skim the fat from the roasting tin, reduce the sediment left to three tablespoons (50 ml) and strain into the prepared sauce.

To prepare the duck for serving, first remove the trussing string only. Cut the breast meat of the duck off the bone and slice in long thin slices. Remove the breast bone carefully with scissors and replace the sliced breast meat on the stuffing. Place the duck on a serving dish and gently pull out the long piece of thread from underneath. Spoon a little of the prepared sauce over and serve the rest separately.

Poussins Farçis Normande

A good dish for a family party. Poussins (and choose the double ones only) need additional flavouring and substance, so the best dishes are those where the birds are stuffed.

2 double poussins
1 large onion, sliced
1 large cooking apple
1 oz (30 g) butter
1 glass white wine
¼ pint (150 ml) jellied
stock

Farce :
2–3 shallots, finely
chopped
1 oz (30 g) butter
6 oz (185 g) minced pork
1 tablespoon chopped
parsley
1 teaspoon chopped
thyme
2 oz (60 g) fresh white
crumbs

First prepare the farce. Soften the shallot in the butter without colouring, add to the pork with the crumbs and herbs. Season well.

Bone out the carcass and rib cage of the poussins, leaving in the leg and wing bones. Spread the farce over the poussins, sew up and truss into the original shape. Brown carefully all over in the hot butter, lift out and add the onion and sliced apple to the pan. Sauté for three or four minutes and replace the poussins, pour round the wine and stock, cover tightly and cook in a moderate oven, 180°C/ 350°F/Gas Mark 4 for about fifteen to twenty minutes. Take up poussins, remove thread and split in half, trim and dish. Keep warm.

Reduce liquid in the pan, strain (or blend) rubbing the apple and onion through to form a purée. Return to the pan, adjust the seasoning, boil up well, draw aside and add cream and a nut of butter. Spoon over the poussins and garnish with the fried apple rings.

Serves 4

Garnish :
Fried apple rings
Chopped parsley

Galantine de Canard en Gelée

A good way of serving duck for a buffet. Plan to have a chicken chaudfroid or salad, using the white meat only, also on the table, so that the dark meat can be used in a galantine.

1 × 4½–5 lb (2¼–2½ kg) duck
2 tablespoons (35 ml) oil

Farce:
12 oz (339 g) minced pork
3 oz (84 g) fresh breadcrumbs
1 medium sized onion, finely chopped
1 oz (30 g) butter
1 rounded teaspoon chopped sage
1 rounded teaspoon chopped parsley
1 glass (70 ml) sherry
6–8 blanched pistachio nuts, shredded
1 beaten egg
4–5 oz (113–141 g) raw chicken meat, cut from the legs

To finish:
1 pint (600 ml) aspic jelly, flavoured with sherry
Watercress or fine cress

Serves 6–8

Bone the duck, lay flat on a board and season the cut surface.

Prepare farce: put pork and crumbs into a bowl. Soften onion in the butter in a covered pan, turn into the bowl with the herbs, sherry and pistachio nuts. Season well, add the egg and work until smooth. Spread on the duck. Cut the chicken meat into shreds, scatter over the farce. Roll up firmly and sew securely with fine string.

Lay duck on a grid in the roasting tin, rub with the oil, put into a pre-heated oven, 190°C/375°F/Gas Mark 5 and roast, basting occasionally, for about 1–1¼ hours. When well browned take from the oven but leave on the grid and allow to get quite cold.

Remove string and cut into slices ¼–½-inch thick. Arrange on a serving dish and brush well with cool aspic on the point of setting. Give two or three coats to ensure that the slices are well covered. Garnish with the cress.

Poussins Farçis Florentine

For this dish poussins are partially boned out and stuffed with spinach and curd cheese. They are then pot roasted, simmered in tomato sauce and finished with cream.

This is a good dish for a dinner party as there is no last-minute carving and it is easy to serve.

3 poussins
1½ oz (42 g) butter
1 glass (70 ml) Marsala
  or brown sherry
¼ pint (150 ml) cream

Farce:
½ lb (225 g) leaf spinach
1 small onion, finely
  chopped
1 oz (30 g) butter
4 oz (113 g) curd cheese
3 oz or 1 cup (84 g)
  fresh breadcrumbs
1 small beaten egg

Tomato sauce:
1 lb (453 g) red ripe
  tomatoes or 1 × 8-oz
  (225 g) tin Italian
  tomatoes
2 cloves garlic crushed
1 teaspoon dried basil
½ bay leaf
¼ pint (150 ml) jellied
  stock
Salt, freshly ground black
  pepper

Serves 6

Slit the skin of the poussins down the back and, with a small sharp knife, work back the flesh on each side up to the thigh bones. Cut away the carcass bone and rib cage, but leave in the leg, wing and breast bones.

Prepare farce: dip the spinach in boiling salted water, drain and press. Chop finely. Soften onion in the butter, turn into a bowl, add the cheese, crumbs and spinach. Season well and bind with the egg.

Prepare sauce: cut tomatoes in half, squeeze to remove seeds or use canned tomatoes. Add garlic, herbs, seasoning and stock. Cover and simmer to a pulp. Rub through a strainer.

Spread the farce onto the poussins, fold over the cut edges, sew up and reshape. Heat a large cocotte, drop in the butter and when foaming put in the poussins. Brown slowly on all sides, then flame with the Marsala, pour the tomato sauce over and cover tightly. Simmer on cooker top or in the oven at 180°C/350°F/Gas Mark 4 for twenty minutes.

Take up the poussins, remove the trussing string and split the birds in half. Trim away the leg knuckle bone and wing pinions. Dish the halves slightly overlapping. Run the sauce through a strainer into a pan, add cream and boil up well. Adjust seasoning and thicken if necessary with a teaspoon of arrowroot. Spoon over the poussins and serve.

Poussins Farçis au Riz

An excellent dish for a dinner party. It can be prepared and cooked well in advance or come from the deep freeze.

3 double poussins
1½ oz (35 g) butter
2 tablespoons brandy
1½ glasses red wine
18–20 small pickling
 onions
6–8 oz (170–226 g)
 button mushrooms

Stuffing :
4 rashers streaky bacon
4 oz (113 g) rice boiled
 and drained
1 onion
1½ oz (35 g) butter
1 tablespoon chopped
 parsley
½ teaspoon oregano or
 thyme
1 egg

Demi-glace sauce :
2 tablespoons oil
2 tablespoons diced
 carrot, onion and
 celery
¾ oz (20 g) flour
1 pint (568 ml) jellied
 brown stock
1 tablespoon tomato
 purée
A few mushroom peelings
Bouquet garni

Serves 6

Remove the back and carcass bone from each poussin and put on for stock. Prepare the stuffing. Remove the rind from the bacon and fry until brown and very crisp; tip the fat into the rice with the bacon broken into small pieces. Chop the onion very finely, soften in the butter and add to the rice with the herbs and plenty of seasoning; add enough beaten egg to bind. Fill into the birds, sew up and truss neatly.

Blanch and refresh the onions, wash the mushrooms and trim the stalks level with the caps and set aside.

Prepare the demi-glace sauce. Cook the vegetables in oil until soft, then add the flour; continue cooking very slowly to a good russet brown, allow to cool a little, then pour on three-quarters of the stock, return to the fire, stir until boiling, add remaining ingredients and simmer very gently for about thirty minutes.

Add half the reserved stock, bring to the boil, skim and simmer for five minutes. Repeat this process, then strain and return to the rinsed pan. Adjust the seasoning and continue simmering for five to ten minutes, skim if necessary.

Drop 1 oz (15 g) butter into a deep pan and when foaming put in the poussins and brown slowly on all sides, flame with brandy, add the wine and allow to simmer gently until reduced a little. Season lightly and pour on half the demi-glace sauce.

Cover the pan tightly, bring to the boil and then allow to simmer gently on top of the stove or in a very moderate oven, 180°C/350°F/Gas Mark 4 for thirty to forty minutes. Turn and baste the birds once or twice while cooking. Add the prepared onions and mushrooms to the remaining demi-glace, cover and simmer gently for about ten minutes until the onions are tender.

Take up the poussins, remove the string, cut in half and place in an oven-proof casserole. Boil up and reduce the cooking liquor from the poussins and strain into the sauce containing the onions and mushrooms. Adjust the seasoning and pour the sauce and garnish over the birds, cover and replace in the oven for about ten to fifteen minutes before serving.

Galette d'Epinards et Volaille

1 × 2–2½ lb (1–1¼ kg) roasting chicken
A bouquet garni
A plateful sliced root vegetables – onion, carrot, celery
Chicken stock or water
1½ lb (678 g) leaf spinach or 1 packet frozen leaf spinach

Pancake butter made with:
4 oz (113 g) plain flour
1 egg
1 yolk
1 tablespoon melted butter
½ pint (283 ml) milk

Velouté sauce:
1 oz (25 g) butter
1 oz (25 g) flour
10 fluid oz chicken stock
2 tablespoons thick cream
Salt and pepper

Grated cheese
Melted butter

Place the chicken in a deep pan, surround with the vegetables, add bouquet and pour in enough stock or water to come level with the thighs. Salt lightly, cover and simmer for thirty-five to forty minutes. Cool in the liquid. Meantime make up batter in usual way and allow to stand for thirty minutes.

Cook spinach, drain and press. Toss up with a nut of butter. Fry about ten to twelve thin crisp pancakes, stack one on top of another. Set aside.

Take up chicken, skin and shred the meat. Strain stock, removing grease, and measure.

Make velouté sauce in usual way using the stock. Season and finish with the cream. Fold in the chicken. Layer the pancakes one above the other in an oven-proof dish with the spinach, and a generous filling of chicken in between. Cut the 'galette' as for a cake, brush well with melted butter and sprinkle with grated cheese.

Half an hour before serving, slide into a moderately hot oven, 185°C–190°C/360°F–375°F/Gas Mark 4–5 until nicely brown.

Serves 6

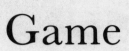

Game

Wild Duck

Widgeon and Teal also come under this category. Their season is from 1 September to 28 February, but they are at their best in October and November. They are best roasted, but keep them underdone, otherwise they tend to have a pronounced fishy flavour.

Wild Duck

Serve with an orange and/or a watercress salad and a good clear gravy or piquante sauce.

Allow a half duck per person.

3 wild duck
3 small onions
3 tablespoons (53 ml) oil
Salt, pepper from the
    mill

3 slices bread, crust
    removed, cut in half
    and fried until golden
    brown in oil

Serves 6

First remove the livers from the ducks and set aside. Put an onion inside each duck and truss. Rub a spoonful of the oil into the breast of each bird and dust lightly with salt.

Roast in a hot oven, 220°C/425°F/Gas Mark 6. Turn and baste the ducks two or three times during the roasting. Allow approximately twenty to twenty-five minutes, but keep them underdone and juicy.

Take up, remove trussing strings, split ducks with a sharp knife and trim away the carcass bones with the scissors, discarding the onion.

Heat the croûtes in the oven and put a half duck on each. Slip them back into the oven for a minute or two then garnish with a sprig or two of watercress and serve very hot with a good gravy or the piquante sauce.

Piquante sauce:
1 medium sized onion, very finely chopped
½ oz (15 g) butter
2 glasses (230 ml) red wine
1 glass (115 ml) jellied brown stock
Grated rind and juice of ½ lemon
2 teaspoons French mustard
Livers of 2 or 3 ducks, finely chopped and sieved
Pepper from the mill
A pinch of arrowroot

Soften onion in the butter, add wine and boil until reduced by a third, then add the stock, lemon rind and juice. Boil gently for three or four minutes while working the mustard into the sieved livers. Season well with pepper and add arrowroot. Draw pan aside. Mix a spoonful or two of the hot liquid with the livers and then stir gradually into the rest of the sauce. Reheat slowly and serve.

Grouse

Season 12 August to 10 December.

Whether young or old, grouse have the finest flavour of all game birds. The only way to eat young grouse is to serve them plainly roasted with the usual accompaniments for roast game, or as a salmis.

For the older birds braise or cook 'en cocotte' to make them tender and improve the flavour.

Braised Grouse

In this recipe beetroot is added to the braising vegetables to give a slight sweetness, as redcurrant jelly does, to the sauce.

2 grouse
1 oz (30 g) dripping or butter
4 oz (113 g) thin rashers of streaky bacon
1 large onion, sliced
1 large carrot, sliced
1 small raw beetroot, peeled and sliced
2 glasses (230 ml) red wine
¼ pint (150 ml) jellied brown stock
Bouquet garni
¼ pint (150 ml) brown or demi-glace sauce (see recipe for *Filet de Boeuf Braisé aux Champignons*, p. 00)
4–5 tablespoons sour cream

Serves 4

Melt the fat in a cocotte, put in the grouse and brown the breasts slowly. Take out.

Line sides and bottom of the cocotte with the bacon, lay the sliced vegetables on top and then the grouse. Season, cover tightly and allow 'to sweat' on a low heat for six to seven minutes. Then draw aside, add wine, stock, seasoning and bouquet. Cover and braise in a slow to moderate oven, 170°C–180°C/325°F–350°F/ Gas Mark 3–4 for 1–1½ hours, or until tender.

Take up the grouse, remove trussing strings and split the birds in two. Trim away the carcass bones with the scissors and lay in the casserole. Cover and keep warm.

Strain the liquid into a saucepan, add the demi-glace and the sour cream. Adjust seasoning and boil gently until syrupy in consistency. Spoon over the grouse and serve very hot.

Grouse 'En Salmis'

2 young grouse
Dripping
1 tablespoon each of
   finely diced carrot,
   onion and celery
1 oz (30 g) butter
¾ oz (21 g) flour (scant)
Bouquet garni
1 pint (600 ml) stock
½ teaspoon tomato purée
1–2 glasses (230 ml) red
   wine
4 oz (113 g) mushrooms
5 croûtes of bread to
   garnish

Serves 4

Roast the grouse lightly, with a little dripping, in a hot oven, 220°C/425°F/Gas Mark 7, for about ten minutes, take out and cool.

Meantime melt ½ oz (15 g) of the butter, add the vegetables and cook slowly until barely coloured. Then add the remainder of the butter, the flour and cook slowly to a good brown. Draw aside, add the stock, purée and bouquet. Season lightly and simmer for thirty minutes, skimming occasionally.

Now carve the grouse and lay the pieces in a casserole. Chop or pound the carcasses, add the wine and turn into a saucepan. Strain the sauce and add the vegetables to the carcasses. Allow this to boil rapidly for a few minutes, then strain back again into the sauce, pressing well to extract all the juice. Simmer until a syrupy consistency. Adjust the seasoning.

Pour half over the grouse in the casserole, and replace in a moderate oven for ten to fifteen minutes. Meantime, sauté the mushrooms in rest of butter. Add the mushrooms with the remaining sauce to the salmis and continue cooking for a further five minutes.

Hare

Season October to late January.

Hare is not to everyone's taste, but so often this dislike is due to indifferent cooking and presentation. Being a dry meat it should be marinaded and then cooked with the marinade and finished in a rich sauce. For example the back can be cooked with wine and cream to make a dinner party dish, and the rest turned into a savoury stew, i.e. Jugged Hare or a 'Civet de Lievre'.

Estouffade de Lièvre

1 medium sized hare
  with the blood

Marinade:
2 shallots, chopped
½ teaspoon salt
Black pepper from the
  mill
2 glasses (100 ml each
  glass) port
1 teaspoon vinegar
1 teaspoon chopped
  thyme
2 teaspoons oil

1 tablespoon oil
½ oz (15 g) butter
1 medium sized onion
  finely chopped
¾ pint (450 ml) stock
1 bay leaf
The blood of the hare
1 teaspoon arrowroot
4–5 tablespoons
  (70–88 ml) double
  cream

Serves 4–6

Have the back and hind legs of the hare cut into moderate sized pieces, trimming away any bits of skin. Lay the joints on a flat dish. Combine ingredients for the marinade and spoon over the hare. Leave for one to two hours.

Pat the pieces dry with a paper towel. Heat the oil in a thick iron casserole, add the butter and put in the hare. Sauté until nicely coloured, turning the pieces frequently. Then lift them out and add the onion. Cook gently for one to two minutes, then add the marinade and stock.

Bring to the boil, replace the hare and add the bay leaf. Cover tightly and cook in a slow to moderate oven, 170°C–180°C/325°F–350°F/Gas Mark 3–4 for 1½ hours or until tender.

Take out the hare. Mix the blood with the arrowroot and strain into the sauce off the heat. Add cream and bring slowly to the boil, stirring well. Adjust seasoning and replace the pieces of hare. Reheat carefully and serve with a chestnut and celery purée.

Chestnut and celery purée:
1 lb (453 g) potatoes
1 tin unsweetened chestnut purée
1 oz (28 g) butter
3–4 sticks of celery heart, chopped
Salt and pepper
A little hot milk if necessary.

Boil the potatoes, drain and dry. Crush well and beat in the chestnut purée over a gentle heat. Add the butter and a little hot milk if necessary.

Stir in the celery and season well. Pile up in a serving dish.

Partridge

Season 1 September to 1 February. Partridge, especially the English or grey partridge, almost equals grouse in flavour. Unfortunately they are difficult and expensive to obtain, certainly in town areas.

If young serve plainly roasted with the proper accompaniments for game. Older birds can be cooked 'en cocotte'.

Perdrix en Cocotte Bourguignon

2 plump partridges
1 oz (30 g) butter
2 glasses (230 ml) Burgundy
½ pint (300 ml) good jellied stock
1 teaspoon tomato purée
Bouquet garni
4 oz (113 g) rasher unsmoked streaky bacon
4 oz (113 g) button mushrooms
2 dozen pickling onions
1 oz (30 g) butter
Kneaded butter made with 1 oz (28 g) butter and ½ oz (15 g) flour

Serves 4

Drop 1 oz (30 g) butter in a heavy casserole and when foaming put in the partridges and colour slowly on all sides. Season with salt and pepper and add the herbs. Flame just one glass of the wine, pour over the birds and add the stock and tomato purée. Cover with paper and lid and place in a moderate oven to cook.

Meantime, remove the rust and rind from the bacon, cut into lardons and blanch to remove the saltpetre; wash the mushrooms in salt water, drain and cut into quarters. Blanch the small onions. Melt the 1 oz butter in a frying pan, put in the bacon and onions and cook until taking colour; then add the mushrooms and continue cooking for two or three minutes. When the partridges have had forty minutes cooking, add the bacon, mushrooms and onions and continue cooking until all are tender, about ten to fifteen minutes.

Take up the partridges, carve and arrange in a serving dish, and keep warm. Flame the remaining glass of wine, add to the juices in the pan and then thicken with the kneaded butter. Spoon the sauce and garnish over the birds.

Pheasant

The meat of pheasant is inclined to be dry so the flavour is improved by various garnishes, a rich gravy or sauce rather than a plain roast.

Of the several recipes we do the following three are considered the best.

Faisan en Cocotte aux Marrons

2 plump pheasants
1½ oz (45 g) clarified butter or bacon fat
1 small onion, finely chopped
2 glasses (230 ml) red wine
½–¾ pint (300–450 ml) brown jellied stock
A bouquet garni
½ lb (225 g) button mushrooms
½ lb (225 g) 'pickling' onions
Kneaded butter

Garnish:
1¼ lb (566 g) sound chestnuts (or 1 lb/453 g when peeled)
A bouquet garni tied to a stick of celery
1 pint (600 ml) brown jellied stock
½ oz (15 g) butter

Serves 4–6

Brown the pheasants slowly all over in the butter or fat until nicely browned. If the pheasants have been larded remove the fat half way through the browning and allow the breasts to colour.

Take out the birds, add the onion and after a minute or two the wine. Boil to reduce by about a third. Add ¼ pint (150 ml) of the stock and the bouquet. Season and cover the cocotte tightly. Braise in a very moderate oven, 170°C–180°C/ 325°F–360°F/Gas Mark 3–4, for forty-five to fifty minutes, turning the birds once or twice.

Meantime blanch the onions for five minutes, then drain. Sauté the mushrooms whole in ½ oz (14 g) butter in the same pan for three minutes. Draw aside.

Have chestnuts peeled then put into a shallow pan with the bouquet and sufficient stock to cover. Add butter, season, bring to the boil and simmer with the lid half on until the nuts are tender and the stock well reduced and to a glaze. Take out the bouquet half way through the cooking. Take up the pheasants.

Strain the gravy and return to the cocotte with the rest of the stock. Thicken with the kneaded butter, reboil and add the onions. Allow to simmer while carving the pheasants. Lay the meat in a deep dish and keep warm. Add the mushrooms to the sauce and adjust seasoning, and the thickening, if necessary. Spoon over the dish and pile the chestnuts at each end.

Ballotine de Faisan

1 good pheasant, if possible one with unbroken skin
1 oz (30 g) butter
1 glass (70 ml) sherry
1 onion
1 carrot
1 glass (115 ml) white wine
¼ pint (150 ml) jellied stock
Bouquet of herbs
Kneaded butter

Farce:

2 shallots, finely chopped
¾ oz (21 g) butter
1 pippin apple such as Cox's
6 oz (169 g) well flavoured sausage meat or skinned sausages
1 egg

Serves 4

First prepare the farce. Peel, core and cut the apple into dice. Melt the butter, add the shallots and apple and cook briskly for one or two minutes, stirring frequently. Turn into a bowl. Work in the sausage meat and egg, lightly beaten. Set aside.

Slit skin down the back of the pheasant then bone out completely, working the meat off the carcass and legs. Flatten out the meat and season. Spread the farce over the surface and roll up. Sew securely. Brown slowly and carefully in a casserole in the butter. When well browned, flame with the sherry, then add the onion and carrot whole, the wine, stock and herbs. Season. Cover tightly and cook in a moderate oven, 180°C/350°F/Gas Mark 4, basting and turning occasionally, for forty-five minutes.

Take up, strain gravy into a small pan. Skim off any surplus butter and work into a level tablespoon flour for the kneaded butter. Add this by degrees to the gravy. Adjust seasoning and reboil.

Remove strings from the 'ballotine' and slice across into about ½-inch slices. Spoon over the dish and garnish at each end with a julienne of vegetables.

Julienne of vegetables:
½ head celery
¾ lb (339 g) carrots
3 medium leeks
1 oz (30 g) butter

Cut the celery and carrots into neat matchlike pieces. Thinly slice the white part of the leek.

Melt the butter, add all the vegetables and cover with buttered greaseproof paper. Cook over a moderate heat for five minutes, turning occasionally and then place in a casserole in a moderate oven, 180°C/350°F/Gas Mark 4 until tender.

Meanwhile, shred and blanch the green part of the leek and, just before serving, scatter it over the vegetables. (A tablespoon (18 ml) of sherry can be added to the vegetables as they go into the oven.)

Faisan en Cocotte Flamande

1 brace pheasant
1 carrot
1 onion
1 oz (28 g) butter
1 glass (70 ml) sherry
6 heads of chicory
½ oz (15 g) butter
A squeeze of lemon juice
1 tablespoon (18 ml)
    water
A pinch of salt
Black pepper from the
    mill
½ pint (300 ml) strong
    jellied stock

To finish:
1 large Cox's apple
½ oz (14 g) butter
¼ pint (150 ml) soured
    cream

Serves 4–6

Heat a large flame-proof casserole, drop in the butter and, while it is foaming, put in the pheasants and colour them slowly on all sides. Put in the onion and carrot, cut in quarters, around, season and pour over the sherry; cover and cook over a moderate flame for five minutes. Reduce the heat and cook on the side of the fire or in a moderate oven, 180°C/350°F/Gas Mark 4 until the bird is almost cooked (about forty minutes).

Meanwhile, trim and wipe and halve the heads of chicory. Lay it in a casserole in which the butter has been melted. Season well with pepper, add the lemon juice. Dissolve the salt in the water and sprinkle it over the chicory. Cover and cook in a moderate oven until the liquid has evaporated and the chicory is tender.

Take up the pheasant and keep warm. Deglaze the pan with the stock, strain, reduce to about half quantity and adjust the seasoning.

Peel and dice the apple. Heat a small heavy frying pan, drop in the butter and fry briskly until golden brown, add the sour cream and bring to the boil.

Arrange the chicory in a gratin dish, carve the pheasant and put on top. Spoon over the apple and cream and put back in the oven for seven or eight minutes before serving. Pour the gravy into a sauce boat and hand separately.

Pigeon

Pigeon are at their best from March to October but there is no closed season for them. Those shot around harvest time near good farm land are as a rule plump and tender. They are not hung like most game but cooked very fresh from 12–24 hours after killing. When young the flesh is very delicate and butter should be used for browning or roasting.

Pigeons Farçis en Casserole

4 pigeons
½ lb (225 g) bacon pieces
1 medium onion, finely
  chopped
4 tablespoons fresh
  breadcrumbs
2 tablespoons chopped
  parsley
Grated lemon rind
½ beaten egg
½–¾ oz (14–21 g) butter
1 tablespoon flour
1 glass (115 ml) white
  wine
¾ pint (450 ml) jellied
  stock
Bouquet garni
½ lb (225 g) 'pickling'
  onions
6 oz (170 g) flat
  mushrooms

Serves 4

Cut the pigeons down the back and remove the back bone and rib cage. Cut the bacon into small pieces with the kitchen scissors and cook slowly until frizzled and brown, remove from the pan with a draining spoon, add the onion and cook slowly until soft. Mix the onion, bacon and parsley together, add just enough crumbs to hold the bacon and bind with the egg. Season with pepper and flavour with the lemon rind.

Fill the pigeons with the stuffing and sew up; brown slowly in the butter in a casserole, blend in the butter, allow to colour then add the wine and stock. Season, add the bouquet of herbs, cover and cook in a moderate oven for one hour.

Meantime blanch the onions for five minutes and drain well. Trim the mushrooms, add to the casserole with the onions and continue cooking for fifteen to twenty minutes.

Take up the pigeons, remove the string, cut each bird in half. Reduce the liquid in the casserole a little and lift out the herbs, and add arrowroot to thicken lightly if necessary. Replace the pigeons in the casserole and reheat. Serve with the gratin of pumpkin.

Potiron Gratiné
2 lb (906 g) pumpkin
1 oz (28 g) butter
¼ pint (150 ml) well reduced fresh tomato
  pulp
4 oz (113 g) cooked rice
1 tablespoon grated Cheddar or
  Parmesan cheese

Peel and cut the pumpkin in pieces and boil gently in light stock or salted water until tender, drain well and rub through a sieve or crush with a potato masher. Dry the pumpkin purée over a gentle heat, add the butter a small piece at a time and continue cooking until all the excess moisture has evaporated. Season with black pepper, add the tomato pulp and cooked rice.

Turn the mixture into a buttered gratin dish, dust with cheese and bake in a hot oven, 200°C/400°F/Gas Mark 6 until brown; allow twenty to thirty minutes.

Pigeons Braisé Allemande

Pigeons can make a 'tasty dish', but, being a dry meat with little fat, need a succulent yet slightly sharp accompaniment. The pickled pork provides this with the sauerkraut. If preferred, a hard white small to medium size cabbage can be used instead.

In this case, shred it finely and layer with the pork in the casserole. Moisten with about $\frac{1}{4}$ pint (150 ml) of stock, seasoning, and a dash of vinegar. Cook for the same amount of time as the sauerkraut.

3–4 plump young
   pigeons, according to
   size
1½ oz (42 g) clarified
   butter
1 small onion, finely
   chopped
1 large glass (150 ml)
   white wine
1 pint (600 ml) brown
   jellied stock
Kneaded butter to bind
Freshly chopped parsley

Sauerkraut:
1 medium sized tin
   sauerkraut
½–¾ lb (225–339 g)
   pickled pork
1–2 oz (28–56 g) butter
½ lb (225 g) pork
   sausages

Serves 4–6

Brown the birds slowly on all sides in the clarified butter. Then add the onion and, when just coloured, add the wine. Cook until the liquid is reduced to about half. This is to deglaze the casserole. Pour in half the stock, cover birds with foil, put on the lid and braise gently in the oven for about one hour.

Meantime drain the sauerkraut, rinse well with cold water and drain thoroughly.

Pressure cook or simmer the pork gently in water with vegetables and a bouquet of herbs until tender. Take up the pork, remove any bones and cut meat into lardons.

Brown the sausages in about half the butter in a casserole. Take out, put in the pork, sauté until lightly brown then mix into the sauerkraut with any fat left in the casserole. Season, moisten if necessary with a spoonful or two of stock. Cover tightly and braise gently for thirty-five to forty minutes.

Take up the pigeons, split and trim away the backbone with the scissors. Slice the sausages and lay on top of the sauerkraut with the pigeons. Add a little of the remaining stock, if necessary, to moisten. Cover and continue to braise for twenty to thirty minutes.

Meantime turn remaining stock into a saucepan, bring to the boil, season and tip on any juice from the casserole. Draw aside and thicken lightly with the kneaded butter. Reboil. Sprinkle parsley over the casserole and serve with the gravy.

Rabbit

Season September to February.

Many people have a prejudice against rabbit but we feel if only they would try any one of the following recipes which have been so popular with the students over the past years, and try the rabbit bred specially for the table — known as Ostend, they might change their minds. This rabbit is larger than the wild kind and can be bought in portions.

Lapin Sauté Chasseur

2 young rabbits, jointed, or 4–5 joints Ostend rabbit
1 tablespoon (18 ml) oil
½ oz (14 g) butter
1 medium sized onion, finely chopped
1 tablespoon flour
1 large glass (125 ml) white wine
½ pint (300 ml) jellied brown stock
2 teaspoons tomato purée
Bouquet garni
3 oz (84 g) button mushrooms, sliced

To garnish:
5–6 triangular croûtes of bread fried in hot oil until golden
Freshly chopped parsley

Serves 4

Trim the joints and if large cut in half to make a moderate sized joint. Soak in cold salted water overnight, then drain, rinse and dry thoroughly.

Heat the oil in a large sauté pan, add butter and put in the rabbit. Sauté gently till nicely coloured, take out and put in the onion. Cook slowly until just brown, sprinkle in the flour, colour lightly and draw aside. Pour in the wine and stock, add purée and bring to the boil. Season, replace the rabbit, tuck in the bouquet, cover and simmer gently for thirty-five to forty minutes. Turn the joints over once and add the mushrooms after twenty minutes cooking.

Dish the rabbit, reduce the sauce a little and spoon over the dish. Sprinkle well with the parsley and surround with the croûtes.

Lapin Moutardé

Most grocers or butchers who slice their bacon sell 'pieces' at a very attractive price and these are good for this recipe.

2 small wild rabbits or 4–5 joints Ostend rabbit

6 oz (170 g) bacon pieces

12 oz (338 g) medium sized onions

1 oz (28 g) flour

1 pint (600 ml) chicken or vegetable stock

Salt and freshly ground white pepper

Bouquet of parsley stalks, sprig of thyme and ½ bay leaf

1 dessertspoon Colman's English mustard *or* Grey-Poupon French mustard

4 tablespoons (70 ml) thick cream

1 dessertspoon chopped parsley

Joint the rabbit, cutting the back in pieces, or divide the joints of the Ostend rabbit if very large, and soak overnight in a large bowl of salted water. Drain, rinse and dry the pieces well.

Remove any rind from the bacon and cut 'the pieces' in even sized strips; place these in a large casserole and fry gently to extract the fat. Meantime roll the rabbit joints in a little of the flour. Lift the bacon from the casserole with a draining spoon and put in the pieces of rabbit; fry gently until golden brown, taking care not to scorch the flour, and remove from the pan.

Add the onions, quartered, and when nicely coloured draw the pan aside and stir in the flour and stock. Return to the heat, stir until boiling, put in the pieces of rabbit, bacon, herbs, salt and pepper. Cover the pan tightly and simmer for 1–1½ hours or until the rabbit is very tender.

Dish the rabbit, remove the herbs and reduce the sauce if necessary for a minute or two over a brisk heat. Draw the pan aside, add the mustard, cream and parsley and spoon over the rabbit.

Serves 4

Game Pie

A mixture of game–grouse, pheasant, hare and pigeon are all suitable

½–¾ oz (14–21 g) butter

1 tablespoon (18 ml) brandy

A pinch of ground mace

1 glass (115 ml) red wine

¾ pint (450 ml) demi-glace sauce – for recipe see recipe for *Filet de Boeuf Braisé aux Champignons*, p. 88

Cut the game into neat joints, removing as much carcass bone as possible and, if using hare, cut the meat from the saddle in long thick slices. Brown the meat slowly in butter, flame with the brandy. Season with salt, freshly ground pepper and the mace and pour over the red wine. Cover the casserole tightly and place in a moderate oven while preparing the demi-glace sauce and the forcemeat balls.

Cook the shallots in the butter, mix the breadcrumbs with one stick of celery, finely chopped, and herbs; add the shallot and bind with a little beaten egg. Shape into balls.

Take up the game, trim the joints as necessary and place in a pie dish. Strain any liquid from

Forcemeat balls:

2 shallots or 1 small
  onion, finely chopped
1½ oz (45 g) butter
2 sticks celery
½ cup (200 ml) fresh
  breadcrumbs
1 teaspoon mixed dried
  herbs
1 dessertspoon parsley
½ beaten egg
6 oz (170 g) flat
  mushrooms
½ lb (225 g) puff pastry

Serves 4–6

the casserole into the sauce and simmer both together for eight to ten minutes. Moisten the game with about half the sauce and leave to cool, then place the mushrooms and forcemeat balls in the dish.

Roll out the pastry in an oval for the top of the pie and set aside. From the trimmings cut a few leaves for decoration and a long strip twice as wide as the edge of the pie dish, and fix this over and under the edge. Damp the pastry and place the oval on top. Press the edge firmly, make a small hole in the top and decorate suitably. Brush with beaten egg and bake in a hot oven 220°C/425°F/Gas Mark 7 for fifteen to twenty minutes until the pastry is risen and brown, then wrap it in a double sheet of dampened greaseproof paper. Lower the heat to 170°C/325°F/Gas Mark 3 and continue to cook for a further thirty to forty minutes.

Before serving reheat the remaining sauce and pour into a gravy boat and trim the pastry away from the under-rim of the pie dish.

Offal

Harvest Pâté

1 large rabbit
2 pigeons
½ lb (225 g) minced pork
1-lb (453 g) piece smoked
  gammon
1 calf's foot or pig's
  trotter
1 clove garlic, crushed
1 dessertspoon chopped
  parsley
1 glass (115 ml) white
  wine
2 tablespoons (35 ml)
  brandy
A pinch ground mace
Bouquet garni

Cut the meat from rabbit and mince coarsely. Cut the fillets from the breast of the pigeon and cut into strips. Set aside. Put the gammon into a pan with the foot, barely cover with water, add half the wine and the bouquet garni. Cover pan and cook gently for forty to forty-five minutes. Then leave to cool in the liquid.

Meantime add the minced rabbit to the pork with the garlic, parsley and ground mace. Pour over the rest of wine and the brandy, cover and leave for one hour.

Lift out the gammon, mince or chop finely, mix with the mince. Layer this mixture with the fillets of pigeon in a terrine, finishing with a layer of farce. Cover with a lid and spread luting paste round the edge. Cook in a bain-marie, 170°C–180°C/325°F–350°F/Gas Mark 3–4 for two hours. Continue simmering the foot in the liquid for another hour to provide a good jelly. Leave the pâté to cool, break away the luting paste and press lightly overnight.

Serve sliced, surrounded with the calf's foot jelly. Hungarian marrow salad makes an excellent accompaniment to this full flavoured pâté.

Hungarian marrow salad:
1 medium sized marrow
Olive oil
2 shallots, finely chopped
1 dessertspoon Hungarian
  paprika

Spicy dressing:
1 teaspoon dill seeds,
  bruised and infused in
  2 tablespoons (35 ml)
  vinegar
1 dessertspoon tomato
  purée
4–5 tablespoons (70–88
  ml) oil
Salt, pepper from the mill
A pinch sugar

Peel marrow, split in two and scoop out the seeds. Cut each half into thin slices. Heat 2–3 tablespoons oil in a large frying pan, put in the marrow with the shallot. Fry, turning frequently with a slice until barely soft, then mix in the paprika and seasoning. After a few seconds turn into a bowl to cool.

Strain the vinegar, add purée to it with the oil and seasonings. Mix well. Add to the marrow and mix carefully. Turn into a salad bowl and chill slightly before serving.

Serves 4–6

Liver

Calves' liver is without doubt considered superior to lambs', but nowadays, except for a special occasion, the price is prohibitive. For many recipes good quality lambs' liver is excellent.

For best results, remove the very fine membrane that lies over the liver and, of course, the ducts. Liver should never be overcooked otherwise it becomes hard, tough and tasteless. If sliced, one minute frying, at most. on each side is enough.

The following recipe is a favourite one in the School and many students who dislike the plain 'liver and bacon' will eat this with enthusiasm.

Foie de Veau à l'Orange

If possible use calves' liver for this dish, and keep it for special guests who would appreciate it.

Pilaff:
1½ oz (42 g) butter
1 medium sized onion, chopped
4 oz (113 g) rice
¾ pint (450 ml) stock
1 oz (28 g) freshly grated Parmesan cheese

1 lb (453 g) calves' liver
3–4 tablespoons flour
1 teaspoon freshly ground black pepper
½ teaspoon salt
2 teaspoons dry mustard
¼ teaspoon cayenne
2 oz (60 g) butter
1 medium sized onion, finely chopped
1 large clove garlic, crushed
1 glass (115 ml) red wine
½ glass (57 ml) jellied stock
1 tablespoon mixed chopped herbs

First prepare the pilaff in the usual way (see recipe for *Rognons Sauté Garibaldi*, p. 172) finishing with the butter and cheese dotted over the surface of the rice. Cover pan and set aside.

Slice orange without peeling. Fry in the butter, dusting well with sugar, until nicely coloured. Take out and keep warm.

Slice the liver thinly with a sharp knife. Mix seasonings with the flour. Dip the slices in this. Heat a large frying pan, drop in two-thirds of the butter, put in the liver and fry quickly on both sides for one minute. Lift onto a hot serving dish and slip into a warm oven.

Add the remaining butter to the pan and when melted add the onion and garlic. Sauté for. two or three minutes, then add the wine. Reduce to half, add stock and herbs. Boil up and spoon over the liver. Garnish with the orange slices. Serve at once.

Stir the pilaff with a fork, turn it into a dish and serve with the liver.

Serves 4

Garnish:
1 orange
½ oz (14 g) butter
Caster sugar

Foie d'Agneau Venitien

1 lb (453 g) lambs'
  liver
Seasoned flour
3 oz (84 g) butter
1 large onion, thinly
  sliced
2 tablespoons (35 ml)
  wine or cider vinegar
1 glass (115 ml) dry
  white wine
1 teaspoon chopped
  thyme or marjoram
1 tablespoon chopped
  parsley

Slice the liver thinly and cut across into finger-shaped pieces. When ready to cook, roll a few pieces at a time in seasoned flour. Heat a large heavy frying pan, drop in 1 oz (28 g) of the butter; when foaming put in the onion and cook slowly until golden. Add vinegar and simmer until the liquid has evaporated.

Drop in the remaining butter, increase the heat, add liver and sauté briskly for two to three minutes, turning frequently. Draw aside, add wine and herbs. Adjust seasoning, bring to the boil and simmer for one minute. Serve at once with a saffron or tomato pilaff.

Serves 4

Foie à la Bonne Femme

In this recipe the liver is braised in the piece before slicing, and has the classic garnish of button onions, mushrooms, ham and potatoes.

Use either calves' or lambs' liver according to choice.

1–1½ lb (453–678 g) liver,
  with the ducts removed
1 oz (30 g) bacon fat
  or dripping
4 oz (113 g) unsmoked
  streaky bacon, in the
  piece
18–20 'pickling' onions
4 oz (113 g) button
  mushrooms
2 medium sized potatoes
  or 8 baby new potatoes
2 teaspoons flour
1 wineglass (115 g) white
  wine or cider
½ pint (300 ml) brown
  stock, jellied for
  preference
Bouquet garni

Heat a thick cocotte or casserole. Drop in the fat; when hot, but not smoking, put in the liver and fry gently turning it over once, allowing three minutes on each side. Draw aside and take out liver.

Cut the bacon into lardons, put into a pan with the peeled onions. Cover with cold water, bring to the boil, strain and rinse with cold water. Drain well. Add to the cocotte with the mushrooms, trimmed but left whole. Sauté for four or five minutes.

Meantime quarter the potatoes lengthways and trim, but leave the new ones whole. Add to the cocotte, continue to cook for a few minutes then stir in the flour and add the wine and stock. Bring to the boil, put in the bouquet and liver, baste well, cover with a piece of foil and the lid. Braise in a moderate oven, 170°C–180°C/325°F–350°F/Gas Mark 3–4 for twenty to twenty-five minutes.

Take up the liver and remove the bouquet. Allow sauce to simmer uncovered while slicing the liver. Lay the liver in a deep dish for serving, adjust seasoning of the sauce, then spoon it over the liver.

Serves 4

Rognons Sauté Garibaldi

Veal or lambs' kidneys can be used for this dish. If veal, two should be enough. They weigh 6–8 oz (170–225 g) each. Skin and cut across into ½-inch slices.

6 lambs' kidneys
2 medium onions
1–1½ oz (28–42 g) butter
1 glass (70 ml) Marsala or brown sherry
6 oz (170 g) 'flat' mushrooms
1 dessertspoon flour
1 dessertspoon tomato purée
8 fluid oz (225 ml) stock
1 bay leaf
Clove garlic
4 tomatoes

Serves 4

Skin and split the kidneys. Sauté in the butter enough to 'seize' them. Flame with the Marsala. Take them out, add the onions finely sliced, and after a few minutes add the mushrooms quartered. Sauté for a few more minutes, then stir in the flour, purée and stock. Add bay leaf, garlic and seasoning. Replace the kidneys and simmer gently for fifteen to twenty minutes.

Skin, pip and quarter the tomatoes. Add them to the pan just before serving. Dish and serve with saffron rice.

Saffron rice:
1 large onion
½ lb (225 g) long grained rice
A good pinch of saffron
2 oz (56 g) butter
1¼–1½ pints (750–900 ml) stock
1½ oz (42 g) cheese

Melt two-thirds of the butter, add the finely sliced onion, cover and cook slowly until soft but not coloured. Add the rice, fry for a few minutes until the rice looks clear, add salt and pepper, the saffron which has been soaked in an eggcupful of hot water for thirty minutes before using, and 1¼ pints (750 ml) of stock. Bring to the boil, cover tightly and put into a moderate oven for twenty to thirty minutes, or until the grains are tender and the stock absorbed.

Add the extra stock if necessary, and with a fork stir in the rest of the butter and cheese.

Rognons Sauté Turbigo

An old favourite and one of the most liked of all kidney dishes.

Kidneys encased in fat are the best to buy as they are firmer and easier to skin. Moreover the fat when rendered down makes the best dripping for frying.

Blanch the onions and drain; quarter the mushrooms and set aside. Skin the kidneys, cut in half lengthways and remove core. Heat a sauté or deep frying pan, drop in the butter, and, when it is foaming, put in the kidneys and sauté briskly until nicely brown. Lift out and put in the chipolatas, lower the heat and brown also.

Take them out, add the onions and mushrooms, shake over a brisk heat for two or

18–20 'pickling' onions
¼ lb (113 g) button
   mushrooms
6 lambs' kidneys
2 oz (60 g) butter
¼ lb (113 g) chipolata
   sausages
1 dessertspoon flour
1 teaspoon tomato purée
1 tablespoon (18 ml)
   sherry
1½ gills (225 ml) brown
   stock
1 bay leaf
Salt and pepper
2 slices stale bread for
   croûtes
Chopped parsley

three minutes, then draw aside. Stir in the flour, purée, sherry and stock and bring to the boil; season. Slice the sausages diagonally into two or three pieces and add to the pan with the bay leaf and kidneys. Cover and simmer gently for twenty to twenty-five minutes.

In the meantime, prepare the croûtes by cutting the bread into triangular pieces and frying in a little hot oil until golden brown. Dish the kidneys, surround with croûtes and sprinkle with parsley.

Serves 4

Pain Farçi au Ris d'Agneau

This is a good way to serve lambs' sweetbreads for a lunch or supper dish. It will keep hot satisfactorily.

1 small Coburg loaf of
   white bread
1 oz (30 g) butter, melted

Salpicon:
1–1½ lb (453–678 g)
   lambs' sweetbreads
1–1½ oz (30–45 g) butter
1 large onion, thinly
   sliced
1 large carrot, thinly
   sliced
1½ glasses (172 ml) red
   wine
3 oz (84 g) button
   mushrooms
A bouquet garni
5–7 fluid oz (150–225 ml)
   jellied chicken stock
1 oz (28 g) butter worked
   to a paste with 1
   tablespoon flour
   (kneaded butter)

Cut the top off the loaf and scoop out the crumb. Brush the outside crust and top well with the melted butter. Set aside. Soak sweetbreads as described on p. 174, then blanch, drain and press until cold between two plates with a weight on top.

Melt the butter in a shallow braising pan or casserole. Add the sweetbreads and sauté gently, stirring frequently until coloured. Lift out the sweetbreads, put in the onion and carrot, cover and sweat gently for five to six minutes. Pour on the wine, increase heat and reduce to about half. Add the mushrooms, whole, and the sweetbreads. Season, tuck in the bouquet and pour over the stock. Cover and braise gently in the oven or simmer on the cooker top for twenty-five to thirty minutes or until the sweetbreads are tender.

Meantime put the loaf and top on a baking tray and into the oven. Take out the bouquet and add the kneaded butter, piece by piece. When dissolved, bring to the boil and simmer for two or three minutes. Well fill the loaf with this mixture and replace the top slantwise. Serve very hot.

Serves 4

Goulash de Ris d'Agneau

1½ lb (678 g) lambs'
    sweetbreads
1½ lb (678 g) Spanish
    onions
3 oz (84 g) butter
2 teaspoons Hungarian
    paprika
½ pint (300 ml) veal or
    chicken stock
½ oz (14 g) flour
2½ fluid oz (70 ml) cream
1 medium sized red
    pepper or 2 caps
    canned pimento

Serves 4

Soak the sweetbreads for several hours in cold salted water. Drain and place in a pan of cold salted water with a slice of lemon. Bring slowly to the boil, simmer for one or two minutes, drain and rinse. Remove any ducts and membrane and press between two plates with a light weight on top.

Melt 2 oz (56 g) butter in a sauté pan, add the finely sliced onions and allow to soften slowly, uncovered, for about twenty minutes. Remove from the pan, add the remaining 1 oz (28 g) butter and quickly brown the well dried sweetbreads. Lower the heat, add the paprika, cook for one to two minutes and then blend in the flour and stock. Season lightly and replace the sweetbreads. Cover and simmer very gently for twenty to thirty minutes until tender. Five minutes before serving, add the cream and the skinned, shredded red pepper or canned pimento. Serve with Pommes Normande.

Pommes Normande:
1½ lb (678 g) potatoes
1½ oz (42 g) butter
¾ pint (450 ml) milk
Seasoning

Cut the potatoes in thin even slices and arrange overlapping in a well buttered fire-proof dish. Season between the layers with salt and freshly ground black pepper, pour over the milk and cover the top with the remaining butter cut into tiny pieces. Bake in a moderately hot oven, 190°C–200°C/375°F–400°F/Gas Mark 5–6 for about fifty to sixty minutes until the potatoes are cooked and the liquid absorbed.

Ris de Veau Tante Marie

Perhaps the best of sweetbread dishes and one where calves' breads should be used. They are a little more difficult to come by than the lambs' and may have to be

Soak the sweetbreads as described in the previous recipe. Put the sweetbreads into a pan, cover with fresh cold water, add lemon, a little salt and bring to the boil. Drain, rinse and press between two plates until quite cold.

Trim away any gristle and return to the pan. Barely cover with stock and simmer for ten to fifteen minutes. Drain well and dry the

ordered previously from the butcher. Calves' sweetbreads are slightly more expensive than lambs, but texture and flavour are excellent.

1–1½ lb (453–678 g) calves' sweetbreads
A slice of lemon
Good veal or chicken stock
1–2 tablespoons (18–35 ml) oil
1 oz (30 g) butter
4 oz (113 g) button onions
1 clove garlic
1 teaspoon flour
1 small glass (65 ml) sherry
¼ pint (150 ml) white wine
8 fluid oz (225 ml) stock
Bouquet garni
4 oz (113 g) button mushrooms
5–6 bread croûtes
1 dessertspoon tomato purée
Kneaded butter
4 tablespoons (75 ml) cream

sweetbreads; reserve 8 fluid oz (225 ml) of the stock.

Heat the oil, add butter and put in the onions and garlic. Cook for two to three minutes, then add the sweetbreads and allow to brown. Dust with the flour, flame with the sherry, add the wine, stock and bouquet garni. Season and simmer for thirty-five minutes.

Meantime, fry the croûtes in butter, lift out and arrange on the serving dish. Sauté the mushrooms briskly in the same pan, leaving them whole; set aside. Take up the sweetbreads, slice thickly and arrange on the croûtes. Add the tomato purée to the liquid in the pan and thicken with a little kneaded butter. Reboil, adjust the seasoning, add the cream and mushrooms. Boil for one or two minutes, then spoon over the sweetbreads.

Serves 6

Ris de Veau Marie-Anne

This recipe incorporates one of the best of sauces for serving with veal or suprêmes of chicken and certain vegetables. Again, it is best done with calves' sweetbreads.

1½–1¾ lb (678–792 g) calves' sweetbreads
Root vegetables to flavour, i.e. onion, carrot, celery

Soak and blanch the sweetbreads, drain, refresh and press between two plates with a weight on top until cold and firm. Trim.

Cover the bottom of a shallow pan or casserole with a layer of thinly sliced vegetables. Lay the sweetbreads on top and barely cover with the stock. Season lightly and put in the bouquet. Cover pan and simmer for thirty-five to forty minutes until tender. Draw aside while preparing the sauce. Keep this warm in a bain-marie.

Lift out the breads with a draining spoon and cut into thick slices. Arrange, slightly over-

Good chicken or veal
stock
A bouquet garni

¾ pint (450 ml) Sauce
Poulette

Garnish:
2½–3 lb (1¼–1½ kg) baby
broad beans
½ lb (225 g) small new
carrots

Fondant or Château
potatoes

Serves 6

lapping, in a hot dish, then coat well with the sauce.

Have ready the beans and baby carrots cooked separately, well drained and tossed up with a knob of butter. Arrange at either end of the dish and serve the potatoes separately.

Sauce Poulette:
1½ oz (45 g) butter
1 oz (30 g) flour
½ pint (300 ml) jellied veal or
chicken stock
¼ pint (150 ml) cream
2 egg yolks
½ teaspoon lemon juice
1 tablespoon freshly chopped parsley

Melt the butter in a thick saucepan. Draw aside and stir in the flour. Cook for two or three seconds. Pour on the stock off the heat, blend, then stir until boiling. Season and add two-thirds of the cream. Boil gently until syrupy.

Blend yolks with rest of cream and add this liaison by degrees to the sauce, off the heat. Finish with the lemon juice and parsley. Cover the pan and stand it in a bain-marie until wanted.

Puddings

Aspic de Pommes

The Cordon Bleu has no other recipe quite like this – layers of carefully poached apples set in a natural apple jelly. Its success does depend on having the right kind of apple and we must admit it takes a great deal of time and care in cooking, but we know of no other sweet that past guests remember so well. Choose an apple of the pippin variety; Cox's Orange Pippin is particularly good.

The preparation and cooking must be spread over two days.

Serves 4

Day 1 :

2 lb (1 kg) tart cooking apples
1¼ pint (750 ml) water

Put ¾ pint (450 ml) of water in shallow pan and heat, while wiping the apples with a clean damp cloth. Slice the apples thinly straight into the hot water, do not core or peel, and simmer until tender crushing them down with a wooden spoon from time to time. Strain through a jelly bag of flannel or felt. When the juice has finished dripping (allow at least four hours for this) turn the pulp back in the pan with ½ pint (300 ml) water and simmer gently for about 1½ hours. Strain this and then add the two strained juices together; measure and reduce, if necessary, to 9 fluid oz (280 ml) by simmering gently.

Day 2 :

10 oz (282 g) lump sugar
Juice ½ lemon
2 lb (906 g) firm fleshed dessert apples
4 oz (113 g) candied fruit (a mixture of angelica, glacé cherries and pineapple, candied orange peel and apricots)

Dissolve the sugar in the apple juice made the day before, add the lemon juice and boil for four to five minutes. Draw aside. Peel, core and quarter the apples and slice them directly into the syrup. Cook the apples *gently* in the covered pan for ten to twelve minutes; stir carefully from time to time. Remove the lid from the pan and continue cooking until the amount of syrup left is just sufficient to moisten the slices. Cover the pan again, draw off the heat and leave until the apple slices are clear.

Meanwhile cut the candied fruits in small pieces and mix them together; add them to the cooked apple and stir carefully. Pour the mixture into a wet cake tin or charlotte mould and put in a cold place to set.

Make a sauce with 3 tablespoons redcurrant or crab apple jelly or apricot jam melted in 3 tablespoons (50 ml) water. Strain if necessary, cool and add 1 tablespoon (18 ml) rum. Unmould the chartreuse, pour the sauce over and serve cold.

Griestorte au Citron

This light and 'short' textured cake is made without flour and is a marvellous vehicle for serving a very little choice fruit and making it go a long way, a small bowl of your first home-grown strawberries or raspberries for example. Here it is filled with a mixture of fresh cream and home-made lemon curd, making it seasonal throughout the year. It will fit into any menu – particularly good for Sunday lunch – and it freezes well.

3 large eggs
4 oz (113 g) caster sugar
½ lemon
2 oz (56 g) fine semolina
Scant 1 oz (25 g) ground almonds

Filling:
¼ pint (150 ml) double
  cream
¼ pint, about 8
  tablespoons, lemon
  curd

To finish:
3 tablespoons sifted icing
  sugar

Serves 6

Butter a shallow 8-inch cake tin, line the base with a disc of buttered greaseproof paper and dust first with caster sugar and then with flour. Set the oven at 180°C/350°F/Gas Mark 4.

Separate the eggs, beat the yolks and sugar together until light in colour and texture, strain on the lemon juice and continue to beat until thick. Fold in the grated lemon rind, semolina and ground almonds. Whip the egg whites until stiff and using a large basting spoon cut and fold them into the mixture. Turn into the prepared tin and bake in the pre-set oven for thirty to forty-five minutes. Cool on a wire rack.

Whip the cream until firm and fold in the lemon curd, leaving it a little streaky. Split the cake, using a serrated knife as the crumb of the cake is very tender; fill with the lemon cream, reshape and dust the top with icing sugar.

Lemon curd:
½ lb (225 g) granulated sugar
¼ lb (113 g) butter
Grated rind and juice of 2 large lemons
3 eggs, well beaten

Put all the ingredients into a double saucepan and stir over low heat until the mixture is thick. Great care must be taken not to let the mixture boil or it will curdle. Pour it into clean dry pots.

Store in a cool place and this will keep for at least a month.

A delicious variation can be made to this cake when *Santa Rosa Plums* are available – this happens twice a year as they are exported from Spain and South Africa. No other plum has quite the same colour and flavour. Poach the plums in a very little sugar syrup and when cold drain them and melt 2 tablespoons redcurrant jelly in the juice and thicken with 1 teaspoon arrowroot. Split the cake and fill with 2 petit suisse cream cheeses mixed with ¼ pint (150 ml) double cream whipped and sweetened with vanilla sugar. Arrange the plums on top of the cake and spoon or brush over the glaze.

Tonille aux Pêches

Serve this sweet for a luncheon party when fresh peaches are in season. The crisp biscuit paste made with toasted hazelnuts complements the tender flesh of a ripe peach to perfection. Use either the English peach with white flesh or the yellow clingstone variety but never tinned peaches, they are too sweet and the juice around them softens the layers of crisp biscuit pastry.

3 oz (85 g) hazelnuts
3¼ oz (90 g) butter
2¼ oz (60 g) caster sugar
4½ oz (125 g) flour

Filling:
½ pint (300 ml) double
   cream
1 orange
5–6 lumps sugar
3–4 fresh peaches

To finish:
3 tablespoons sifted icing
   sugar

Serves 6–8

Toast the nuts in the oven and, when nicely browned, rub them in a thick cloth to remove the skins and grind them through a nut mill, or blender or a food processor. (Nuts with their high fat content are easily burnt, so watch them carefully and allow about five minutes in a moderately hot oven.)

Work the butter and sugar together until light and soft then work in the sifted flour and prepared nuts. Chill in the fridge for at least 30 minutes.

Divide the pastry into three pieces and shape very carefully, on a floured board, into balls. Place each piece in turn on an ungreased baking sheet and roll or pat out with the fingers – if the paste starts to crack pinch together with fingers – into a very thin round 8 inches across. Bake in a moderate oven 190°C/375°F/Gas Mark 5 for about ten minutes. Check the rounds after about eight minutes as ovens can vary and, as the nuts have been baked once, if the pastry browns it will taste scorched and bitter.

Trim the rounds as you take them from the oven but do not attempt to remove them from the baking sheet. Cut one round only into six to eight even portions and slide a thin palette knife under each piece to release it from the tin; do the same under each plain round. After two or three minutes the pastry should be firm enough to slide onto cooling racks.

Meantime rub the sugar lumps over the orange to remove all the oil and zest, crush them with a wooden spoon and add the juice of half the orange. Stir well, adding extra fine sugar to make a thick syrup. Peel and slice the peaches onto a plate, spoon over the orange syrup and cover to exclude the air.

Partially whip the cream, add the syrup from the peaches, a little at a time, and continue whipping until firm. Sandwich the layers with the cream and peaches, arrange the cut sections on top and dust with the icing sugar. This is best done on the serving plate. Just before serving cut through the two bottom layers.

Austrian Cheese Cake with Raisins

Among the teaching staff of the Cordon Bleu Cookery School and Winkfield Place where favourite recipes for cheese cakes are collected and swopped, this has always been voted the best. Search for the brand of fine seedless raisins packed without mineral oil or preservatives of any kind.

2 oz (56 g) butter
4 oz (113 g) caster sugar
8 oz (225 g) curd or
    cream cheese
2 large eggs
2 oz (56 f) fine semolina
2 oz (56 g) ground
    almonds
Grated rind and juice
    ½ lemon

To finish:
3 tablespoons sifted icing
    sugar

Serves 6

Grease and prepare an 8-inch shallow cake tin as described in the previous recipe and set the oven at 190°C/375°F/Gas Mark 5.

Beat the butter and sugar in a warm basin until very soft, add the curd or cream cheese gradually. Beat in the egg yolks one at a time and continue to beat until creamy in colour and texture; stir in the semolina, ground almonds and lemon. Whip the egg whites until stiff and using a large basting spoon cut and fold them carefully into the mixture. Turn at once into the prepared tin and bake for forty-five to sixty minutes in the pre-set oven.

If you are in any doubt as to whether the mixture is done at the end of one hour, turn the heat off and leave the cake to cool in the oven. Serve dusted with icing sugar.

In the summer months omit the raisins and serve the cheese cake masked with whipped cream with a bowl of fresh raspberries handed separately.

Here is what we consider to be the best method of serving raspberries to accompany a cake, meringue or pudding of any kind.

Take one quarter of the raspberries you have to hand and rub these through a nylon strainer. Beat in slowly, one tablespoon at a time, sifted icing sugar – when the fruit purée thickens it will be sweet enough – the amount of icing sugar needed will depend on the variety of fruit and the season.

Pour this purée or 'Melba Sauce' over the whole berries and allow to stand for at least two hours before serving. The flavour is best if the raspberries are kept at room temperature and not in the refrigerator.

Gâteau au Chocolat Montmorency

This dark chocolate cake filled with cherries and cream is decorated with large curls of chocolate. As this 'caraque' keeps

Line, grease, sugar and flour the sandwich tin. Sift the flour with a pinch of salt and set aside. Mix the cocoa in a saucepan to a smooth paste with the water and cook to a heavy cream; allow to cool.

well (at least two to three weeks) in an airtight container, make more than you need. Prepare it early in the day before the kitchen gets warm and use a good quality dessert chocolate, not a cooking variety.

Cake:
3 eggs
4½ oz (127 g) caster sugar
2½ oz (70 g) flour
2 oz (56 g) cocoa
¼ pint (150 ml) water

Filling:
1 lb (453 g) red cherries
2 tablespoons caster sugar
1 teaspoon arrowroot
1 tablespoon (18 ml) Kirsch
½ pint (300 ml) double cream

To finish:
2 oz (56 g) plain dessert chocolate
2 tablespoons sifted icing sugar

8½- to 9-inch deep sandwich tin. Oven setting: 180°C/350°F/ Gas Mark 4.

Note: The cocoa should be the consistency of well-creamed butter; if too thick add a few drops of cold water.

Whisk the eggs a little, add the sugar and whisk at high speed until thick and mousse-like. If using a wheel whisk set the basin over a pan of hot water to hasten the process. Fold two-thirds of the flour into the mixture, add the prepared cocoa and the remaining flour. Turn into the prepared tin and bake for forty-five to fifty minutes.

Meantime stone the cherries and place them in a pan with the sugar, cover and set over gentle heat until the juices run freely. Mix the arrowroot and 1 tablespoon (18 ml) water, add to the cherries and stir until boiling; turn into a bowl to cool. Add the Kirsch.

Whip the cream, sweeten lightly with vanilla sugar and place about 4 tablespoonsful on a piping bag fitted with a vegetable rose nozzle. When the cake is cold, split and fill with the remaining cream and the cherries. Dust the top of the cake with icing sugar and decorate with rosettes of cream and caraque.

Chocolate caraque:
Shred or grate 2 oz (56 g) chocolate and melt it on a plate over a pan of hot water. Do not allow the plate to get too hot and work the chocolate continually with a palette knife. Lift the plate off the pan and, still working the chocolate with the knife, allow it to cool a little and so thicken. When about the consistency of mud put the plate back on the pan and rewarm until the chocolate runs freely.

Spread the chocolate thinly on a marble slab or formica topped table and when almost set curl it off with a thin sharp knife.

The same chocolate cake is used for another great favourite called:

Gâteau Belle Hélène:
The method is exactly the same as for Gâteau au Chocolat Montmorency, but *perfectly ripe* dessert pears are used to replace the cherries and a chocolate sauce is served separately.

Serves 8

Bakewell Tart

This seems to have little in common with the tarts sold in Derbyshire but we think the combination of the homemade lemon curd and strawberry jam make this Cordon Bleu version extra good. Serve it at Saturday or Sunday lunch; it is a family favourite everywhere.

Rich shortcrust pastry:
8 oz (225 g) flour
6 oz (170 g) butter
1 dessertspoon caster
 sugar
1 egg yolk
About 1½ tablespoons
 (27 ml) cold water

Filling:
2 tablespoons strawberry
 jam
2 tablespoons lemon curd
2 oz (56 g) butter
4 oz (113 g) caster sugar
Grated rind and juice
 1 small lemon
2 eggs
4 oz (113 g) ground
 almonds
2 oz (56 g) stale cake
 crumbs

Line an 8-inch sandwich tin with the pastry and use the trimmings to make a double lining to the sides of the tin. Press firmly, cut the two layers together with back of a small knife and scallop the edge with the thumb. Prick the bottom lightly and spread the pastry first with jam and then with the lemon curd.

Work the butter until soft, add the lemon rind and the sugar gradually and beat until light. Add the beaten eggs a little at a time and then stir in the ground almonds, cake crumbs and lemon juice. Spread the mixture over the lemon curd and bake in a moderate oven, 190°C/375°F/Gas Mark 5 for about forty-five minutes, until set and golden brown.

Serves 6

Butterscotch Cream Flan

Rich shortcrust pastry:
6 oz (169 g) flour
4 oz (113 g) butter
1 dessertspoon caster
 sugar
1 egg yolk
1 tablespoon (18 ml) cold
 water

Prepare the pastry, chill and line into an 8-inch flan ring and bake bind. Cool on a rack.

Meantime melt the butter in a heavy saucepan and when golden brown add the sugar; stir until foaming and cook for two or three minutes. Remove from the heat and stir in the boiling water. Place the cornflour, flour and salt in another pan and mix to a smooth

Filling:
2 oz (56 g) butter
4 oz (113 g) dark brown
 sugar
¼ pint (150 ml) boiling
 water
2 tablespoons cornflour
1 tablespoon flour
Good pinch of salt
½ pint (300 ml) milk
2 egg yolks
2 drops vanilla essence

Decoration:
3½ fluid oz (100 ml)
 cream
2 tablespoons finely
 chopped browned nuts

paste with the milk; add the brown sugar mixture. Stir over gentle heat until boiling and then cook for one minute.

Pour half the mixture onto the beaten egg yolks, return to the pan and continue cooking for one minute. Add the vanilla essence. Pour the mixture into the pastry case and chill.

Whip the cream, spread carefully over the top and mark with a palette knife. Decorate with the nuts.

Serves 4–6

Tarte aux Pommes Grillé

Pâte Sucrée
(French flan pastry):
6 oz (169 g) flour
3 oz (84 g) butter
3 oz (84 g) sugar
3 egg yolks
2 drops vanilla essence

Filling:
2 lb (1 kg) cooking
 apples
½ oz (14 g) butter
1 tablespoon (18 ml)
 water
3 oz (84 g) granulated
 sugar
2 tablespoons orange
 marmalade

To finish:
A little beaten egg and
 caster sugar

Serves 6

Make up and chill the pastry as given in the recipe on p. 187.

Meantime prepare the filling. Wipe the apples, remove the stalk and 'eye' but not the core. Rub the butter over the bottom of a heavy saucepan, quarter the apples and slice directly into the pan; add the water, press a butter wrapper or greaseproof paper on top and cover with the lid. Cook slowly to a pulp and rub through a nylon strainer. Return the purée to the rinsed pan, add the sugar and cook until very thick. Stir in the marmalade and turn onto a plate to cool.

Roll out two-thirds of the pastry and line into an 8-inch flan ring, prick the bottom of the flan several times and fill with the apple purée. Roll the remaining pastry to an oblong and cut into ½-inch wide strips. Damp the edge of the flan and place the pastry strips in a lattice over the top of apple; press the strips firmly to the edge. Brush the flan with the egg, dust with sugar and bake at 190°C/375°F/Gas Mark 5 for thirty to thirty-five minutes. Slide onto a rack and leave to cool a little before lifting off the flan ring.

Mincemeat Flan 'Cordon Bleu'

Do not wait for Christmas to make this flan but try it as soon as English Cox's Orange Pippins are in season. No other apple has the same flavour.

Rich shortcrust pastry:
½ lb (225 g) plain flour
6 oz (180 g) butter
1 dessertspoon caster sugar
1 egg yolk
About 2 tablespoons (35 ml) cold water

Fresh mincemeat:
2 Cox's apples
3 oz (84 g) each currants, raisins and sultanas
3 oz (84 g) grapes, peeled and pipped
1 ripe banana
1 tablespoon finely chopped candied orange peel
1 oz (28 g) blanched, shredded almonds
Grated rind and juice ½ lemon
¼ teaspoon grated nutmeg
3 oz (84 g) demerara or raw cane sugar
1 oz (28 g) butter, melted
2 tablespoons (35 ml) rum or brandy

To finish:
3½ fluid oz (100 ml) cream
1 teaspoon caster sugar
1–2 tablespoons (18–35 ml) rum or brandy

8- to 9-inch flan ring. Oven setting 190°C/380°F/Gas Mark 5.

Prepare the pastry and chill.

Peel, core and chop the apples and mix with the dry fruit, which has been previously washed and dried. Add the halved grapes and diced banana and all the other ingredients and mix well. This mincemeat can be stored in a covered container in the refrigerator for one week.

Roll out one-third of the pastry to a round the same size as the flan ring. Stamp out a round 2½ inches in diameter from the centre. Set aside the ring and add the small round to the rest of the pastry. Roll out and line into the flan ring; fill with the fresh mincemeat, damp the edges and cover with the ring of pastry. Press firmly and cut the two edges together using the back of the blade of a table knife.

Protect the exposed mincemeat with a small disc of foil and bake in the pre-set oven to a pale golden brown, about twenty-five minutes. Brush the flan with a little lightly beaten egg white and quickly dust with caster sugar; lift off the flan ring and return the flan to the oven for five to seven minutes 'to frost' the top.

Allow to cool a little on the baking sheet then slide carefully onto a serving platter, remove the disc of foil and spoon the whipped flavoured cream into the middle. Serve freshly baked.

Serves 8

Tarte aux Fruits à la Crème

This flan is a good way of serving a mixture of dessert fruits. It is excellent for luncheon or for a buffet supper party.

The mixture of strawberries and banana is just a suggestion but the combination of firm yellow fleshed peaches and raspberries is equally good. Have the redcurrant glaze prepared and cooled somewhat before preparing the banana or peaches; if these fruits are peeled and sliced and brushed immediately with the glaze they will not discolour.

French flan pastry
  Pâté Sucrée :
6 oz (169 g) plain flour
3 oz (84 g) butter
3 oz (84 g) caster sugar
3 egg yolks
2 drops vanilla essence

Filling :
¼ pint (150 ml) double cream
4 lumps sugar
1 orange
½ lb (225 g) strawberries
2 bananas
½ lb (225 g) redcurrant jelly

8-inch flan ring. Oven setting 190°C/375°F/ Gas Mark 5.

Serves 6

Prepare the pastry. Sift the flour with a small pinch of salt onto a marble slab or formica table, make a well in the middle and in this put the other ingredients. It is best to have the butter at room temperature and not straight from the refrigerator; if this is not possible cut the butter into walnut sized pieces to make the job easier. Take a palette knife in one hand and with the finger tips of the other work the butter, sugar and yolks together until they have lost their separate identities. Use the palette knife to clear your fingers and prevent the mixture reaching the palm of your hand at this stage.

Now work in the flour as quickly as possible and knead lightly to a smooth dough. Wrap and chill for one hour before rolling out and lining the flan ring; bake blind in the pre-set oven for about fifteen minutes. Remove the paper, beans and flan ring and return to the oven for about three to five minutes to dry.

Whisk the redcurrant jelly well and rub through a strainer into a saucepan. Heat gently without stirring until clear, then bring to the boil; allow to cool but not set.

Hull the strawberries. Rub the sugar lumps over the orange to remove the zest, crush and add very little orange juice to make a thick syrup. Whip the cream and flavour with the orange syrup. When the flan case is cold, fill with the cream and arrange the strawberries on the top. Peel and slice the bananas and arrange overlapping in circles beween the strawberries. Brush at once with the glaze and allow to set before serving.

Tarte aux Chocolat et Poires

The chocolate pastry for this flan is made by the same method as the pastry in the recipe on p. 187, the cocoa being sifted with the flour. The pears must be ripe and full of flavour, there is no point in attempting this recipe with hard unripe pears as they will not soften while baking and to cook them first makes them too sweet.

Make this for a luncheon party around Christmas time when English Comice pears are at their very best and again when you can find Australian Packhams and English, French or Italian Williams.

Chocolate pastry:
6 oz (170 g) plain flour
1 oz (28 g) cocoa
3 oz (84 g) butter
3 oz (84 g) caster sugar
3 egg yolks
2–3 drops vanilla essence

Filling:
3–4 ripe dessert pears
1 tablespoon vanilla
  sugar
2 tablespoons (35 ml)
  brandy

To finish:
Egg white and caster
  sugar or 6 tablespoons
  (105 ml) apricot glaze

8- to 9-inch flan ring.
  Oven setting 190°C/
  375°F/Gas Mark 5.

Serves 6–8

Prepare the pastry and chill for one hour. Peel, quarter and core the pears, sprinkle with the sugar and brandy and leave to macerate for 30 minutes.

Roll out two-thirds of the pastry and line into the flan ring. Drain the pears, arrange in the flan and reserve the juice. Roll out the remaining pastry with any trimmings and cut into ½-inch strips; arrange these lattice fashion over the pears. Bake for about thirty-five minutes.

Five minutes before the tart is cooked, remove from the oven and brush lightly with egg white and dust with caster sugar. Return to the oven for a few minutes to frost the top. Serve with a bowl of whipped cream flavoured with the reserved pear juice.

If preferred, the dry glaze of egg white and sugar can be replaced by an apricot glaze flavoured with the pear juice; this is brushed on after the flan has cooled a little.

Galette Montmorency

A rich almond pastry flan especially suitable for a lunch party.

Morellos can still be bought in shops (or grown in your garden), otherwise use canned fruit as directed. Late July/August is the season for fresh cherries.

Almond pastry:

6 oz (170 g) plain flour
2½ oz (70 g) ground almonds
4 oz (113 g) butter
3 oz (84 g) caster sugar
2 egg yolks
Grated rind of ½ lemon or vanilla essence or Kirsch to flavour

Filling:

1 can (450 g) pitted Morello cherries
¼ pint (142 ml) juice from the cherries
1 dessertspoon redcurrant jelly
A level dessertspoon sago
1 teaspoon Kirsch
Sugar to taste

¼ pint (142 ml) double cream, lightly whipped, sweetened and flavoured with Kirsch

8-inch shallow flan ring

Serves 6

Prepare pastry: sift the flour with a pinch of salt onto a pastry board or slab; make a small well in the centre and sprinkle the almonds on the flour. Place the butter, sugar, eggs and flavouring in the middle of the flour and work these ingredients together with the fingertips of one hand. When blended, draw in the flour and almonds and knead lightly until smooth. Wrap and chill for one hour before using.

Drain and measure the juice from the cherries, making up the quantity with water if necessary. Sweeten to taste. Bring to the boil with the redcurrant jelly, draw aside, stir in the sago and simmer for four to five minutes until clear. Remove from heat, add Kirsch and allow to cool.

Roll out a third of the pastry to a round the size of the top of the flan ring. Stamp out a round 2½ inches in diameter from the centre. Set aside the ring and add the small round to the rest of the pastry. Roll out and line into the flan ring. Fill with the cherry mixture. Cover with the ring of pastry, press round the edges, brush with water and dust with caster sugar. Bake in a pre-set oven, 190°C/380°F/ Gas Mark 5 until pale golden. Cool a little before removing flan ring.

To serve, slide onto serving dish and spoon the whipped flavoured cream into the centre. Serve the Galette slightly warm.

Apple and Almond Jalousie

Puff pastry made with:
½ lb (225 g) flour
½ lb (225 g) butter
4–5 fluid oz
(104–140 ml) ice cold
water and good
squeeze lemon juice

Filling:
3–4 sharp dessert apples
(Granny Smiths,
Sturmer or Cox's
Orange Pippins)
2 oz (56 g) sultanas
½ oz (14 g) flaked
almonds

To finish:
½ lb (225 g) apricot jam
Squeeze lemon

Serves 8

Roll out the pastry to an oblong just under a ¼-inch thick and about 4-inches wide. Cut it into two portions, one a little larger than the other. Roll the smaller piece to the same size as the other, trim the edges and place it on a damp baking sheet. Damp a 1-inch band on all four sides and cover the centre with a layer of thinly cut apple slices, scatter the sultanas on top and cover these with another layer of apple.

Fold the first piece of pastry in two lengthways. With a sharp knife, cut it into ¼-inch strips across the fold, starting and finishing 1-inch from each end and leaving a similar 1-inch band opposite the fold. Open out the cut portion and lift it onto the base. Press the edges firmly and 'cut up' with the back of a knife. Chill for five to ten minutes.

Brush the pastry with the egg, dust lightly with sugar and then scatter over the nuts. Bake at 220°C/425°F/Gas Mark 7 for about twenty-five minutes then reduce the heat to 190°C/375°F/Gas Mark 5 and continue baking until brown and crisp, about ten minutes. Cover the top with greaseproof paper if necessary to prevent the almonds burning.

Remove to a cooling rack and brush copiously with the hot glaze which should fill between the slits of pastry and run into the apple. Allow to cool and cut into slices for serving.

For a special occasion add a teaspoon of rum to the apricot glaze.

Strawberry Torte

Strawberries are disappointing to freeze but when plentiful and 'a good buy' it is worth crushing a few with a fork and packing them in ½-pint (300-ml) quantities to make a few special sweets. They have all the flavour of summer if not the texture of the fresh fruit and are

Work the butter until soft, add the sugar by degrees and beat until light and fluffy; beat in the yolks one at a time and the hot milk by degrees. The butter must retain its natural appearance and never oil; the hot milk if added as advised will cook the egg yolk but not spoil the butter.

Partially whip the cream and fold in half the strawberry pulp. Stir the prepared nuts into the butter mixture and carefully fold in the strawberry cream.

Line the cake tin with the biscuits and fill

excellent not only for the following recipe but for a soufflé, mousse, fool and ices.

4 oz (113 g) unsalted
   butter
3 oz (84 g) caster sugar
2 egg yolks
4 tablespoons (70 ml)
   hot milk
2 oz (56 g) freshly
   ground brazil nuts
½ pint (300 ml)
   strawberry pulp
½ pint (300 ml) double
   cream
1 packet Boudoir biscuits

7½-inch loose bottom
   cake tin

with the strawberry mixture. Cover with foil and leave in the refrigerator overnight or place in the freezer for two to three hours.

Turn onto a plate and serve the remaining strawberry pulp as an accompanying sauce, adding extra sugar to it if necessary.

Serves 6–8

Charlotte au Chocolat et Cognac

This very rich sweet will serve eight or more, so if you are in the habit of offering a choice of sweets at a dinner party, it is wise to prepare this in two smaller tins as the mixture freezes well.

½ lb (225 g) unsalted
   butter
½ lb (225 g) soft dark
   brown sugar
½ lb (225 g) plain dessert
   chocolate
¼ pint (150 ml) hot
   strong black coffee
4 egg yolks
2–3 tablespoons brandy
½ pint (300 ml) double
   cream
2 packets Boudoir biscuits

9-inch diameter or 2
   spring-form moulds
   with centre tube fitted.

Cream the butter until soft, add the sugar a little at a time and continue beating until soft and fluffy. Melt the chocolate in the coffee and beat in the yolks one at a time while the mixture is hot; allow to cool a little, then beat into the butter and sugar mixture.

Whip the cream and fold into the chocolate mixture with the brandy. Line the bottom and sides of the tin with the biscuits, moisten if liked with a little extra brandy and pour in the filling.

Cover with foil and chill for twelve hours in the refrigerator. Turn out and decorate with extra cream if liked.

Serves 8 plus

191

Vacherin Brazilienne

This is a good addition to a buffet table, especially around Christmas time.

Meringue:
4 egg whites
½ lb (225 g) soft brown sugar

Filling:
½ pint (300 ml) double cream
1 rounded teaspoon instant coffee
2–3 small ripe bananas
4 pieces glacé ginger

Decoration:
3 tablespoons sifted icing sugar
4 fluid oz cream, whipped

Serves 8

Set the oven at 140°C/275°F/Gas Mark 1 and line two baking sheets with Bakewell paper.

Beat the egg whites in a bowl until stiff and quickly fold in the sugar with a large metal spoon. Divide the mixture in two and spread carefully in circles 8 inches in diameter or use a forcing bag with a plain ½-inch tube and pipe the meringue in a spiral pattern on the baking sheets.

Bake the meringue in the pre-heated oven for about sixty to seventy minutes or until they are dry and lightly coloured. Cool on a wire rack and when almost cold, peel off the paper.

Flavour the cream with the coffee dissolved in a very little water and sweeten lightly; cut the glacé ginger into fine shreds and slice the bananas. Fill the meringue rounds with the coffee flavoured cream, ginger and bananas, making sure the bananas are well coated with cream to prevent discolouration. Dust the top of the vacherin with icing sugar and decorate with rosettes of whipped cream.

If, however, you wish to freeze this sweet fill with the coffee flavoured cream only, dust with the icing sugar and decorate with the plain sweetened cream. Pack in a box and freeze.

Serve the following mixture of Fruits Rafraichis separately. Prepare this on the day it is to be served.

4 Clementines
4 slices fresh pineapple
3 oz (84 g) granulated sugar
5 tablespoons (100 ml) water
2–3 small ripe bananas
4 pieces glacé ginger
2 tablespoons (35 ml) ginger syrup

Peel the Clementines, remove all the pith and cut in slices; slice the pineapple, remove skin and core and cut each slice in half.

Dissolve the sugar slowly in the water and then boil for one minute; allow to cool and add the syrup from the glacé ginger.

Slice the bananas into a bowl, cover with the prepared Clementines and pineapple, add the finely sliced ginger and spoon over the cold sugar syrup. Put a plate on the fruit to hold it in the syrup, cover with film wrap and chill for one to two hours.

The Vacherin should be removed from the freezer three to four hours before serving. It might need a little extra icing sugar dusted over the top before placing on the buffet.

Vacherin Panaché

Serve this on a buffet; it will give ten to twelve portions. It is another of these useful meringue sweets which are especially suitable for freezing.

Chocolate and raspberry flavours marry well together, but of course other combinations can be used.

Meringue:
6 egg whites
12 oz (338 g) caster sugar

Filling and decoration:
2 oz (56 g) plain dessert chocolate
3 tablespoons (53 ml) water
½ teaspoon instant coffee
2 tablespoons ground praline
4 tablespoons (70 ml) fresh raspberry purée
Vanilla sugar
1½ pints (900 ml) double cream
3 tablespoons sifted icing sugar

Serves 10–12

Line four baking sheets with Bakewell paper and mark each with circles 9 inches (23 cm) in diameter, and set the oven at 140°C/275°F/Gas Mark 1.

Prepare the meringue. Whisk the egg whites until stiff but not dry – start with a wheel or electric beater but finish by hand using a ballon whisk. Add six teaspoons of the measured sugar and continue to whisk for one minute. Fold in the remaining sugar carefully, using a basting spoon.

Spread or pipe out the meringue on the prepared baking sheets and bake for 1 to 1½ hours in the pre-set oven until dry and crisp. When cool peel off the paper carefully.

Dissolve the chocolate slowly in water, add the coffee and allow to cool. Partially whip the cream and divide in half. Add a little vanilla sugar to one portion and continue beating until the cream will just hold shape; put a third of this vanilla cream in a piping bag fitted with a vegetable rose pipe and keep in the refrigerator.

Divide the unflavoured cream into two basins, whisk each until stiff, mix in the chocolate and praline to one portion and the raspberry purée into the other.

Layer the meringue rounds starting with the chocolate praline cream, then the vanilla and lastly the raspberry. Top with the remaining round of meringue and press lightly. Dust the top with icing sugar and pipe with the reserved vanilla cream. Fill one to two hours before it is to be cut or, better still, freeze and remove from the freezer and leave at room temperature for four hours before serving.

Roulage de Chocolat

Make the day before a special party and use the finest plain dessert chocolate you can find; mixed with fresh eggs and sugar the mixture is baked and the result is magic!

This freezes beautifully and if you propose doing so use foil for the rolling operation. Allow to thaw for at least five hours at room temperature as the flavour and texture of chocolate is more mellow if not too cold.

6 oz (170 g) plain chocolate
3–4 fluid oz water or strong black coffee
5 large eggs
8 oz (225 g) caster sugar

Filling:
½ pint (300 ml) cream
½ teaspoon caster sugar
2–3 drops pure essence of vanilla or 1 teaspoon rum or brandy
4–6 tablespoons icing sugar

Make a case with a double sheet of Bakewell paper 13½ inches × 11 inches (34 cm × 28 cm) and 1 inch (25 cm) deep

Serves 8–10

Set the oven at 180°C/350°F/Gas Mark 4.

Separate the eggs, work the egg yolks with a wooden spoon or electric beater, add the sugar gradually and continue to beat until thick and pale in colour.

Grate the chocolate or slice finely with a knife, place in a saucepan with the water or coffee and stir gently over a low heat until melted to a thick cream; set aside.

Whip the egg whites with a ballon whisk until stiff but not dry. Add the warm chocolate to the egg yolk mixture and beat for half a minute. Cut and fold the egg whites into the chocolate mixture and turn at once into the paper case; smooth into the corners with a palette knife.

Bake in the pre-set oven for ten to fifteen minutes or until firm to the touch. Have ready a clean cloth wrung out in cold water. Take the roulage from the oven, leave to cool a little then cover the top with the damp cloth. (This will help to soften the sugary crust and make the roulage easier to roll.) When quite cold leave in the refrigerator overnight.

The next day partially whip the cream, add the sugar and flavouring and continue to whip until firm.

Lay a piece of greaseproof paper on the kitchen table and dust it well with sifted icing sugar. Remove the cloth from the top of the roulage and the paper clips or sellotape from the corners of the paper-case and turn the roulage up-side down on to the greaseproof paper. Remove the paper-case by tearing it away in long narrow strips. Spread with the whipped cream.

Lift the greaseproof paper carefully along the length and roll up the roulage away from you. Keep it in the paper for a minute or two then lift it carefully on to a serving dish. Dust again with icing sugar if necessary to hide any cracks.

Caramel Mousse

This recipe shows the difference between a cold soufflé and a mousse. If

Prepare the caramel. Put the lump sugar and half the water in a pan and dissolve slowly, do not stir but tap the bottom of the pan

the students of the School put *Lemon Soufflé* at the top of their list of 'the best pudding' it must be because they find a *Caramel Mousse* more difficult to make. There was no doubt about the favourite with the customers of our restaurant over the twenty-one years it flourished. In summer time the mousse was served with fresh strawberries and at other times with a caramel sauce full of thickly sliced bananas.

It must be said that it is not easy to make but if the advice given in the recipe is understood and followed you will soon master the technique of mousse making.

6 oz (169 g) lump sugar
¼ pint (150 ml) cold
    water
1 teaspoon liquid glucose
    or a pinch cream of
    tartar
3 whole eggs
2 egg yolks
2 oz (56 g) caster sugar
½ oz gelatine
Juice 2 lemons
3½ fluid oz (100 ml)
    double cream

Decoration:
3½ fluid oz (100 ml)
    double cream
½ lb (225 g) strawberries
    or 2 large bananas
    according to season.

Serves 6

from time to time. Add the glucose or the cream of tartar melted in a teaspoon water, increase the heat and boil steadily, without stirring, to a dark brown caramel.

Cover your hand holding the pan, remove it from heat and immediately pour in the rest of the cold water. Stir and pour into a bowl to cool. When cold the caramel should be the consistency of heavy cream, not as thick as treacle.

Whisk the whole eggs, yolks and caster sugar at high speed until thick; the mixture when allowed to drop from the whisk should remain in a thick ribbon or rope on itself. If only a hand whisk is available the bowl containing the mixture should sit over a pan of hot water.

Meantime strain the lemon juice into a small pan or ramekin, sprinkle in the gelatine and, when well soaked, dissolve it over gentle heat. Partially whip the cream – it is important that this is much the same consistency as the egg and sugar mousse.

Stir in the caramel, cream and gelatine to the egg mixture. If not in a stainless steel bowl turn the mixture into a clean metal pan and stir most carefully over a bowl of ice until on the point of setting. Pour at once into a lightly oiled ring mould. Put in a cool place to set.

Unmould onto a serving plate, mask and decorate with rosettes of cream and fill the centre of the mould with the hulled strawberries.

When strawberries are out of season, make a second batch of caramel, add a squeeze of lemon and a dash of water if too thick and slice directly into this sauce the two ripe bananas. Serve separately in a sauce bowl with ladle.

Dacquoise

This almond meringue should be slightly soft in the centre; the cream of tartar in the recipe helps to achieve this result but the almonds play their part too – they must be freshly blanched and ground. Serve this for a dinner party or any special occasion. Both dacquoise and sauce will freeze well.

5 egg whites
10 oz (282 g) caster sugar
4 oz (113 g) almonds
⅛ teaspoon cream of
  tartar

Filling and sauce :
½ pint (300 ml) double
  cream
½ lb (225 g) fresh
  apricots or Santa Rosa
  plums
¼ pint (150 ml) sugar
  syrup made with:
  3 oz (84 g) granulated
    sugar
  3 tablespoons (53 ml)
    water

To finish :
A little extra cream
3 tablespoons sifted icing
  sugar

Line two baking sheets with Bakewell paper and set the oven at 150°C/300°F/Gas Mark 1.

Blanch the almonds, dry well on paper towelling and grind through a nut mill or food processer.

Whip the egg whites until stiff but not dry, add two tablespoons of the measured sugar sifted with the cream of tartar and whisk for about ten seconds. Fold in the remaining sugar and ground almonds. Spread or pipe the mixture in two rounds 9 inches (23 cm) in diameter. Bake for about 1 to 1¼ hours, reducing the heat of the oven to 130°C/250°F/Gas Mark ½ after forty-five minutes.

Slide onto a wire rack and after fifteen minutes turn over and pull off the paper. Meantime halve the apricots or plums, remove the stones and stew with 1 tablespoon sugar and 5 tablespoons water until soft and pulpy; rub through a nylon strainer.

Whip the cream until thick, fold in a little of the fruit purée to flavour and sweeten to taste. Sandwich the dacquoise with the fruit flavoured cream, dust the top with icing sugar and decorate with rosettes of whipped cream. Thin the remaining fruit purée with the cold sugar syrup to make a sauce.

Serves 8

Soufflé Cappuccino

½ pint (300 ml) creamy
  milk
1 oz (28 g) fécule or
  arrowroot and flour
  mixed
3 oz (84 g) granulated
  sugar

Take 3 tablespoons of the milk and blend into the fécule. Pour the rest of the milk into a pan, bring just to boiling point, draw aside and add the sugar and coffee; cover and leave for ten minutes.

Meantime prepare the soufflé cases. Rub ¼ oz (7 g) butter over the bottom and sides of the

1 rounded teaspoon
   instant coffee
1 oz (28 g) butter
1 oz (28 g) light brown
   sugar
3 egg yolks
4 egg whites
2 tablespoons sifted icing
   sugar

3 × 4½-inch (11-cm)
   soufflé cases
Oven setting 190°C/
   380°F/Gas Mark 5

Serves 6

soufflé cases, dust thickly with soft brown sugar and tie bands of Bakewell paper around the outside to stand one inch above the top. Sit the cases in a roasting tin.

Stir the warm milk to make sure the sugar is dissolved and add the fécule in a thin steady stream. Place over gentle heat and stir until boiling. Allow to cook for five seconds, remove from the heat and cover the surface of the 'sauce' with the butter divided in small pieces.

Replace the lid on the pan and leave for ten to fifteen minutes. Mix the butter into the sauce, add the egg yolks one at a time and beat well. Whisk the egg whites with a balloon whisk until very stiff, stir one tablespoonful into the mixture with a wooden spoon; cut and fold in the remainder with a basting spoon.

Divide the mixture between the three soufflé dishes and smooth the top with a palette knife. Pour very hot water in the roasting tin to come well up the sides of the soufflé cases and put on the middle shelf of the pre-set oven.

Bake for about eighteen minutes then draw the soufflés to the mouth of the oven and dust with the icing sugar. Return the soufflés gently into position and bake a few extra minutes until nicely glazed and firm to the touch on the outside. Remove the papers and serve at once.

Serve a bowl of whipped cream sweetened and flavoured with instant coffee and a little brandy. This should be firm and well chilled. The cold cream should be spooned into the hot soufflé when served.

Crêpes aux Cerises

Batter:
3 oz (84 g) flour
2 eggs
1 teaspoon caster sugar
1 tablespoon (18 ml)
   melted butter
Approx. 8 fluid oz
   (220 ml) milk
3–4 tablespoons crushed
   macaroons

Sift the flour and sugar with a pinch of salt into a bowl. Make a well in the centre of the flour, add 1 egg, 1 yolk and the butter and gradually beat in the milk. Cover and stand in a cool place.

Meantime toast the crushed macaroons in the oven until golden brown. Stone the cherries, place in a pan with the sugar and orange rind or Kirsch, cover and set over a low heat and cook carefully until the juices run freely; add the redcurrant jelly, stir carefully until melted then cover and cook very gently for five to eight minutes.

Filling:
1 lb (453 g) red cherries
1 tablespoon caster sugar
Grated rind ½ orange or
 1 tablespoon (18 ml)
 Kirsch
2 tablespoons redcurrant
 jelly

To finish:
3½ fluid oz (100 ml)
 cream
A pinch ground
 cinnamon

Whip the remaining egg white and fold into the batter with the macaroons.

Fry the pancakes as thinly as possible, put a spoonful of cherries on each, roll up and lay in a buttered fire-proof dish. Dust well with caster sugar and put in a hot oven, 200°C/400°F/Gas Mark 6 for three or four minutes. Boil the cream with the cinnamon, pour over the pancakes and serve at once.

Serves 6

Crêpes aux Noisettes

These pancakes may be fried and filled in the morning before a dinner party or even deep frozen weeks earlier. Remove from the freezer two to three hours before needed and bake for fifteen minutes at 190°C 375°F/Gas Mark 5.

Batter:
3 oz (84 g) flour
1 teaspoon caster sugar
1 tablespoon melted
 butter
1 egg
1 yolk
Approx. 8 fluid oz
 (220 ml) milk

Filling:
3 oz (84 g) hazelnuts
3 oz (84 g) butter
2 oz (56 g) caster sugar
1 teaspoon instant coffee
 dissolved in 1
 tablespoon (18 ml)
 freshly boiled water *or*
1 tablespoon brandy

Prepare the batter and leave to stand for about one hour.

Brown the hazelnuts in a moderate oven for about fifteen minutes and rub in a thick cloth to remove the skins. Chop finely. Cream the butter and sugar together until soft and light, work in the prepared hazelnuts and flavour with either coffee essence or brandy.

Fry paper thin pancakes, spread with the filling and fold in three like a 'tricorne'; place in a buttered fire-proof dish and dust with icing sugar. Slip into a hot oven, 200°C/400°F/Gas Mark 6 for about five minutes just before serving.

While delicious on their own these pancakes are even better served with a fresh apricot compote.

Serves 4–6

Baked Orange Soufflé

4 oz (113 g) lump sugar
2 oranges
1 oz (28 g) butter
9 fluid oz (260 ml)
  creamy milk
¾ oz (21 g) flour
3 egg yolks
4 egg whites
2 tablespoons sifted icing
  sugar

Serves 4

Rub some of the sugar lumps over the rind of the oranges to remove all the zest – the oranges should look quite bald! Take 1 oz (28 g) of the lump sugar, using only two to three pieces of the flavoured sugar, and crush with a wooden spoon or rolling pin. Set aside.

Take 3 tablespoons (53 ml) of the milk and mix with the flour. Set aside. Put the remainder into a large pan, bring to the boil and add the sugar. Draw the pan aside, cover and leave for twelve minutes.

Set the oven at 190°C/375°F/Gas Mark 5 and prepare a 7-inch (2-pint capacity) soufflé case. Rub ¼ oz (7 g) of the butter over the bottom and sides of the soufflé case, sprinkle with crushed sugar and dust with a little extra caster sugar. Tie a band of Bakewell paper around the outside of the case to stand 1½ inches (4 cm) above the rim.

Stir the warm milk until all the sugar has dissolved and blend in the flour mixture in a thin steady stream. Stir over gentle heat to boiling point, draw the pan aside and cover the surface of the sauce with the butter divided into small pieces. Replace the lid on the pan and leave for ten to fifteen minutes.

Stand the prepared soufflé case in a roasting tin containing hot water. Now mix the butter into the sauce and beat the egg yolks in one at a time. Whip the egg whites with a balloon whisk to a firm snow, add one tablespoon to the orange mixture and stir in gently with a wooden spoon.

Cut and fold in the rest of the egg whites using a basting spoon. Turn quickly into the prepared case, piling the mixture up in the centre. Smooth top with a palette knife and make a few cuts round the sides to settle the mixture evenly and to let in the heat of the oven.

Put the soufflé on the middle shelf of the oven and bake for about twenty-five minutes. Draw the soufflé gently to the front of the oven and dredge the top with icing sugar. Replace and cook a further two to three minutes to glaze the top. Remove the paper and serve at once. Remember a hot soufflé should be firm to the touch on top but soft and creamy in the middle; if overbaked it will fall rapidly when removed from the oven!

Hot Chocolate Soufflé

3 oz (84 g) plain block
  chocolate
1 tablespoon (18 ml)
  water
9 fluid oz (260 ml)
  creamy milk
1 oz (28 g) fécule or
  arrowroot and flour
  mixed
1 oz (28 g) butter
1 oz (28 g) caster sugar
2–3 drops vanilla essence
3 egg yolks
4 egg whites
2 tablespoons sifted icing
  sugar

7-inch (2-pint capacity)
  soufflé case
Oven setting 190°C/
  380°F/Gas Mark 5

Serves 4

Grate the chocolate into a large saucepan, add the water and melt over gentle heat until smooth. Meantime mix the fécule with 3 tablespoons (53 ml) of the measured milk. Add the rest of the milk to the chocolate, bring to the boil, add the sugar, draw aside, cover and leave for ten minutes.

Rub the bottom and sides of the soufflé case with ¼ oz (7 g) of the butter and dust with the caster sugar. Tie a band of Bakewell paper around the outside of the soufflé case to stand one inch above the top. Add the fécule and follow the instructions given in the previous recipe. Add the vanilla with the egg yolks.

Serve the soufflé with a hot chocolate sauce and a bowl of chilled vanilla flavoured cream.

Hot chocolate sauce:
4 oz (113 g) dark dessert chocolate
3 oz (84 g) granulated sugar
½ pint (300 ml) water
Small piece vanilla pod or 2–3 drops vanilla
  essence

Grate the chocolate finely into a small pudding basin. Put the sugar and water in a pan over gentle heat, sit the bowl of chocolate on the top and work with a palette knife until melted to a smooth cream. Remove from the saucepan and set aside. When the sugar has dissolved, add the vanilla pod and boil gently for five minutes; remove the vanilla pod.

Pour the sugar syrup into the chocolate, mix well and return to the saucepan. Simmer gently for about ten minutes until the sauce coats the back of a wooden spoon.

Cold Lemon Soufflé

The Cordon Bleu Cookery School in London has been teaching students to make this recipe for the last thirty-four years and it is still the most popular cold sweet of all. Light

Prepare a 6-inch, 1¾-pint (1-l) capacity soufflé case. Tie a band of doubled greaseproof paper round the outside of the soufflé case to stand 1¼ inches above the top.

Separate the eggs, whisk the yolks and sugar together for two to three minutes, add the strained lemon juice and whisk at high speed until all the sugar is dissolved and the mixture

as a feather and 'fresh' tasting, it is very straighforward to make. Serve it for any special occasion or when you want 'to spoil' someone.

This soufflé will freeze well but because of its delicate nature must be carefully packed, either in a rigid container with a lid or a cardboard box wrapped in a polythene bag to exclude air and prevent other flavours contaminating the cream.

4 eggs, if *extra* large, 3
   will do
½ lb (225 g) caster sugar
2½ lemons
½ oz (15 g) gelatine
5 tablespoons (75 ml)
   water
½ pint (300 ml) double
   cream

Decoration:
A little extra cream – 3½
   fluid oz (110 ml)
1 tablespoon finely
   chopped pistachio nuts
   or browned almonds

is light in colour and texture. Meantime remove the zest from the lemon rinds on the finest part of the grater, put the gelatine to soak in the water and partially whip the cream. Fold the cream carefully into the lemon mixture using a large basting spoon. The mixture will thicken considerably as you do this. Dissolve the gelatine over a low heat.

Whisk the egg whites to a firm snow, start them with a wheel or electric whisk until foamy but finish with a ballon whisk if you want perfection. Blend the hot gelatine into the egg and sugar mixture; set the bowl on ice, add the whipped whites, cut and fold into the mixture and as it begins to thicken creamily pour quickly into the prepared soufflé case. Put in a cold place to set.

Remove the band of greaseproof paper, spread a thin layer of whipped cream over the top and decorate with rosettes of cream. Sprinkle the rosettes with the finely chopped nuts. If the weather is very hot turn the band of greaseproof paper inside out, re-tie around the soufflé and keep in the refrigerator until wanted.

Serves 6

Cakes

Walnut Bread

This recipe was a tea-time speciality for twenty-one years in the Cordon Bleu Kitchen Restaurant; it was served very thinly sliced and spread with unsalted butter.

It is easy to make and freezes so well it is worth while investing in extra loaf tins and baking as many as your oven will hold. The recipe fills a 1-lb loaf tin.

4 oz (113 g) granulated
    sugar
6 oz (170 g) golden syrup
8 fluid oz milk
2 oz (56 g) sultanas
8 oz (225 g) plain flour
3 teaspoons baking powder
A pinch of salt
2 oz (56 g) chopped
    walnuts
1 beaten egg

Grease and flour a 1-lb loaf tin and set the oven at 180°C/350°F/Gas Mark 4. Place the sugar, syrup, milk and sultanas in a saucepan over a low heat and stir until the sugar has dissolved; tip into a basin and allow to cool.

Sift the flour with the baking powder and salt into a mixing bowl and add the walnuts. Add the beaten egg to the cooled syrup mixture, blend together and pour into the flour. Mix quickly to a smooth batter, pour immediately into the prepared tin and bake for about 1–1½ hours. Turn the oven to 170°C/325°F/Gas Mark 3 after forty-five minutes.

Fruit Cake for Everyday

This is a good cut-and-come-again cake.

6 oz (170 g) butter
Grated rind and juice
    ½ orange
6 oz (170 g) soft light
    brown sugar
3 large eggs
12 oz (340 g) self-raising
    flour
6 oz (170 g) currants
6 oz (170 g) sultanas
3 oz (84 g) candied peel
2 tablespoons (35 ml)
    milk
8-inch cake tin
Oven setting 180°C/
    350°F/Gas Mark 4

Line the cake tin with greaseproof paper unless it has a non-stick surface; if so, follow the manufacturer's instructions. Pick over and clean the fruit if necessary and finely chop the candied peel. Sift the flour with a pinch of salt and set aside.

Work the butter with the orange rind until soft, add the sugar and beat well until light and fluffy. Beat in the eggs one at a time and stir in a tablespoonful of the flour if the mixture shows signs of curdling. Cut and fold the flour, fruit and candied peel into the mixture with the orange juice. Add the milk if necessary to give a mixture that will just drop from the mixing spoon. Turn into the prepared tin and bake in the middle of the pre-set oven and bake for about 1 to 1½ hours.

Belvoir Ginger Cake

This rich, sticky ginger cake is good not only at tea time but excellent served at lunch buttered, with a slice of Wensleydale cheese. It keeps very well and should always be made two to three days before it is to be eaten to allow it to mature.

4 oz (113 g) butter
4 oz (113 g) soft brown sugar
2 eggs
10 oz (280 g) black treacle
8 oz (225 g) plain flour
Pinch of salt
1 teaspoon ground ginger
4 oz (113 g) sultanas
½ teaspoon bicarbonate of soda
2–3 tablespoons (35–53 ml) milk

Line a 7½- to 8-inch cake tin with Bakewell paper and set the oven at 170°C/325°F/Gas Mark 3. Soften the butter, add the sugar and beat thoroughly until soft. Sift the flour with the salt and ground ginger; add half to the sultanas and set aside. Stir the treacle into the butter and sugar mixture, beat in the eggs one at a time, adding each one with half the remaining flour. Mix well.

Warm the milk to blood heat only and dissolve the baking soda in this. Add to the cake mixture with the remaining flour and sultanas. Turn into the prepared tin and bake for 1½ to 2 hours, reducing the heat to 150°C/300°F/Gas Mark 2 after one hour.

Orange Cake

4 oz (114 g) self-raising flour
A pinch salt
4 oz (113 g) butter
1 small orange
4 oz (113 g) caster sugar
2 eggs

To finish:
3 tablespoons sifted icing sugar for dredging or glacé icing

Line the bottom of an 8-inch sandwich tin with Bakewell paper, butter lightly and dust with flour. Set the oven at 190°C/375°F/Gas Mark 5. Sift the flour with the salt and set aside. Soften the butter, add the finely grated orange rind and sugar and beat well until light and fluffy. Separate the eggs and add the yolks one at a time.

Squeeze and strain the juice from the orange and whip the egg whites with a balloon whisk until stiff. Cut and fold the sifted flour into the mixture with the orange juice, using a basting spoon. Lastly add the egg whites and turn at once into the prepared tin. Bake for about thirty to forty minutes in the pre-set oven.

Loosen the cake from the sides of the tin with a round-bladed knife. Turn the cake onto a clean folded tea cloth on the palm of the hand, remove the paper and cool the cake on a wire rack. When cool either dredge with the sifted icing sugar or coat with the following icing:

8–12 oz (300 g) icing sugar
3 strips orange peel
3 tablespoons (53 ml) water

Sift the icing sugar twice through a nylon strainer and set aside. Remove the strips of orange rind with a potato peeler – these strips should be no more than a ½-inch/15-mm wide – and cut across in the finest shreds; drop in boiling water for one minute. Strain and leave on kitchen paper.

Place the water in a small saucepan and add the sieved icing sugar a spoonful at a time. Beat thoroughly with a wooden spatula. The icing should coat the spatula quite thickly and look very glossy. Place the saucepan over a *very* low heat, warm carefully beating all the time. Remember the pan must not get hot and it is wise to test the bottom frequently with the palm of the hand. Add the prepared rind to the icing and pour quickly over the cake.

Gâteau de Savoie

This lemon sponge has a marvellous texture quite unlike conventional recipes. Serve it for tea or to accompany a compote of fruit at a luncheon party. It is best made with fécule, that is potato flour, but if this is difficult to find use a mixture of the finest plain flour and arrowroot.

2½ oz (70 g) fécule or
1¼ oz (35 g) each arrowroot and plain flour
3 eggs
5 oz (140 g) caster sugar
Grated rind and juice ½ lemon

Line the bottom of an 8½-inch moule à manqué or deep sandwich tin with greaseproof paper, butter lightly and dust first with caster sugar and then with flour. Set the oven at 185°C/370°F/Gas Mark 4–5.

If using the mixture of flours, sift well together. Separate the eggs. Beat the egg yolks, sugar and lemon juice together at high speed until very thick and white then add the fécule and lemon rind and mix well. Whip the egg whites to a firm snow with a balloon whisk and fold them into the mixture with a large basting spoon. Turn into the prepared tin and bake in the moderate oven for about forty-five minutes. When cool, dust with icing sugar.

Gingerbread

This is a light sponge variety of gingerbread; serve freshly baked for tea.

4 oz (113 g) butter
½ lb (225 g) golden syrup
3 oz (84 g) granulated sugar
¼ pint (150 ml) milk
4 oz (113 g) self-raising flour
Pinch of salt
2 teaspoons ground ginger
1 teaspoon mixed spice
1 teaspoon bicarbonate of soda
2 eggs
4 oz (113 g) wholemeal flour
1 tablespoon marmalade

Line an 8-inch square cake tin and set the oven at 170°C/325°F/Gas Mark 4. Place the butter, syrup, sugar and milk in a saucepan and stir over gentle heat until the sugar is dissolved; allow to cool.

Sift the self-raising flour with salt, spices, and baking soda into a mixing bowl and add the wholemeal flour. Beat the eggs well and add to the flours with the cooled syrup mixture and marmalade. Beat with a wooden spoon to a smooth batter. Pour into the prepared tin and bake for about 1½ hours. When cool cut into squares for serving.

Chocolate and Orange Cake

For a rich dark cake that keeps well, this cannot be bettered but you must use the very best unsweetened chocolate. An American brand called *Bakers* will give the best result.

2 oz (56 g) unsweetened chocolate
5–6 tablespoons (80–90 ml) water
3 large eggs
4½ oz (127 g) caster sugar
Grated rind ½ orange
2¼ oz (64 g) plain flour

Prepare a 9- to 9½-inch moule à manqué or deep sandwich tin and set the oven at 180°C/350°F/Gas Mark 4. Melt the chocolate with the water to a thick cream and put aside to cool. Whisk the eggs, sugar and orange rind at high speed until thick and mousse-like. Sift the flour with a pinch of salt and check the consistency of the chocolate – if too thick or oily stir in a few drops of cold water. Fold the flour and chocolate into the egg mixture and turn carefully into the prepared tin and bake for about forty to fifty minutes in the pre-set oven.

Prepare the filling. Mix the chocolate powder and orange rind to a smooth paste with the water in a small saucepan and cook over gentle heat to a thick cream; remove from the fire and beat in the egg yolk. Allow this mixture to cool slightly and beat in the butter a little at a time.

Filling:
2 oz (56 g) sweetened
    chocolate powder
Grated rind ½ orange
3 tablespoons (53 ml)
    water
1 egg yolk
2 oz (56 g) butter

Chocolate glacé icing:
3 oz (84 g) plain dessert
    chocolate
4 tablespoons (70 ml)
    stock syrup or water
8 oz (225 g) icing sugar
½ teaspoon salad oil

When the cake is cool split and fill with filling, reshape and cover the top with a chocolate glacé icing.

Icing:
Cut the chocolate into small pieces and place in a saucepan with the sugar syrup or water. Dissolve over gentle heat and bring *just* to the boil; allow to cool slightly. Beat in the sifted icing sugar, a spoonful at a time, add the oil and rewarm gently.

If this cake is to be served as a luncheon party sweet use the following filling:

Grated rind ½ orange
1 tablespoon caster sugar
1 tablespoon (18 ml) brandy
¼ pint (150 ml) double cream

Mix the orange rind, sugar and a little orange juice to give a thick syrup. Whip the cream and add the orange syrup and brandy.

Dundee Cake

½ lb (225 g) butter
Grated rind 1 lemon
½ lb (225 g) caster sugar
2 oz (56 g) ground
    almonds
4 eggs
11 oz (312 g) self-raising
    flour
Pinch of salt
½ lb (225 g) sultanas
½ lb (225 g) currants
3 oz (84 g) candied peel,
    finely shredded
2 tablespoons (35 ml)
    milk

For top:
2 oz (84 g) Valencia
    almonds blanched and
    split
1 tablespoon (18 ml)
    milk

Line an 8-inch cake tin with Bakewell paper and set the oven at 170°C/325°F/Gas Mark 3. Work the butter and lemon rind until soft, add the sugar and beat thoroughly until light in colour and texture. Work in the ground almonds and beat again. Beat in the eggs one at a time adding one tablespoon of flour after the last egg if the mixture shows any sign of curdling.

Sift the flour with the salt and, using a metal spoon, fold one-third into the mixture; add the fruit and candied peel. Fold in the remaining flour with the milk. Turn the mixture into the tin, smooth the top with a palette knife, cover with the almonds and brush with the milk. Bake in the pre-set oven for about 2–2¼ hours.

Luncheon Plum Cake

This is a super cake for a
picnic or indeed for any
occasion that calls for a
moist fruit cake that is not
as rich as a Christmas
cake.

¾ lb (340 g) butter
¾ lb (340 g) caster sugar
4 oz (113 g) ground
  almonds
5 eggs
1 tablespoon (18 ml)
  black treacle
1 lb (453 g) plain flour
1 lb (453 g) seedless
  raisins
½ lb (225 g) currants
½ lb (225 g) sultanas
4 oz (113 g) candied peel
1 teaspoon mixed spice
Pinch of salt
1 teaspoon bicarbonate
  of soda
4–5 fluid oz cider, orange
  squash or milk

Line a 12-inch *or* 2 × 7½-inch cake tins with
Bakewell paper and set the oven at 170°C/
325°F/Gas Mark 3. Cream the butter, add
sugar and beat thoroughly. Work in the ground
almonds and continue to beat until light in
colour and texture.

Clean the dried fruit and finely chop the
candied peel. Divide the flour into three
portions; sift one part on to the prepared fruit,
sift a second part with the salt and spice and the
remaining portion sift with the baking soda.

Beat the eggs, one at a time, into the butter
and sugar mixture, then add the black treacle.
Fold in the flour with the spice, followed by the
fruit. Add the cider alternately with the flour
sifted with the baking soda to give a mixture
that will drop from the spoon. Bake in the pre-
set oven for 1½ hours for the small cakes, 2–2½
hours for one large cake.

Devil's Food Cake with Fudge Icing

An American cake with
a soft crumb; it is dark
and sweet and is made
with cocoa.

6 oz (170 g) plain flour
½ teaspoon baking
  powder
1 teaspoon bicarbonate
  of soda
Pinch of salt
2 oz (56 g) cocoa
8 fluid oz water
4 oz (113 g) butter or
  shortening
10 oz (284 g) caster sugar
2 eggs

Prepare two 8-inch sandwich tins and set the
oven at 180°C/350°F/Gas Mark 4. Sift the flour
with the baking powder, baking soda and salt;
blend the cocoa with the cold water and set on
one side.

Soften the butter, add the sugar and beat well
until white. Whip the eggs until frothy, add to
the mixture a little at a time and beat again
for two to three minutes. Stir in the sifted
flour alternately with the cocoa and water.
Divide the mixture between the two tins and
bake for thirty to thirty-five minutes in the pre-
set oven.

When cold sandwich and cover the cakes
with Chocolate Fudge Icing.

Chocolate fudge icing:
1 lb (453 g) granulated sugar
¼ pint (150 ml) water
1 tablespoon golden syrup
2 oz (56 g) butter
2 oz (56 g) cocoa

Place all the ingredients in a large saucepan and stir very gently over a low heat until all the sugar has dissolved. Bring to the boil and cook steadily *without* stirring to the soft ball stage, 234°F on a sugar/jam thermometer. Remove from the heat and leave to cool.

Beat steadily with a wooden spatula until the mixture thickens and holds shape.

Gâteau Pain de Genes

It is only within recent years that ground almonds have been available in France and this cake was always made with almonds freshly blanched and pounded to a paste with the sugar first and the other ingredients added after.

The cake is rich and close textured and is good served for tea or to accompany a fruit suedoise or any fruit compote where the fruit kernel has an almond flavour, e.g., apricot, cherry and plum.

4 oz (113 g) butter
5 oz (140 g) caster sugar
3½ oz (100 g) ground almonds
3 eggs
1 tablespoon (18 ml) Kirsch or orange flower water
1½ oz (45 g) fécule

Line the bottom of an 8- to 8½-inch moule à manqué or deep sandwich tin with Bakewell paper, butter the sides of the tin and dust with flour. Set the oven at 180°C/350°F/Gas Mark 4.

Soften the butter, add the sugar gradually and beat at high speed until white. Beat the eggs to a froth and add them gradually with the ground almonds and continue beating for three minutes. Fold the fécule and Kirsch into the mixture using a basting spoon and turn into the prepared tin. Bake in the pre-set oven for about one hour.

Rich Pound Cake

Good for a birthday cake.

½ lb (225 g) butter
½ lb (225 g) soft brown
  sugar
4 eggs
3 tablespoons (53 ml)
  sherry, brandy or rum
½ lb (225 g) plain flour
Pinch of salt
1 teaspoon mixed spice
½ teaspoon grated
  nutmeg
½ lb (225 g) each
  currants, raisins and
  sultanas
2 oz (56 g) glacé cherries
2 oz (56 g) almonds,
  blanched and shredded
2 oz (56 g) candied peel,
  finely shredded

Line an 8-inch cake tin with Bakewell paper and set the oven at 170°C/325°F/Gas Mark 3. Soften the butter with a wooden spoon, add the sugar and beat thoroughly until soft and light. Separate the eggs and beat in the yolks with the sherry or spirit. Sift the flour with the salt and spices; divide into three portions, fold one into the cake mixture very lightly and mix another with the cleaned fruit, halved cherries, almonds and peel.

Whisk the egg whites until stiff; add the fruit to the mixture and then fold in the remaining flour and egg whites. Turn the mixture into the tin and bake in the pre-set oven for about two hours or until the cake tests done.

Menu
Suggestions

January

New Year's Luncheon Party
Smoked Salmon Pâté (No. 2)
Jugged Hare or Garrick Steak
Vegetable Garnish (see Plaice Durand)
Apple and Almond Jalousie

February

A Dinner Party
Potage de Tomates à l'Orange or Pineapple
    with Tarragon Cream Dressing
Poussins Farçis au Riz
Spinach 'en branche'
New Dutch Carrots 'Vichy'
Dacquoise

March

Sunday Brunch Party
Salade d'Avocats et Poires
Oeufs en Cocotte Arnold Bennett
Rognons Sauté Turbigo
Galette d'Epinards et Volaille
Aspic de Pommes
Austrian Cheese Cake with Raisins

April

Two Fork Luncheon Parties
(1) Tomates Farçis Carmel
     Coquilles St Jacques Mornay
     Orange Cake
(2) Salmagundy
     Tarte aux Chocolat et Poires

May

A Celebration Lunch
Tartelettes de Champignons Bonne Femme
Truites Farçis au Saumon
New Potatoes – Cucumber Salad
Griestorte

June

Midsummer Party
Asparagus Mousse
Jambon au Blanc or Galantine de Canard
    en Gelée
Potato Salad
Lettuce hearts filled with stoned cherries,
    moistened with French dressing and finished
    with chopped walnuts and chives
Vacherin Brazilienne

July	*Dinner Party* Potage Crème de Cresson Cold Salmon with Mayonnaise and Cucumber Salad or Mousse de Saumon Nantua Hot New Potatoes Crêpes aux Cerises

August	*Dishes for a holiday week-end*
	Flageolet, Tunny and Tomato Salad served
	  with Hot Herb Loaf
	Luncheon Plum Cake
	Poulet en Cocotte Bonne Femme
	Tonille aux Pêches or Chocolate and Orange
	  Cake

September	*Lunch Party*
	Oeufs Florentine
	Harvest Pâté or Epaule d'Agneau aux Fines
	  Herbes
	Butterscotch Cream Flan or Belvoir Ginger
	  Cake and Cheese

October	*Autumn Dinner Party* Artichauts Vinaigrette Provençale or Spicy Tomato Soup Soles Fourées aux Crevettes Roses Pommes Sauté Cold Lemon Souffié
November	*Dinner Party* Potage Crème d'Oignon or Coquilles St Jacques Sauté Bercy Ragoût de Veau Créole Calabresse Strawberry Torte
December	*Dishes for the Christmas Buffet* Oeufs Pochés aux Crevettes Mousse au Jambon Game Pie Salads Roulage au Chocolat Mincemeat Flan 'Cordon Bleu'

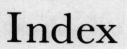

Index